ŚRĪMAD-BHĀGAVATAM

Ninth Canto

"Liberation"

(Part Two—Chapters 9–16)

With the Original Sanskrit Text,
Its Roman Transliteration, Synonyms,
Translation and Elaborate Purports

by

His Divine Grace
A.C. Bhaktivedanta Swami Prabhupāda
Founder-*Ācārya* of the International Society for Krishna Consciousness

THE BHAKTIVEDANTA BOOK TRUST
New York · Los Angeles · London · Bombay

Readers interested in the subject matter of this book
are invited by the International Society for Krishna Consciousness
to correspond with its Secretary.

International Society for Krishna Consciousness
3764 Watseka Avenue
Los Angeles, California 90034

First Printing, 1977: 20,000 copies

Library of Congress Cataloging in Publication Data (Revised)

Puranas. Bhāgavatapurāna.
Śrīmad-Bhāgavatam.

Includes bibliographical references and indexes.
CONTENTS: Canto 1. Creation. 3 v.—Canto 2. The cosmic manifestation. 2 v.—Canto 3. The status quo. 4 v.—Canto 4. The creation of the Fourth Order. 4 v.—Canto 5. The creative impetus. 2 v.
1. Chaitanya, 1486-1534. I. Bhaktivedanta Swami, A. C., 1896- II. Title.
BL1135.P7A22 1972 73-169353
ISBN 0-912776-95-1

ALL GLORY TO ŚRĪ GURU AND GAURĀṄGA

ŚRĪMAD BHĀGAVATAM

of

KṚṢṆA-DVAIPĀYANA VYĀSA

अथेशमायारचितेषु सङ्गं
गुणेषु गन्धर्वपुरोपमेषु ।
रूढं प्रकृत्यात्मनि विश्वकर्तु-
र्भावेन हित्वा तमहं प्रपद्ये ॥

atheśa-māyā-raciteṣu saṅgaṁ
guṇeṣu gandharva-puropameṣu
rūḍhaṁ prakṛtyātmani viśva-kartur
bhāvena hitvā tam ahaṁ prapadye

(p. 42)

BOOKS by
His Divine Grace A. C. Bhaktivedanta Swami Prabhupāda

Bhagavad-gītā As It Is
Śrīmad-Bhāgavatam, Cantos 1–9 (27 Vols.)
Śrī Caitanya-caritāmṛta (17 Vols.)
Teachings of Lord Caitanya
The Nectar of Devotion
The Nectar of Instruction
Śrī Īśopaniṣad
Easy Journey to Other Planets
Kṛṣṇa Consciousness: The Topmost Yoga System
Kṛṣṇa, the Supreme Personality of Godhead (3 Vols.)
Perfect Questions, Perfect Answers
Dialectic Spiritualism—A Vedic View of Western Philosophy
Transcendental Teachings of Prahlād Mahārāja
Kṛṣṇa, the Reservoir of Pleasure
Life Comes from Life
The Perfection of Yoga
Beyond Birth and Death
On the Way to Kṛṣṇa
Geetār-gan (Bengali)
Rāja-vidyā: The King of Knowledge
Elevation to Kṛṣṇa Consciousness
Kṛṣṇa Consciousness: The Matchless Gift
Back to Godhead Magazine (Founder)

A complete catalog is available upon request

The Bhaktivedanta Book Trust
3764 Watseka Avenue
Los Angeles, California 90034

Table of Contents

CHAPTER FIFTEEN
Paraśurāma, the Lord's Warrior Incarnation

CHAPTER SIXTEEN
Lord Paraśurāma Destroys the World's Ruling Class

Preface

We must know the present need of human society. And what is that need? Human society is no longer bounded by geographical limits to particular countries or communities. Human society is broader than in the Middle Ages, and the world tendency is toward one state or one human society. The ideals of spiritual communism, according to *Śrīmad-Bhāgavatam*, are based more or less on the oneness of the entire human society, nay, of the entire energy of living beings. The need is felt by great thinkers to make this a successful ideology. *Śrīmad-Bhāgavatam* will fill this need in human society. It begins, therefore, with the aphorism of Vedānta philosophy *janmādy asya yataḥ* to establish the ideal of a common cause.

Human society, at the present moment, is not in the darkness of oblivion. It has made rapid progress in the field of material comforts, education and economic development throughout the entire world. But there is a pinprick somewhere in the social body at large, and therefore there are large-scale quarrels, even over less important issues. There is need of a clue as to how humanity can become one in peace, friendship and prosperity with a common cause. *Śrīmad-Bhāgavatam* will fill this need, for it is a cultural presentation for the re-spiritualization of the entire human society.

Śrīmad-Bhāgavatam should be introduced also in the schools and colleges, for it is recommended by the great student-devotee Prahlāda Mahārāja in order to change the demoniac face of society.

kaumāra ācaret prājño
dharmān bhāgavatān iha
durlabhaṁ mānuṣaṁ janma
tad apy adhruvam arthadam
(*Bhāg.* 7.6.1)

Disparity in human society is due to lack of principles in a godless civilization. There is God, or the Almighty One, from whom everything emanates, by whom everything is maintained and in whom everything is merged to rest. Material science has tried to find the ultimate source of creation very insufficiently, but it is a fact that there is one ultimate source of everything that be. This ultimate source is explained rationally and authoritatively in the beautiful *Bhāgavatam* or *Śrīmad-Bhāgavatam.*

Śrīmad-Bhāgavatam is the transcendental science not only for knowing the ultimate source of everything but also for knowing our relation with Him and our duty towards perfection of the human society on the basis of this perfect knowledge. It is powerful reading matter in the Sanskrit language, and it is now rendered into English elaborately so that simply by a careful reading one will know God perfectly well, so much so that the reader will be sufficiently educated to defend himself from the onslaught of atheists. Over and above this, the reader will be able to convert others to accepting God as a concrete principle.

Śrīmad-Bhāgavatam begins with the definition of the ultimate source. It is a bona fide commentary on the *Vedānta-sūtra* by the same author, Śrīla Vyāsadeva, and gradually it develops into nine cantos up to the highest state of God realization. The only qualification one needs to study this great book of transcendental knowledge is to proceed step by step cautiously and not jump forward haphazardly like with an ordinary book. It should be gone through chapter by chapter, one after another. The reading matter is so arranged with its original Sanskrit text, its English transliteration, synonyms, translation and purports so that one is sure to become a God-realized soul at the end of finishing the first nine cantos.

The Tenth Canto is distinct from the first nine cantos because it deals directly with the transcendental activities of the Personality of Godhead Śrī Kṛṣṇa. One will be unable to capture the effects of the Tenth Canto without going through the first nine cantos. The book is complete in twelve cantos, each independent, but it is good for all to read them in small installments one after another.

I must admit my frailties in presenting *Śrīmad-Bhāgavatam*, but still I am hopeful of its good reception by the thinkers and leaders of society on the strength of the following statement of *Śrīmad-Bhāgavatam* (1.5.11):

tad-vāg-visargo janatāgha-viplavo
yasmin prati-ślokam abaddhavaty api

nāmāny anantasya yaśo 'ṅkitāni yac
chṛṇvanti gāyanti gṛṇanti sādhavaḥ

"On the other hand, that literature which is full with descriptions of the transcendental glories of the name, fame, form and pastimes of the unlimited Supreme Lord is a transcendental creation meant to bring about a revolution in the impious life of a misdirected civilization. Such transcendental literatures, even though irregularly composed, are heard, sung and accepted by purified men who are thoroughly honest."

Oṁ tat sat

A. C. Bhaktivedanta Swami

Introduction

"This *Bhāgavata Purāṇa* is as brilliant as the sun, and it has arisen just after the departure of Lord Kṛṣṇa to His own abode, accompanied by religion, knowledge, etc. Persons who have lost their vision due to the dense darkness of ignorance in the age of Kali shall get light from this *Purāṇa.*" (*Śrīmad-Bhāgavatam* 1.3.43)

The timeless wisdom of India is expressed in the *Vedas*, ancient Sanskrit texts that touch upon all fields of human knowledge. Originally preserved through oral tradition, the *Vedas* were first put into writing five thousand years ago by Śrīla Vyāsadeva, the "literary incarnation of God." After compiling the *Vedas*, Vyāsadeva set forth their essence in the aphorisms known as *Vedānta-sūtras. Śrīmad-Bhāgavatam* is Vyāsadeva's commentary on his own *Vedānta-sūtras.* It was written in the maturity of his spiritual life under the direction of Nārada Muni, his spiritual master. Referred to as "the ripened fruit of the tree of Vedic literature," *Śrīmad-Bhāgavatam* is the most complete and authoritative exposition of Vedic knowledge.

After compiling the *Bhāgavatam*, Vyāsa impressed the synopsis of it upon his son, the sage Śukadeva Gosvāmī. Śukadeva Gosvāmī subsequently recited the entire *Bhāgavatam* to Mahārāja Parīkṣit in an assembly of learned saints on the bank of the Ganges at Hastināpura (now Delhi). Mahārāja Parīkṣit was the emperor of the world and was a great *rājarṣi* (saintly king). Having received a warning that he would die within a week, he renounced his entire kingdom and retired to the bank of the Ganges to fast until death and receive spiritual enlightenment. The *Bhāgavatam* begins with Emperor Parīkṣit's sober inquiry to Śukadeva Gosvāmī: "You are the spiritual master of great saints and devotees. I am therefore begging you to show the way of perfection for all persons, and especially for one who is about to die. Please let me know what a man should hear, chant, remember and worship, and also what he should not do. Please explain all this to me."

Śukadeva Gosvāmī's answer to this question, and numerous other questions posed by Mahārāja Parīkṣit, concerning everything from the nature of the self to the origin of the universe, held the assembled sages in rapt attention continuously for the seven days leading to the King's death. The sage Sūta Gosvāmī, who was present on the bank of the Ganges when Śukadeva Gosvāmī first recited *Śrīmad-Bhāgavatam*, later repeated the *Bhāgavatam* before a gathering of sages in the forest of Naimiṣāraṇya. Those sages, concerned about the spiritual welfare of the people in general, had gathered to perform a long, continuous chain of sacrifices to counteract the degrading influence of the incipient age of Kali. In response to the sages' request that he speak the essence of Vedic wisdom, Sūta Gosvāmī repeated from memory the entire eighteen thousand verses of *Śrīmad-Bhāgavatam*, as spoken by Śukadeva Gosvāmī to Mahārāja Parīkṣit.

The reader of *Śrīmad-Bhāgavatam* hears Sūta Gosvāmī relate the questions of Mahārāja Parīkṣit and the answers of Śukadeva Gosvāmī. Also, Sūta Gosvāmī sometimes responds directly to questions put by Śaunaka Ṛṣi, the spokesman for the sages gathered at Naimiṣāraṇya. One therefore simultaneously hears two dialogues: one between Mahārāja Parīkṣit and Śukadeva Gosvāmī on the bank of the Ganges, and another at Naimiṣāraṇya between Sūta Gosvāmī and the sages at Naimiṣāraṇya Forest, headed by Śaunaka Ṛṣi. Furthermore, while instructing King Parīkṣit, Śukadeva Gosvāmī often relates historical episodes and gives accounts of lengthy philosophical discussions between such great souls as the saint Maitreya and his disciple Vidura. With this understanding of the history of the *Bhāgavatam*, the reader will easily be able to follow its intermingling of dialogues and events from various sources. Since philosophical wisdom, not chronological order, is most important in the text, one need only be attentive to the subject matter of *Śrīmad-Bhāgavatam* to appreciate fully its profound message.

The translator of this edition compares the *Bhāgavatam* to sugar candy—wherever you taste it, you will find it equally sweet and relishable. Therefore, to taste the sweetness of the *Bhāgavatam*, one may begin by reading any of its volumes. After such an introductory taste, however, the serious reader is best advised to go back to Volume One of the First Canto and then proceed through the *Bhāgavatam*, volume after volume, in its natural order.

This edition of the *Bhāgavatam* is the first complete English translation of this important text with an elaborate commentary, and it is the first widely available to the English-speaking public. It is the product of the scholarly and devotional effort of His Divine Grace A. C. Bhaktivedanta Swami Prabhupāda, the world's most distinguished teacher of Indian religious and philosophical thought. His consummate Sanskrit scholarship and intimate familiarity with Vedic culture and thought as well as the modern way of life combine to reveal to the West a magnificent exposition of this important classic.

Readers will find this work of value for many reasons. For those interested in the classical roots of Indian civilization, it serves as a vast reservoir of detailed information on virtually every one of its aspects. For students of comparative philosophy and religion, the *Bhāgavatam* offers a penetrating view into the meaning of India's profound spiritual heritage. To sociologists and anthropologists, the *Bhāgavatam* reveals the practical workings of a peaceful and scientifically organized Vedic culture, whose institutions were integrated on the basis of a highly developed spiritual world view. Students of literature will discover the *Bhāgavatam* to be a masterpiece of majestic poetry. For students of psychology, the text provides important perspectives on the nature of consciousness, human behavior and the philosophical study of identity. Finally, to those seeking spiritual insight, the *Bhāgavatam* offers simple and practical guidance for attainment of the highest self-knowledge and realization of the Absolute Truth. The entire multivolume text, presented by the Bhaktivedanta Book Trust, promises to occupy a significant place in the intellectual, cultural and spiritual life of modern man for a long time to come.

—The Publishers

His Divine Grace
A. C. Bhaktivedanta Swami Prabhupāda
Founder-Ācārya of the International Society for Krishna Consciousness

PLATE ONE

By performing very severe austerities, King Bhagīratha received the benediction from mother Ganges that she would descend to the earth planet. But she was afraid that her forceful waters would pierce the surface of the earth and continue down to the lower planetary system. King Bhagīratha reassured her: "Like a cloth woven of threads extending for its length and breadth, this entire universe, in all its latitude and longitude, is situated under different potencies of the Supreme Personality of Godhead. Lord Śiva is the incarnation of the Lord, and thus he represents the Supersoul in the embodied soul. He can sustain your forceful waves on his head." After saying this, King Bhagīratha performed further austerities and very quickly satisfied Lord Śiva. Thus, when the King approached Lord Śiva and requested him to sustain the forceful waves of the Ganges, Lord Śiva accepted the proposal, saying, "Let it be so." Then, with great attention, Śiva sustained on his head the torrent of Ganges water, which is purifying, having emanated from the toes of Lord Viṣṇu. *(pp. 3–11)*

PLATE TWO

Being prayed for by the demigods, the Supreme Personality of Godhead, the Absolute Truth Himself, directly appeared with His expansion and expansions of the expansion. Their holy names were Rāma, Lakṣmaṇa, Bharata and Śatrughna. These celebrated incarnations thus appeared in four forms as the sons of Mahārāja Daśaratha. Carrying out the order of His father, who was bound by a promise to his wife, Lord Rāmacandra left behind His kingdom, opulence, friends, well-wishers, residents and everything else and went to the forest with His wife, mother Sītā, and His younger brother Lord Lakṣmaṇa. Carrying His invincible bow and arrows in His hand, Lord Rāma wandered throughout the forest for fourteen years, accepting a life of hardship. *(pp. 49–50)*

PLATE THREE

In the assembly where mother Sītā was to choose her husband, in the midst of the heroes of this world, Lord Rāmacandra broke the bow belonging to Lord Śiva. This bow was so heavy that it was carried by three hundred men, but the Lord bent it, strung it and broke it in the middle, just as a baby elephant breaks a stick of sugar cane. Thus the Lord achieved the hand of mother Sītā, who was endowed with transcendental qualities of form, beauty, behavior, age and nature. *(p. 55)*

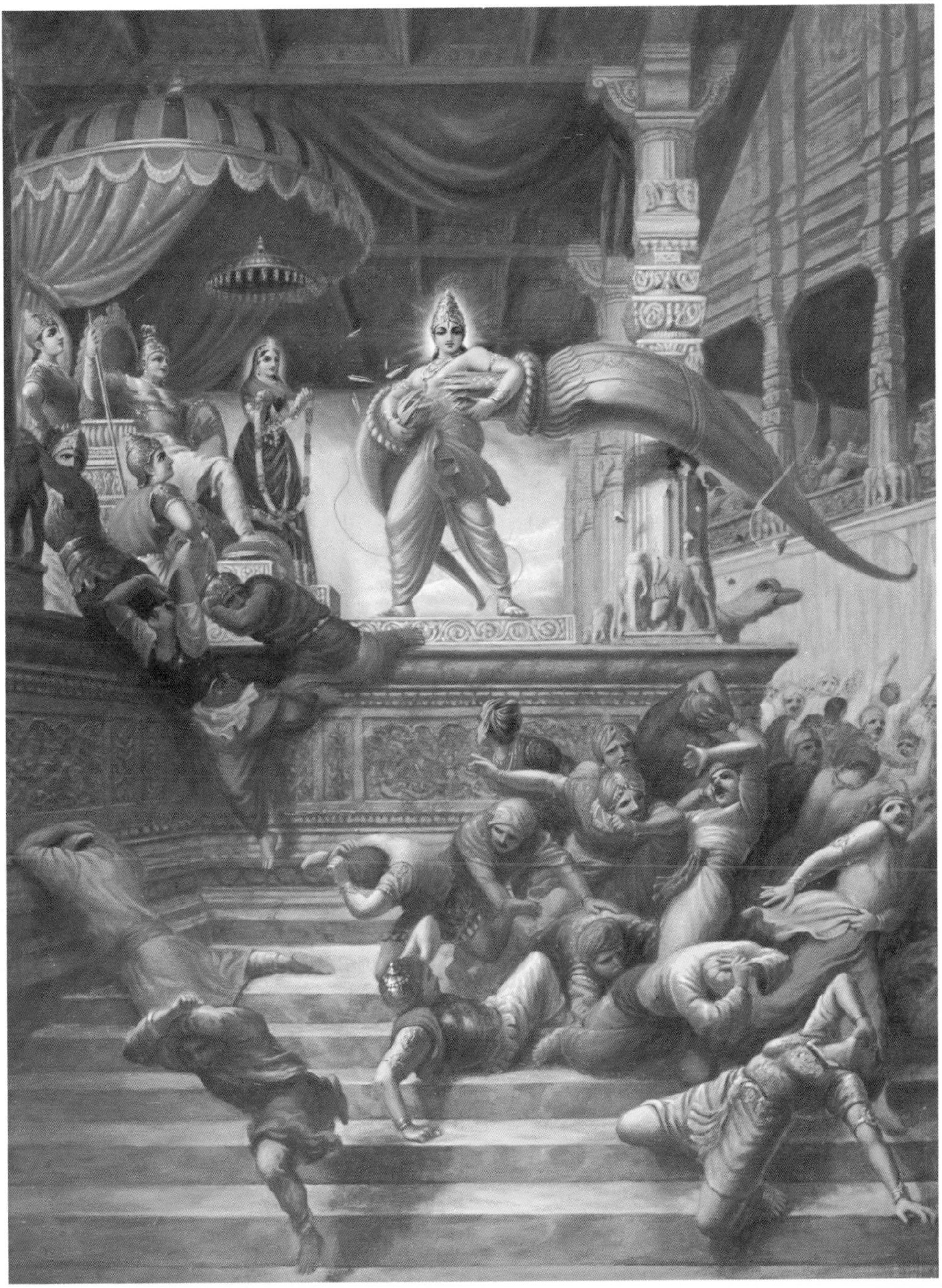

PLATE FOUR

The Personality of Godhead, Lord Rāmacandra, being aggrieved for His kidnapped wife, Sītā, glanced over the city of Rāvaṇa with red-hot eyes. Then the great ocean, trembling in fear, gave Him His way, because its family members, the aquatics like the sharks, snakes and crocodiles, were being burned. The personified ocean said, "O great hero, although my water presents no impediment to Your going to Laṅkā, please construct a bridge over it to spread Your transcendental fame. Upon seeing this wonderfully uncommon deed of Your Lordship, all the great heroes and kings in the future will glorify You." Thereupon the Lord had His faithful monkey servants, like Hanumān and Sugrīva, hurl huge boulders into the sea, and, by the Lord's supreme potency, they floated on the water, forming a bridge to Laṅkā. *(pp. 63–68)*

PLATE FIVE

After killing the demon Rāvaṇa and rescuing mother Sītā, Lord Rāmacandra returned to His capital, Ayodhyā. He was greeted on the road by the princely order, who showered His body with beautiful, fragrant flowers, while great personalities like Brahmā and other demigods glorified His activities in great jubilation. When the Lord's brother Bharata understood that Lord Rāmacandra was returning to Ayodhyā, He immediately took upon His own head Lord Rāmacandra's wooden shoes and came out from His camp at Nandigrāma. Lord Bharata was accompanied by ministers, priests and other respectable citizens, by professional musicians vibrating pleasing musical sounds, and by learned *brāhmaṇas* loudly chanting Vedic hymns. Following in the procession were chariots drawn by beautiful horses with harnesses of golden rope. These chariots were decorated by flags with golden embroidery and by other flags of various sizes and patterns. There were soldiers bedecked with golden armor, servants bearing betel nut, and many well-known and beautiful prostitutes. Many servants followed on foot, bearing an umbrella, wisks, different grades of precious jewels, and other paraphernalia befitting a royal reception. Accompanied in this way, Lord Bharata, His heart softened in ecstasy and His eyes full of tears, approached Lord Rāmacandra and fell at His lotus feet in great ecstatic love. *(p. 87)*

PLATE SIX

Lord Rāmacandra's ancestral palace, which He occupied with His consort, Sītādevī, was full of various treasures and valuable wardrobes. The sitting places on the two sides of the entrance door were made of coral, the yards were surrounded by pillars of *vaidūrya-maṇi*, the floor was made of highly polished emeralds, and the foundation was made of marble. The entire palace was decorated with flags and garlands and bedecked with valuable stones, shining with a celestial effulgence. In addition, the palace was fully decorated with pearls and surrounded by lamps and incense. Sitting upon a magnificent throne, Lord Rāmacandra would receive the citizens of Ayodhyā. Not having seen the Lord for a very long time, they would eagerly approach Him with the paraphernalia of worship and pray: "O Lord, as You have rescued the earth from the bottom of the sea in Your incarnation as a boar, may You now maintain it. Thus we beg Your blessings." *(pp. 131–133)*

PLATE SEVEN

Upon seeing Lord Paraśurāma, Kārtavīryārjuna immediately feared him and sent many elephants, chariots and horses, along with nearly two million soldiers equipped with clubs, swords, arrows and many other weapons to fight against him. But Lord Paraśurāma killed all of them. Being expert in killing the enemy, the Lord worked with the speed of the mind and wind, slashing his enemies with his chopper. Wherever he went, the enemies fell, their legs, arms and shoulders being severed, their chariot drivers killed, and their carriers, the elephants and horses, all annihilated. By manipulating his axe and arrows, Lord Paraśurāma cut to pieces the shields, flags, bows and bodies of Kārtavīryārjuna's soldiers, who fell on the battlefield, muddying the ground with their blood. *(pp. 236–239)*

The site of Ayodhyā, the capital of the kingdom of Lord Rāmacandra. *(Chapter 10)*

CHAPTER NINE

The Dynasty of Aṁśumān

This chapter describes the history of the dynasty of Aṁśumān, up to Khaṭvāṅga, and it also describes how Bhagīratha brought the water of the Ganges to this earth.

The son of Mahārāja Aṁśumān was Dilīpa, who tried to bring the Ganges to this world but who died without success. Bhagīratha, the son of Dilīpa, was determined to bring the Ganges to the material world, and for this purpose he underwent severe austerities. Mother Ganges, being fully satisfied by his austerities, made herself visible to him, wanting to give him a benediction. Bhagīratha then asked her to deliver his forefathers. Although mother Ganges agreed to come down to earth, she made two conditions: first, she wanted some suitable male to be able to control her waves; second, although all sinful men would be freed from sinful reactions by bathing in the Ganges, mother Ganges did not want to keep all these sinful reactions. These two conditions were subject matters for consideration. Bhagīratha replied to mother Ganges, "The Personality of Godhead Lord Śiva will be completely able to control the waves of your water, and when pure devotees bathe in your water, the sinful reactions left by sinful men will be counteracted." Bhagīratha then performed austerities to satisfy Lord Śiva, who is called Āśutoṣa because he is naturally satisfied very easily. Lord Śiva agreed to Bhagīratha's proposal to check the force of the Ganges. In this way, simply by the touch of the Ganges, Bhagīratha's forefathers were delivered and allowed to go to the heavenly planets.

The son of Bhagīratha was Śruta, the son of Śruta was Nābha, and Nābha's son was Sindhudvīpa. The son of Sindhudvīpa was Ayutāyu, and the son of Ayutāyu was Ṛtūparṇa, who was a friend of Nala. Ṛtūparṇa gave Nala the art of gambling and learned from him the art of *aśva-vidyā.* The son of Ṛtūparṇa was known as Sarvakāma, the son of Sarvakāma was Sudāsa, and his son was Saudāsa. The wife of Saudāsa was named Damayantī or Madayantī, and Saudāsa was also known as

Kalmāṣapāda. Because of some defect in his fruitive activities, Saudāsa was cursed by Vasiṣṭha to become a Rākṣasa. While walking through the forest, he saw a *brāhmaṇa* engaged in sex with his wife, and because he had become a Rākṣasa he wanted to devour the *brāhmaṇa.* Although the *brāhmaṇa's* wife pleaded with him in many ways, Saudāsa devoured the *brāhmaṇa,* and the wife therefore cursed him, saying, "As soon as you engage in sex you will die." After twelve years, therefore, even though Saudāsa was released from the curse of Vasiṣṭha Muni, he remained sonless. At that time, with Saudāsa's permission, Vasiṣṭha impregnated Saudāsa's wife, Madayantī. Because Madayantī bore the child for many years but still could not give birth, Vasiṣṭha struck her abdomen with a stone, and thus a son was born. The son was named Aśmaka.

The son of Aśmaka was known as Bālika. He was protected from the curse of Paraśurāma because of being surrounded by many women, and therefore he is also known as Nārīkavaca. When the entire world was devoid of *kṣatriyas,* he became the original father of more *kṣatriyas.* He is therefore sometimes called Mūlaka. From Bālika, Daśaratha was born, from Daśaratha came Aiḍaviḍi, and from Aiḍaviḍi came Viśvasaha. The son of Viśvasaha was Mahārāja Khaṭvāṅga. Mahārāja Khaṭvāṅga joined the demigods in fighting the demons and was victorious, and the demigods therefore wanted to give him a benediction. But when the King inquired how long he would live and understood that his life would last only a few seconds more, he immediately left the heavenly planets and returned to his own abode by airplane. He could understand that everything in this material world is insignificant, and thus he fully engaged in worshiping the Supreme Personality of Godhead, Hari.

TEXT 1

श्रीशुक उवाच

अंशुमांश्च तपस्तेपे गङ्गानयनकाम्यया ।
कालं महान्तं नाशक्नोत् ततः कालेन संस्थितः ॥ १ ॥

śrī-śuka uvāca
aṁśumāṁś ca tapas tepe
gaṅgānayana-kāmyayā

kālaṁ mahāntaṁ nāśaknot
tataḥ kālena saṁsthitaḥ

śrī-śukaḥ uvāca—Śrī Śukadeva Gosvāmī said; *aṁśumān*—the king named Aṁśumān; *ca*—also; *tapaḥ tepe*—executed austerity; *gaṅgā*—the Ganges; *ānayana-kāmyayā*—with a desire to bring the Ganges to this material world to deliver his forefathers; *kālam*—time; *mahāntam*—for a long duration; *na*—not; *aśaknot*—was successful; *tataḥ*—thereafter; *kālena*—in due course of time; *saṁsthitaḥ*—died.

TRANSLATION

Śukadeva Gosvāmī continued: King Aṁśumān, like his grandfather, performed austerities for a very long time. Nonetheless, he could not bring the Ganges to this material world, and thereafter, in due course of time, he died.

TEXT 2

दिलीपस्तत्सुतस्तद्वदशक्तः कालमेयिवान् ।
भगीरथस्तस्य सुतस्तेपे स सुमहत् तपः ॥ २ ॥

dilīpas tat-sutas tadvad
aśaktaḥ kālam eyivān
bhagīrathas tasya sutas
tepe sa sumahat tapaḥ

dilīpaḥ—named Dilīpa; *tat-sutaḥ*—the son of Aṁśumān; *tat-vat*—like his father; *aśaktaḥ*—being unable to bring the Ganges to the material world; *kālam eyivān*—became a victim of time and died; *bhagīrathaḥ tasya sutaḥ*—his son Bhagīratha; *tepe*—executed penance; *saḥ*—he; *su-mahat*—very great; *tapaḥ*—austerity.

TRANSLATION

Like Aṁśumān himself, Dilīpa, his son, was unable to bring the Ganges to this material world, and he also became a victim of death in due course of time. Then Dilīpa's son, Bhagīratha, performed very severe austerities to bring the Ganges to this material world.

TEXT 3

दर्शयामास तं देवी प्रसन्ना वरदास्मि ते ।
इत्युक्तः स्वमभिप्रायं शशंसावनतो नृपः ॥ ३ ॥

darśayām āsa taṁ devī
prasannā varadāsmi te
ity uktaḥ svam abhiprāyaṁ
śaśaṁsāvanato nṛpaḥ

darśayām āsa—appeared; *tam*—unto him, King Bhagīratha; *devī*—mother Ganges; *prasannā*—being very much satisfied; *varadā asmi*—I shall bless with my benediction; *te*—unto you; *iti uktaḥ*—thus being addressed; *svam*—his own; *abhiprāyam*—desire; *śaśaṁsa*—explained; *avanataḥ*—very respectfully bowing down; *nṛpaḥ*—the King (Bhagīratha).

TRANSLATION

Thereafter, mother Ganges appeared before King Bhagīratha and said, "I am very much satisfied with your austerities and am now prepared to give you benedictions as you desire." Being thus addressed by Gaṅgādevī, mother Ganges, the King bowed his head before her and explained his desire.

PURPORT

The King's desire was to deliver his forefathers, who had been burnt to ashes because of disrespecting Kapila Muni.

TEXT 4

कोऽपि धारयिता वेगं पतन्त्या मे महीतले ।
अन्यथा भूतलं भित्त्वा नृप यास्ये रसातलम् ॥ ४ ॥

ko 'pi dhārayitā vegaṁ
patantyā me mahī-tale
anyathā bhū-talaṁ bhittvā
nṛpa yāsye rasātalam

kaḥ—who is that person; *api*—indeed; *dhārayitā*—who can sustain; *vegam*—the force of the waves; *patantyāḥ*—while falling down; *me*—of me; *mahī-tale*—upon this earth; *anyathā*—otherwise; *bhū-talam*—the surface of the earth; *bhittvā*—piercing; *nṛpa*—O King; *yāsye*—I shall go down; *rasātalam*—to Pātāla, the lower part of the universe.

TRANSLATION

Mother Ganges replied: When I fall from the sky to the surface of the planet earth, the water will certainly be very forceful. Who will sustain that force? If I am not sustained, I shall pierce the surface of the earth and go down to Rasātala, the Pātāla area of the universe.

TEXT 5

किं चाहं न भुवं यास्ये नरा मय्यामृजन्त्यघम् ।
मृजामि तदघं क्वाहं राजंस्तत्र विचिन्त्यताम् ॥ ५ ॥

kiṁ cāham na bhuvaṁ yāsye
narā mayy āmṛjanty agham
mṛjāmi tad aghaṁ kvāhaṁ
rājaṁs tatra vicintyatām

kim ca—also; *aham*—I; *na*—not; *bhuvam*—to the planet earth; *yāsye*—shall go; *narāḥ*—the people in general; *mayi*—in me, in my water; *āmṛjanti*—cleanse; *agham*—the reactions of their sinful activity; *mṛjāmi*—I shall wash; *tat*—that; *agham*—accumulation of sinful reactions; *kva*—unto whom; *aham*—I; *rājan*—O King; *tatra*—on this fact; *vicintyatām*—please consider carefully and decide.

TRANSLATION

O King, I do not wish to go down to the planet earth, for there the people in general will bathe in my water to cleanse themselves of the reactions of their sinful deeds. When all these sinful reactions accumulate in me, how shall I become free from them? You must consider this very carefully.

PURPORT

The Supreme Personality of Godhead says:

sarva-dharmān parityajya
mām ekaṁ śaraṇaṁ vraja
ahaṁ tvāṁ sarva-pāpebhyo
mokṣayiṣyāmi mā śucaḥ

"Abandon all varieties of religion and just surrender unto Me. I shall deliver you from all sinful reaction. Do not fear." (Bg. 18.66) The Supreme Personality of Godhead can accept the reactions of anyone's sinful deeds and neutralize them because He is *pavitra*, pure, like the sun, which is never contaminated by any worldly infection. *Tejīyasāṁ na doṣāya vahneḥ sarva-bhujo yathā* (*Bhāg.* 10.33.29). One who is very powerful is not affected by any sinful activity. But here we see that mother Ganges fears being burdened with the sins of the people in general who would bathe in her waters. This indicates that no one but the Supreme Personality of Godhead is able to neutralize the reactions of sinful deeds, whether one's own or those of others. Sometimes the spiritual master, after accepting a disciple, must take charge of that disciple's past sinful activities and, being overloaded, must sometimes suffer—if not fully, then partially—for the sinful acts of the disciple. Every disciple, therefore, must be very careful not to commit sinful activities after initiation. The poor spiritual master is kind and merciful enough to accept a disciple and partially suffer for that disciple's sinful activities, but Kṛṣṇa, being merciful to His servant, neutralizes the reactions of sinful deeds for the servant who engages in preaching His glories. Even mother Ganges feared the sinful reactions of the people in general and was anxious about how she would counteract the burden of these sins.

TEXT 6

श्रीभगीरथ उवाच
साधवो न्यासिनः शान्ता ब्रह्मिष्ठा लोकपावनाः ।
हरन्त्यघं तेऽङ्गसङ्गात् तेष्वास्ते ह्यघभिद्धरिः ॥ ६ ॥

śrī-bhagīratha uvāca
sādhavo nyāsinaḥ śāntā
brahmiṣṭhā loka-pāvanāḥ
haranty aghaṁ te 'ṅga-saṅgāt
teṣv āste hy agha-bhid dhariḥ

śrī-bhagīrathaḥ uvāca—Bhagīratha said; *sādhavaḥ*—saintly persons; *nyāsinaḥ*—*sannyāsīs; śāntāḥ*—peaceful, free from material disturbances; *brahmiṣṭhāḥ*—expert in following the regulative principles of Vedic scripture; *loka-pāvanāḥ*—who are engaged in delivering the entire world from a fallen condition; *haranti*—shall remove; *agham*—the reactions of sinful life; *te*—of you (mother Ganges); *aṅga-saṅgāt*—by bathing in the Ganges water; *teṣu*—within themselves; *āste*—there is; *hi*—indeed; *agha-bhit*—the Supreme Personality, who can vanquish all sinful activities; *hariḥ*—the Lord.

TRANSLATION

Bhagīratha said: Those who are saintly because of devotional service and are therefore in the renounced order, free from material desires, and who are pure devotees, expert in following the regulative principles mentioned in the Vedas, are always glorious and pure in behavior and are able to deliver all fallen souls. When such pure devotees bathe in your water, the sinful reactions accumulated from other people will certainly be counteracted, for such devotees always keep in the core of their hearts the Supreme Personality of Godhead, who can vanquish all sinful reactions.

PURPORT

Mother Ganges is available to everyone for bathing. Therefore, not only will sinful persons bathe in the Ganges water, but in Hardwar and other holy places where the Ganges flows, saintly persons and devotees will also bathe in the waters of the Ganges. Devotees and saintly persons advanced in the renounced order can deliver even the Ganges. *Tīrthī-kurvanti tīrthāni svāntaḥ-sthena gadābhṛtā* (*Bhāg.* 1.13.10). Because saintly devotees always keep the Lord within the core of their hearts, they can perfectly cleanse the holy places of all sinful reactions.

Therefore, people in general must always respectfully honor saintly persons. It is ordered that as soon as one sees a Vaiṣṇava, or even a *sannyāsī*, one should immediately offer respects to such a holy man. If one forgets to show respect in this way, one must observe a fast for that day. This is a Vedic injunction. One must be extremely careful to refrain from committing offenses at the lotus feet of a devotee or saintly person.

There are methods of *prāyaścitta*, or atonement, but they are inadequate to cleanse one of sinful reactions. One can be cleansed of sinful reactions only by devotional service, as stated in regard to the history of Ajāmila:

kecit kevalayā bhaktyā
vāsudeva-parāyaṇāḥ
aghaṁ dhunvanti kārtsnyena
nīhāram iva bhāskaraḥ

"Only a rare person who has adopted complete, unalloyed devotional service to Kṛṣṇa can uproot the weeds of sinful actions with no possibility that they will revive. He can do this simply by discharging devotional service, just as the sun can immediately dissipate fog by its rays." (*Bhāg.* 6.1.15) If one is under the protection of a devotee and sincerely renders service unto him, by this process of *bhakti-yoga* one is certainly able to counteract all sinful reactions.

TEXT 7

धारयिष्यति ते वेगं रुद्रस्त्वात्मा शरीरिणाम् ।
यस्मिन्नोतमिदं प्रोतं विश्वं शाटीव तन्तुषु ॥ ७ ॥

dhārayiṣyati te vegaṁ
rudras tv ātmā śarīriṇām
yasminn otam idaṁ protaṁ
viśvaṁ śāṭīva tantuṣu

dhārayiṣyati—will sustain; *te*—your; *vegam*—force of the waves; *rudraḥ*—Lord Śiva; *tu*—indeed; *ātmā*—the Supersoul; *śarīriṇām*—of all embodied souls; *yasmin*—in whom; *otam*—is situated in its longitude; *idam*—this whole universe; *protam*—latitude; *viśvam*—the whole universe; *śāṭī*—a cloth; *iva*—as; *tantuṣu*—in threads.

TRANSLATION

Like a cloth woven of threads extending for its length and breadth, this entire universe, in all its latitude and longitude, is situated under different potencies of the Supreme Personality of Godhead. Lord Śiva is the incarnation of the Lord, and thus he represents the Supersoul in the embodied soul. He can sustain your forceful waves on his head.

PURPORT

The water of the Ganges is supposed to rest on the head of Lord Śiva. Lord Śiva is an incarnation of the Supreme Personality of Godhead, who sustains the entire universe by different potencies. Lord Śiva is described in the *Brahma-saṁhitā* (5.45):

kṣīraṁ yathā dadhi vikāra-viśeṣa-yogāt
sañjāyate na hi tataḥ pṛthag asti hetoḥ
yaḥ śambhutām api tathā samupaiti kāryād
govindam ādi-puruṣaṁ tam ahaṁ bhajāmi

"Milk changes into yogurt when mixed with a yogurt culture, but actually yogurt is constitutionally nothing but milk. Similarly, Govinda, the Supreme Personality of Godhead, assumes the form of Lord Śiva for the special purpose of material transactions. I offer my obeisances at Lord Govinda's lotus feet." Lord Śiva is the Supreme Personality of Godhead in the same sense that yogurt is also milk although at the same time it is not milk. For the maintenance of the material world there are three incarnations—Brahmā, Viṣṇu and Maheśvara (Lord Śiva). Lord Śiva is Viṣṇu in an incarnation for the mode of ignorance. The material world exists predominantly in the mode of ignorance. Therefore Lord Śiva is compared here to the longitude and latitude of the entire universe, which resembles a cloth woven of threads extending for both its length and breadth.

TEXT 8

इत्युक्त्वा स नृपो देवं तपसातोषयच्छिवम् ।
कालेनाल्पीयसा राजंस्तस्येशश्चाश्वतुष्यत ॥ ८ ॥

ity uktvā sa nṛpo devaṁ
tapasātoṣayac chivam
kālenālpīyasā rājaṁs
tasyeśaś cāśv atuṣyata

iti uktvā—after saying this; *saḥ*—he; *nṛpaḥ*—the King (Bhagīratha); *devam*—unto Lord Śiva; *tapasā*—by executing austerities; *atoṣayat*—pleased; *śivam*—Lord Śiva, the all-auspicious; *kālena*—by time; *alpīyasā*—which was not very long; *rājan*—O King; *tasya*—upon him (Bhagīratha); *īśaḥ*—Lord Śiva; *ca*—indeed; *āśu*—very soon; *atuṣyata*—became satisfied.

TRANSLATION

After saying this, Bhagīratha satisfied Lord Śiva by performing austerities. O King Parīkṣit, Lord Śiva was very quickly satisfied with Bhagīratha.

PURPORT

The words *āśv atuṣyata* indicate that Lord Śiva was satisfied very soon. Therefore another name for Lord Śiva is Āśutoṣa. Materialistic persons become attached to Lord Śiva because Lord Śiva bestows benedictions upon anyone and everyone very quickly, not caring to know how his devotees prosper or suffer. Although materialistic persons know that material happiness is nothing but another side of suffering, they want it, and to get it very quickly they worship Lord Śiva. We find that materialists are generally devotees of many demigods, especially Lord Śiva and mother Durgā. They do not actually want spiritual happiness, for it is almost unknown to them. But if one is serious about being happy spiritually, he must take shelter of Lord Viṣṇu, as the Lord personally demands:

sarva-dharmān parityajya
mām ekaṁ śaraṇaṁ vraja

ahaṁ tvāṁ sarva-pāpebhyo
mokṣayiṣyāmi mā śucaḥ

"Abandon all varieties of religion and just surrender unto Me. I shall deliver you from all sinful reaction. Do not fear." (Bg. 18.66)

TEXT 9

तथेति राज्ञाभिहितं सर्वलोकहितः शिवः ।
दधारावहितो गङ्गां पादपूतजलां हरेः ॥ ९ ॥

tatheti rājñābhihitaṁ
sarva-loka-hitaḥ śivaḥ
dadhārāvahito gaṅgāṁ
pāda-pūta-jalāṁ hareḥ

tathā—(let it be) so; *iti*—thus; *rājñā abhihitam*—having been addressed by the King (Bhagīratha); *sarva-loka-hitaḥ*—the Personality of Godhead, who is always auspicious to everyone; *śivaḥ*—Lord Śiva; *dadhāra*—sustained; *avahitaḥ*—with great attention; *gaṅgām*—the Ganges; *pāda-pūta-jalām hareḥ*—whose water is transcendentally pure because of emanating from the toes of the Supreme Personality of Godhead Viṣṇu.

TRANSLATION

When King Bhagīratha approached Lord Śiva and requested him to sustain the forceful waves of the Ganges, Lord Śiva accepted the proposal by saying, "Let it be so." Then, with great attention, he sustained the Ganges on his head, for the water of the Ganges is purifying, having emanated from the toes of Lord Viṣṇu.

TEXT 10

भगीरथः स राजर्षिर्निन्ये भुवनपावनीम् ।
यत्र स्वपितॄणां देहा भस्मीभूताः स्म शेरते ॥१०॥

bhagīrathaḥ sa rājarṣir
ninye bhuvana-pāvanīm

yatra sva-pitṝṇāṁ dehā
bhasmībhūtāḥ sma śerate

bhagīrathaḥ—King Bhagīratha; *saḥ*—he; *rāja-ṛṣiḥ*—the great saintly king; *ninye*—carried or brought; *bhuvana-pāvanīm*—mother Ganges, who can deliver the whole universe; *yatra*—in that place where; *sva-pitṝṇām*—of his forefathers; *dehāḥ*—the bodies; *bhasmībhūtāḥ*—having been burnt to ashes; *sma śerate*—were lying.

TRANSLATION

The great and saintly king Bhagīratha brought the Ganges, which can deliver all the fallen souls, to that place on earth where the bodies of his forefathers lay burnt to ashes.

TEXT 11

रथेन वायुवेगेन प्रयान्तमनुधावती ।
देशान् पुनन्ती निर्दग्धानासिञ्चत् सगरात्मजान् ॥११॥

rathena vāyu-vegena
prayāntam anudhāvatī
deśān punantī nirdagdhān
āsiñcat sagarātmajān

rathena—on a chariot; *vāyu-vegena*—driving at the speed of the wind; *prayāntam*—Mahārāja Bhagīratha, who was going in front; *anudhāvatī*—running after; *deśān*—all the countries; *punantī*—sanctifying; *nirdagdhān*—who had been burnt to ashes; *āsiñcat*—sprinkled over; *sagara-ātmajān*—the sons of Sagara.

TRANSLATION

Bhagīratha mounted a swift chariot and drove before mother Ganges, who followed him, purifying many countries, until they reached the ashes of Bhagīratha's forefathers, the sons of Sagara, who were thus sprinkled with water from the Ganges.

TEXT 12

यज्जलस्पर्शमात्रेण ब्रह्मदण्डहता अपि ।
सगरात्मजा दिवं जग्मुः केवलं देहभस्मभिः ॥१२॥

yaj-jala-sparśa-mātreṇa
brahma-daṇḍa-hatā api
sagarātmajā divaṁ jagmuḥ
kevalaṁ deha-bhasmabhiḥ

yat-jala—whose water; *sparśa-mātreṇa*—simply by touching; *brahma-daṇḍa-hatāḥ*—those who were condemned for offending *brahma,* the self; *api*—although; *sagara-ātmajāḥ*—the sons of Sagara; *divam*—to the heavenly planets; *jagmuḥ*—went; *kevalam*—only; *deha-bhasmabhiḥ*—by the remaining ashes of their burnt bodies.

TRANSLATION

Because the sons of Sagara Mahārāja had offended a great personality, the heat of their bodies had increased, and they were burnt to ashes. But simply by being sprinkled with water from the Ganges, all of them became eligible to go to the heavenly planets. What then is to be said of those who use the water of mother Ganges to worship her?

PURPORT

Mother Ganges is worshiped by the water of the Ganges: a devotee takes a little water from the Ganges and offers it back to the Ganges. When the devotee takes the water, mother Ganges does not lose anything, and when the water is offered back, mother Ganges does not increase, but in this way the worshiper of the Ganges is benefited. Similarly, a devotee of the Lord offers the Lord *patraṁ puṣpaṁ phalaṁ toyam*—a leaf, flower, fruit or water—in great devotion, but everything, including the leaf, flower, fruit and water, belongs to the Lord, and therefore there is nothing to renounce or to accept. One must simply take advantage of the *bhakti* process because by following this process one does not lose anything but one gains the favor of the Supreme Person.

TEXT 13

भस्मीभूताङ्गसङ्गेन स्वर्याताः सगरात्मजाः ।
किं पुनः श्रद्धया देवीं सेवन्ते ये धृतव्रताः ॥१३॥

bhasmībhūtāṅga-saṅgena
svar yātāḥ sagarātmajāḥ
kiṁ punaḥ śraddhayā devīṁ
sevante ye dhṛta-vratāḥ

bhasmībhūta-aṅga—by the body which had been burnt to ashes; *saṅgena*—by contacting the water of the Ganges; *svaḥ yātāḥ*—went to the heavenly planets; *sagara-ātmajāḥ*—the sons of Sagara; *kim*—what to speak of; *punaḥ*—again; *śraddhayā*—with faith and devotion; *devīm*—unto mother Ganges; *sevante*—worship; *ye*—those persons who; *dhṛta-vratāḥ*—with vows of determination.

TRANSLATION

Simply by having water from the Ganges come in contact with the ashes of their burnt bodies, the sons of Sagara Mahārāja were elevated to the heavenly planets. Therefore, what is to be said of a devotee who worships mother Ganges faithfully with a determined vow? One can only imagine the benefit that accrues to such a devotee.

TEXT 14

न ह्येतत् परमाश्चर्यं स्वर्धुन्या यदिहोदितम् ।
अनन्तचरणाम्भोजप्रसूताया भवच्छिदः ॥१४॥

na hy etat param āścaryaṁ
svardhunyā yad ihoditam
ananta-caraṇāmbhoja-
prasūtāyā bhava-cchidaḥ

na—not; *hi*—indeed; *etat*—this; *param*—ultimate; *āścaryam*—wonderful thing; *svardhunyāḥ*—of the water of the Ganges; *yat*—which;

iha—herewith; *uditam*—has been described; *ananta*—of the Supreme Lord; *caraṇa-ambhoja*—from the lotus of the feet; *prasūtāyāḥ*—of that which emanates; *bhava-chidaḥ*—which can liberate from material bondage.

TRANSLATION

Because mother Ganges emanates from the lotus toe of the Supreme Personality of Godhead, Anantadeva, she is able to liberate one from material bondage. Therefore whatever is described herewith about her is not at all wonderful.

PURPORT

It has actually been seen that anyone who regularly worships mother Ganges simply by bathing in her water keeps very good health and gradually becomes a devotee of the Lord. This is the effect of bathing in the water of the Ganges. Bathing in the Ganges is recommended in all Vedic *śāstras*, and one who takes to this path will certainly be completely freed from all sinful reactions. The practical example of this is that the sons of Mahārāja Sagara went to the heavenly planets when water from the Ganges merely touched the ashes of their burnt bodies.

TEXT 15

संनिवेश्य मनो यस्मिञ्छ्रद्धया मुनयोऽमलाः ।
त्रैगुण्यं दुस्त्यजं हित्वा सद्यो यातास्तदात्मताम् ॥१५॥

sanniveśya mano yasmiñ
chraddhayā munayo 'malāḥ
traiguṇyaṁ dustyajaṁ hitvā
sadyo yātās tad-ātmatām

sanniveśya—giving full attention; *manaḥ*—the mind; *yasmin*—unto whom; *śraddhayā*—with faith and devotion; *munayaḥ*—great saintly persons; *amalāḥ*—freed from all contamination of sins; *traiguṇyam*—the three modes of material nature; *dustyajam*—very difficult to give up; *hitvā*—they can nonetheless give up; *sadyaḥ*—immediately; *yātāḥ*—achieved; *tat-ātmatām*—the spiritual quality of the Supreme.

TRANSLATION

Great sages, completely freed from material lusty desires, devote their minds fully to the service of the Lord. Such persons are liberated from material bondage without difficulty, and they become transcendentally situated, acquiring the spiritual quality of the Lord. This is the glory of the Supreme Personality of Godhead.

TEXTS 16–17

श्रुतो भगीरथाज्जज्ञे तस्य नाभोऽपरोऽभवत् ।
सिन्धुद्वीपस्ततस्तस्मादयुतायुस्ततोऽभवत् ॥१६॥
ऋतुपर्णो नलसखो योऽश्वविद्यामयान्नलात् ।
दत्त्वाक्षहृदयं चास्मै सर्वकामस्तु तत्सुतम् ॥१७॥

śruto bhagīrathāj jajñe
tasya nābho 'paro 'bhavat
sindhudvīpas tatas tasmād
ayutāyus tato 'bhavat

ṛtūparṇo nala-sakho
yo 'śva-vidyām ayān nalāt
dattvākṣa-hṛdayaṁ cāsmai
sarvakāmas tu tat-sutam

śrutaḥ—a son named Śruta; *bhagīrathāt*—from Bhagīratha; *jajñe*—was born; *tasya*—of Śruta; *nābhaḥ*—by the name Nābha; *aparaḥ*—different from the Nābha previously described; *abhavat*—was born; *sindhudvīpaḥ*—by the name Sindhudvīpa; *tataḥ*—from Nābha; *tasmāt*—from Sindhudvīpa; *ayutāyuḥ*—a son named Ayutāyu; *tataḥ*—thereafter; *abhavat*—was born; *ṛtūparṇaḥ*—a son named Ṛtūparṇa; *nala-sakhaḥ*—who was a friend of Nala; *yaḥ*—one who; *aśva-vidyām*—the art of controlling horses; *ayāt*—achieved; *nalāt*—from Nala; *dattvā*—after giving in exchange; *akṣa-hṛdayam*—the secrets of the art of gambling; *ca*—and; *asmai*—unto Nala; *sarvakāmaḥ*—by the name Sarvakāma; *tu*—indeed; *tat-sutam*—his son (the son of Ṛtūparṇa).

TRANSLATION

Bhagīratha had a son named Śruta, whose son was Nābha. This son was different from the Nābha previously described. Nābha had a son named Sindhudvīpa, from Sindhudvīpa came Ayutāyu, and from Ayutāyu came Ṛtūparṇa, who became a friend of Nalarāja. Ṛtūparṇa taught Nalarāja the art of gambling, and Nalarāja gave Ṛtūparṇa lessons in controlling and maintaining horses. The son of Ṛtūparṇa was Sarvakāma.

PURPORT

Gambling is also an art. *Kṣatriyas* are allowed to exhibit talent in this art of gambling. By the grace of Kṛṣṇa, the Pāṇḍavas lost everything by gambling and were deprived of their kingdom, wife, family and home because they were not expert in the gambling art. In other words, a devotee may not be expert in materialistic activities. It is therefore advised in the *śāstra* that materialistic activities are not at all suitable for the living entities, especially the devotees. A devotee should therefore be satisfied to eat whatever is sent as *prasāda* by the Supreme Lord. A devotee remains pure because he does not take to sinful activities such as gambling, intoxication, meat-eating and illicit sex.

TEXT 18

ततः सुदासस्तत्पुत्रो दमयन्तीपतिर्नृपः ।
आहुर्मित्रसहं यं वै कल्माषाङ्घ्रिमुत क्वचित् ।
वसिष्ठशापाद्र रक्षोऽभूदनपत्यः स्वकर्मणा ॥१८॥

tataḥ sudāsas tat-putro
damayantī-patir nṛpaḥ
āhur mitrasahaṁ yaṁ vai
kalmāṣāṅghrim uta kvacit
vasiṣṭha-śāpād rakṣo 'bhūd
anapatyaḥ sva-karmaṇā

tataḥ—from Sarvakāma; *sudāsaḥ*—Sudāsa was born; *tat-putraḥ*—the son of Sudāsa; *damayantī-patiḥ*—the husband of Damayantī; *nṛpaḥ*—

he became king; *āhuḥ*—it is said; *mitrasaham*—Mitrasaha; *yam vai*—also; *kalmāṣāṅghrim*—by Kalmāṣapāda; *uta*—known; *kvacit*—sometimes; *vasiṣṭha-śāpāt*—being cursed by Vasiṣṭha; *rakṣaḥ*—a man-eater; *abhūt*—became; *anapatyaḥ*—without any son; *sva-karmaṇā*—by his own sinful act.

TRANSLATION

Sarvakāma had a son named Sudāsa, whose son, known as Saudāsa, was the husband of Damayantī. Saudāsa is sometimes known as Mitrasaha or Kalmāṣapāda. Because of his own misdeed, Mitrasaha was sonless and was cursed by Vasiṣṭha to become a man-eater [Rākṣasa].

TEXT 19

श्रीराजोवाच

किंनिमित्तो गुरोः शापः सौदासस्य महात्मनः ।
एतद् वेदितुमिच्छामः कथ्यतां न रहो यदि ॥१९॥

śrī-rājovāca
kiṁ nimitto guroḥ śāpaḥ
saudāsasya mahātmanaḥ
etad veditum icchāmaḥ
kathyatāṁ na raho yadi

śrī-rājā uvāca—King Parīkṣit said; *kim nimittaḥ*—for what reason; *guroḥ*—of the spiritual master; *śāpaḥ*—curse; *saudāsasya*—of Saudāsa; *mahā-ātmanaḥ*—of the great soul; *etat*—this; *veditum*—to know; *icchāmaḥ*—I wish; *kathyatām*—please tell me; *na*—not; *rahaḥ*—confidential; *yadi*—if.

TRANSLATION

King Parīkṣit said: O Śukadeva Gosvāmī, why did Vasiṣṭha, the spiritual master of Saudāsa, curse that great soul? I wish to know of this. If it is not a confidential matter, please describe it to me.

TEXTS 20–21

श्रीशुक उवाच
सौदासो मृगयां किञ्चिच्चरन् रक्षो जघान ह ।
मुमोच भ्रातरं सोऽथ गतः प्रतिचिकीर्षया ॥२०॥
सञ्चिन्तयन्नघं राज्ञः सूदरूपधरो गृहे ।
गुरवे भोक्तुकामाय पक्त्वा निन्ये नरामिषम् ॥२१॥

śrī-śuka uvāca
saudāso mṛgayāṁ kiñcic
caran rakṣo jaghāna ha
mumoca bhrātaraṁ so 'tha
gataḥ praticikīrṣayā

sañcintayann aghaṁ rājñaḥ
sūda-rūpa-dharo gṛhe
gurave bhoktu-kāmāya
paktvā ninye narāmiṣam

śrī-śukaḥ uvāca—Śrī Śukadeva Gosvāmī said; *saudāsaḥ*—King Saudāsa; *mṛgayām*—in hunting; *kiñcit*—sometimes; *caran*—wandering; *rakṣaḥ*—a Rākṣasa, or man-eater; *jaghāna*—killed; *ha*—in the past; *mumoca*—released; *bhrātaram*—the brother of that Rākṣasa; *saḥ*—that brother; *atha*—thereafter; *gataḥ*—went; *praticikīrṣayā*—for taking revenge; *sañcintayan*—he thought; *agham*—to do some harm; *rājñaḥ*—of the King; *sūda-rūpa-dharaḥ*—disguised himself as a cook; *gṛhe*—in the house; *gurave*—unto the King's spiritual master; *bhoktu-kāmāya*—who came there to take dinner; *paktvā*—after cooking; *ninye*—gave him; *nara-āmiṣam*—the flesh of a human being.

TRANSLATION

Śukadeva Gosvāmī said: Once Saudāsa went to live in the forest, where he killed a man-eater [Rākṣasa] but forgave and released the man-eater's brother. That brother, however, decided to take revenge. Thinking to harm the King, he became the cook at the

King's house. One day, the King's spiritual master, Vasiṣṭha Muni, was invited for dinner, and the Rākṣasa cook served him human flesh.

TEXT 22

परिवेक्ष्यमाणं भगवान् विलोक्याभक्ष्यमञ्जसा ।
राजानमशपत् क्रुद्धो रक्षो ह्येवं भविष्यसि ॥२२॥

pariveksyamāṇaṁ bhagavān
vilokyābhakṣyam añjasā
rājānam aśapat kruddho
rakṣo hy evaṁ bhaviṣyasi

pariveksyamāṇam—while examining the eatables; *bhagavān*—the most powerful; *vilokya*—when he saw; *abhakṣyam*—unfit for consumption; *añjasā*—very easily by his mystic power; *rājānam*—unto the King; *aśapat*—cursed; *kruddhaḥ*—being very angry; *rakṣaḥ*—a man-eater; *hi*—indeed; *evam*—in this way; *bhaviṣyasi*—you shall become.

TRANSLATION

While examining the food given to him, Vasiṣṭha Muni, by his mystic power, could understand that it was unfit to eat, being the flesh of a human being. He was very angry at this and immediately cursed Saudāsa to become a man-eater.

TEXTS 23–24

रक्षःकृतं तद् विदित्वा चक्रे द्वादशवार्षिकम् ।
सोऽप्यपोऽञ्जलिमादाय गुरुं शप्तुं समुद्यतः ॥२३॥
वारितो मदयन्त्यापो रुशतीः पादयोर्जहौ ।
दिशः खमवनीं सर्वं पश्यञ्जीवमयं नृपः ॥२४॥

rakṣaḥ-kṛtaṁ tad viditvā
cakre dvādaśa-vārṣikam
so 'py apo-'ñjalim ādāya
guruṁ śaptuṁ samudyataḥ

vārito madayantyāpo
ruśatīḥ pādayor jahau
diśaḥ kham avanīṁ sarvaṁ
paśyañ jīvamayaṁ nṛpaḥ

rakṣaḥ-kṛtam—having been done by the Rākṣasa only; *tat*—that serving of human flesh; *viditvā*—after understanding; *cakre*—(Vasiṣṭha) performed; *dvādaśa-vārṣikam*—twelve years of penance for atonement; *saḥ*—that Saudāsa; *api*—also; *apaḥ-añjalim*—a palmful of water; *ādāya*—taking; *gurum*—his spiritual master, Vasiṣṭha; *śaptum*—to curse; *samudyataḥ*—was preparing; *vāritaḥ*—being forbidden; *madayantyā*—by his wife, who was also known as Madayantī; *apaḥ*—water; *ruśatīḥ*—strong by chanting of a *mantra; pādayoḥ jahau*—threw on his legs; *diśaḥ*—all directions; *kham*—in the sky; *avanīm*—on the surface of the world; *sarvam*—everywhere; *paśyan*—seeing; *jīvamayam*—full of living entities; *nṛpaḥ*—the King.

TRANSLATION

When Vasiṣṭha understood that the human flesh had been served by the Rākṣasa, not by the King, he undertook twelve years of austerity to cleanse himself for having cursed the faultless King. Meanwhile, King Saudāsa took water and chanted the śapa-mantra, preparing to curse Vasiṣṭha, but his wife, Madayantī, forbade him to do so. Then the King saw that the ten directions, the sky and the surface of the globe were full of living entities everywhere.

TEXT 25

राक्षसं भावमापन्नः पादे कल्माषतां गतः ।
व्यवायकाले ददृशे वनौकोदम्पती द्विजौ ॥२५॥

rākṣasaṁ bhāvam āpannaḥ
pāde kalmāṣatāṁ gataḥ
vyavāya-kāle dadṛśe
vanauko-dampatī dvijau

rākṣasam—man-eating; *bhāvam*—propensity; *āpannaḥ*—having gotten; *pāde*—on the leg; *kalmāṣatām*—a black spot; *gataḥ*—obtained; *vyavāya-kāle*—at the time of sexual intercourse; *dadṛśe*—he saw; *vana-okaḥ*—living in the forest; *dam-patī*—a husband and wife; *dvijau*—who were *brāhmaṇas.*

TRANSLATION

Saudāsa thus acquired the propensity of a man-eater and received on his leg a black spot, for which he was known as Kalmāṣapāda. Once King Kalmāṣapāda saw a brāhmaṇa couple engaged in sexual intercourse in the forest.

TEXTS 26–27

क्षुधार्तो जगृहे विप्रं तत्पत्न्याहाकृतार्थवत् ।
न भवान् राक्षसः साक्षादिक्ष्वाकूणां महारथः ॥२६॥
मदयन्त्याः पतिर्वीर नाधर्मं कर्तुमर्हसि ।
देहि मेऽपत्यकामाया अकृतार्थं पतिं द्विजम् ॥२७॥

kṣudhārto jagṛhe vipraṁ
tat-patny āhākṛtārthavat
na bhavān rākṣasaḥ sākṣād
ikṣvākūṇāṁ mahā-rathaḥ

madayantyāḥ patir vīra
nādharmaṁ kartum arhasi
dehi me 'patya-kāmāyā
akṛtārthaṁ patiṁ dvijam

kṣudhā-ārtaḥ—being aggrieved by hunger; *jagṛhe*—caught; *vipram*—the *brāhmaṇa; tat-patnī*—his wife; *āha*—said; *akṛta-artha-vat*—being unsatisfied, poor and hungry; *na*—not; *bhavān*—yourself; *rākṣasaḥ*—a man-eater; *sākṣāt*—directly or factually; *ikṣvākūṇām*—among the descendants of Mahārāja Ikṣvāku; *mahā-rathaḥ*—a great fighter; *madayantyāḥ*—of Madayantī; *patiḥ*—the husband; *vīra*—O hero; *na*—not; *adharmam*—irreligious act; *kartum*—to do; *arhasi*—you deserve; *dehi*—please deliver; *me*—my; *apatya-kāmāyāḥ*—desiring to get a son; *akṛta-artham*—whose desire has not been fulfilled; *patim*—husband; *dvijam*—who is a *brāhmaṇa.*

TRANSLATION

Being influenced by the propensity of a Rākṣasa and being very hungry, King Saudāsa seized the brāhmaṇa. Then the poor woman, the brāhmaṇa's wife, said to the King: O hero, you are not actually a man-eater; rather, you are among the descendants of Mahārāja Ikṣvāku. Indeed, you are a great fighter, the husband of Madayantī. You should not act irreligiously in this way. I desire to have a son. Please, therefore, return my husband, who has not yet impregnated me.

TEXT 28

देहोऽयं मानुषो राजन् पुरुषस्याखिलार्थदः ।
तस्मादस्य वधो वीर सर्वार्थवध उच्यते ॥२८॥

deho 'yaṁ mānuṣo rājan
puruṣasyākhilārthadaḥ
tasmād asya vadho vīra
sarvārtha-vadha ucyate

dehaḥ—body; *ayam*—this; *mānuṣaḥ*—human; *rājan*—O King; *puruṣasya*—of the living being; *akhila*—universal; *artha-daḥ*—beneficial; *tasmāt*—therefore; *asya*—of the body of my husband; *vadhaḥ*—the killing; *vīra*—O hero; *sarva-artha-vadhaḥ*—killing all beneficial opportunities; *ucyate*—it is said.

TRANSLATION

O King, O hero, this human body is meant for universal benefits. If you kill this body untimely, you will kill all the benefits of human life.

PURPORT

Śrīla Narottama dāsa Ṭhākura has sung:

hari hari viphale janama goṅāinu
manuṣya-janama pāiyā, rādhā-kṛṣṇa nā bhajiyā,
jāniyā śuniyā viṣa khāinu

The body of a human being is extremely valuable because in this body one can understand the instructions of Kṛṣṇa and attain the ultimate destination of the living entity. The living entity is within the material world to fulfill the mission of going back home, back to Godhead. In the material world, one hankers for happiness, but because one does not know the ultimate destination, one changes bodies one after another. However, if one gets the opportunity to possess a human form of body, in this body he can fulfill the four principles of *dharma, artha, kāma* and *mokṣa*, and if one is properly regulated he makes further progress, after liberation, to engage in the service of Rādhā and Kṛṣṇa. This is the success of life: to stop the process of repeated birth and death and go back home, back to Godhead (*mām eti*), to be engaged in the service of Rādhā and Kṛṣṇa. Therefore, taking a human body is meant for completing one's progress in life. Throughout human society, killing of a human being is taken very seriously. Hundreds and thousands of animals are killed in slaughterhouses, and no one cares about them, but the killing of even one human being is taken very seriously. Why? Because the human form of body is extremely important in executing the mission of life.

TEXT 29

एष हि ब्राह्मणो विद्वांस्तपःशीलगुणान्वितः ।
आरिराधयिषुर्ब्रह्म महापुरुषसंज्ञितम् ।
सर्वभूतात्मभावेन भूतेष्वन्तर्हितं गुणैः ॥२९॥

eṣa hi brāhmaṇo vidvāṁs
tapaḥ-śīla-guṇānvitaḥ
ārirādhayiṣur brahma
mahā-puruṣa-saṁjñitam

sarva-bhūtātma-bhāvena
bhūteṣv antarhitaṁ guṇaiḥ

eṣaḥ—this; *hi*—indeed; *brāhmaṇaḥ*—a qualified *brāhmaṇa; vidvān*—learned in Vedic knowledge; *tapaḥ*—austerity; *śīla*—good behavior; *guṇa-anvitaḥ*—endowed with all good qualities; *āri-rādhayiṣuḥ*—desiring to be engaged in worshiping; *brahma*—the Supreme Brahman; *mahā-puruṣa*—the Supreme Person, Kṛṣṇa; *saṁjñitam*—known as; *sarva-bhūta*—of all living entities; *ātma-bhāvena*—as the Supersoul; *bhūteṣu*—in every living entity; *antarhitam*—within the core of the heart; *guṇaiḥ*—by qualities.

TRANSLATION

Here is a learned, highly qualified brāhmaṇa, engaged in performing austerity and eagerly desiring to worship the Supreme Lord, the Supersoul who lives within the core of the heart in all living entities.

PURPORT

The wife of the *brāhmaṇa* did not regard her husband as a superficial *brāhmaṇa* who was called a *brāhmaṇa* merely because he was born of a *brāhmaṇa* family. Rather, this *brāhmaṇa* was actually qualified with the brahminical symptoms. *Yasya yal lakṣaṇaṁ proktam* (*Bhāg.* 7.11.35). The symptoms of a *brāhmaṇa* are stated in the *śāstra:*

śamo damas tapaḥ śaucaṁ
kṣāntir ārjavam eva ca
jñānaṁ vijñānam āstikyaṁ
brahma-karma svabhāvajam

"Peacefulness, self-control, austerity, purity, tolerance, honesty, wisdom, knowledge, and religiousness—these are the qualities by which the *brāhmaṇas* work." (Bg. 18.42) Not only must a *brāhmaṇa* be qualified, but he must also engage in actual brahminical activities. Simply to be qualified is not enough; one must engage in a *brāhmaṇa's* duties. The duty of a *brāhmaṇa* is to know the *paraṁ brahma,* Kṛṣṇa (*paraṁ brahma paraṁ dhāma pavitraṁ paramaṁ bhavān*). Because this *brāhmaṇa* was actually qualified and was also engaged in brahminical activities (*brahma-karma*), killing him would be a greatly sinful act, and the *brāhmaṇa's* wife requested that he not be killed.

TEXT 30

सोऽयं ब्रह्मर्षिवर्यस्ते राजर्षिप्रवराद् विभो ।
कथमर्हति धर्मज्ञ वधं पितुरिवात्मजः ॥३०॥

so 'yaṁ brahmarṣi-varyas te
rājarṣi-pravarād vibho
katham arhati dharma-jña
vadhaṁ pitur ivātmajaḥ

saḥ—he, the *brāhmaṇa; ayam*—this; *brahma-ṛṣi-varyaḥ*—not only a *brāhmaṇa* but the best of great sages, or *brahmarṣis; te*—also from you; *rāja-ṛṣi-pravarāt*—who are the best of all saintly kings, or *rājarṣis; vibho*—O master of the state; *katham*—how; *arhati*—he deserves; *dharma-jña*—O you, who are quite aware of religious principles; *vadham*—killing; *pituḥ*—from the father; *iva*—like; *ātmajaḥ*—the son.

TRANSLATION

My lord, you are completely aware of the religious principles. As a son never deserves to be killed by his father, here is a brāhmaṇa who should be protected by the king, and never killed. How does he deserve to be killed by a rājarṣi like you?

PURPORT

The word *rājarṣi* refers to a king who behaves like a *ṛṣi*, or sage. Such a king is also called *naradeva* because he is considered a representative of the Supreme Lord. Because his duty is to rule the kingdom to maintain brahminical culture, he never desires to kill a *brāhmaṇa*. Generally, a *brāhmaṇa*, woman, child, old man or cow is never regarded as punishable. Thus the wife of the *brāhmaṇa* requested the King to refrain from this sinful act.

TEXT 31

तस्य साधोरपापस्य भ्रूणस्य ब्रह्मवादिनः ।
कथं वधं यथा बभ्रोर्मन्यते सन्मतो भवान् ॥३१॥

tasya sādhor apāpasya
bhrūṇasya brahma-vādinaḥ
kathaṁ vadhaṁ yathā babhror
manyate san-mato bhavān

tasya—of him; *sādhoḥ*—of the great saintly person; *apāpasya*—of one who has no sinful life; *bhrūṇasya*—of the embryo; *brahma-vādinaḥ*—of one who is well versed in Vedic knowledge; *katham*—how; *vadham*—the killing; *yathā*—as; *babhroḥ*—of a cow; *manyate*—you are thinking; *sat-mataḥ*—well recognized by higher circles; *bhavān*—your good self.

TRANSLATION

You are well known and worshiped in learned circles. How dare you kill this brāhmaṇa, who is a saintly, sinless person, well versed in Vedic knowledge? Killing him would be like destroying the embryo within the womb or killing a cow.

PURPORT

As stated in the *Amara-kośa* dictionary, *bhrūṇo 'rbhake bāla-garbhe:* the word *bhrūṇa* refers either to the cow or to the living entity in embryo. According to Vedic culture, destroying the undeveloped embryo of the soul in the womb is as sinful as killing a cow or a *brāhmaṇa.* In the embryo, the living entity is present in an undeveloped stage. The modern scientific theory that life is a combination of chemicals is nonsense; scientists cannot manufacture living beings, even like those born from eggs. The idea that scientists can develop a chemical situation resembling that of an egg and bring life from it is nonsensical. Their theory that a chemical combination can have life may be accepted, but these rascals cannot create such a combination. This verse refers to *bhrūṇasya vadham*—the killing of a *bhrūṇa* or destruction of the embryo. Here is a challenge from the Vedic literature. The crude, atheistic understanding that the living entity is a combination of matter belongs to the grossest ignorance.

TEXT 32

यद्ययं क्रियते भक्ष्यस्तर्हि मां खाद पूर्वतः ।
न जीविष्ये विना येन क्षणं च मृतकं यथा ॥३२॥

yady ayaṁ kriyate bhakṣyas
tarhi māṁ khāda pūrvataḥ
na jīviṣye vinā yena
kṣaṇaṁ ca mṛtakaṁ yathā

yadi—if; *ayam*—this *brāhmaṇa; kriyate*—is accepted; *bhakṣyaḥ*—as eatable; *tarhi*—then; *mām*—me; *khāda*—eat; *pūrvataḥ*—before that; *na*—not; *jīviṣye*—I shall live; *vinā*—without; *yena*—whom (my husband); *kṣaṇam ca*—even for a moment; *mṛtakam*—a dead body; *yathā*—like.

TRANSLATION

Without my husband, I cannot live for a moment. If you want to eat my husband, it would be better to eat me first, for without my husband I am as good as a dead body.

PURPORT

In the Vedic culture there is a system known as *satī* or *saha-maraṇa*, in which a woman dies with her husband. According to this system, if the husband dies, the wife will voluntarily die by falling in the blazing funeral pyre of her husband. Here, in this verse, the feelings inherent in this culture are expressed by the wife of the *brāhmaṇa*. A woman without a husband is like a dead body. Therefore according to Vedic culture a girl must be married. This is the responsibility of her father. A girl may be given in charity, and a husband may have more than one wife, but a girl must be married. This is Vedic culture. A woman is supposed to be always dependent—in her childhood she is dependent on her father, in youth on her husband, and in old age on her elderly sons. According to *Manu-saṁhitā*, she is never independent. Independence for a woman means miserable life. In this age, so many girls are unmarried and falsely imagining themselves free, but their life is miserable. Here is an instance in which a woman felt that without her husband she was nothing but a dead body.

TEXT 33

एवं करुणभाषिण्या विलपन्त्या अनाथवत् ।
व्याघ्रः पशुमिवाखादत् सौदासः शापमोहितः ॥३३॥

evaṁ karuṇa-bhāṣiṇyā
vilapantyā anāthavat
vyāghraḥ paśum ivākhādat
saudāsaḥ śāpa-mohitaḥ

evam—in this way; *karuṇa-bhāṣiṇyāḥ*—while the *brāhmaṇa's* wife was speaking very pitiably; *vilapantyāḥ*—lamenting severely; *anātha-vat*—exactly like a woman who has no protector; *vyāghraḥ*—a tiger; *paśum*—prey animal; *iva*—like; *akhādat*—ate up; *saudāsaḥ*—King Saudāsa; *śāpa*—by the curse; *mohitaḥ*—because of being condemned.

TRANSLATION

Being condemned by the curse of Vasiṣṭha, King Saudāsa devoured the brāhmaṇa, exactly as a tiger eats its prey. Even though the brāhmaṇa's wife spoke so pitiably, Saudāsa was unmoved by her lamentation.

PURPORT

This is an example of destiny. King Saudāsa was condemned by the curse of Vasiṣṭha, and therefore even though he was well qualified he could not restrain himself from becoming a tigerlike Rākṣasa, for this was his destiny. *Tal labhyate duḥkhavad anyataḥ sukham* (*Bhāg.* 1.5.18). As one is put into distress by destiny, destiny can also put one in a happy situation. Destiny is extremely strong, but one can change destiny if one comes to the platform of Kṛṣṇa consciousness. *Karmāṇi nirdahati kintu ca bhakti-bhājām* (*Brahma-saṁhitā* 5.54).

TEXT 34

ब्राह्मणी वीक्ष्य दिधिषुं पुरुषादेन भक्षितम् ।
शोचन्त्यात्मानमुर्वीशमशपत् कुपिता सती ॥३४॥

brāhmaṇī vīkṣya didhiṣuṁ
puruṣādena bhakṣitam
śocanty ātmānam urvīśam
aśapat kupitā satī

brāhmaṇī—the wife of the *brāhmaṇa; vīkṣya*—after seeing; *didhiṣum*—her husband, who was about to give the seed of a child; *puruṣa-adena*—by the man-eater (Rākṣasa); *bhakṣitam*—having been eaten up; *śocantī*—lamenting very much; *ātmānam*—for her body or her self; *urvīśam*—unto the King; *aśapat*—cursed; *kupitā*—being angry; *satī*—the chaste woman.

TRANSLATION

When the chaste wife of the brāhmaṇa saw that her husband, who was about to discharge semen, had been eaten by the man-eater, she was overwhelmed with grief and lamentation. Thus she angrily cursed the King.

TEXT 35

यस्मान्मे भक्षितः पाप कामार्तायाः पतिस्त्वया ।
तवापि मृत्युराधानादकृतप्रज्ञ दर्शितः ॥३५॥

yasmān me bhakṣitaḥ pāpa
kāmārtāyāḥ patis tvayā
tavāpi mṛtyur ādhānād
akṛta-prajña darśitaḥ

yasmāt—because; *me*—my; *bhakṣitaḥ*—was eaten up; *pāpa*—O sinful one; *kāma-ārtāyāḥ*—of a woman very much bereaved because of sexual desire; *patiḥ*—husband; *tvayā*—by you; *tava*—your; *api*—also; *mṛtyuḥ*—death; *ādhānāt*—when you try to discharge semen in your wife; *akṛta-prajña*—O foolish rascal; *darśitaḥ*—this curse is placed upon you.

TRANSLATION

O foolish, sinful person, because you have eaten my husband when I was sexually inclined and desiring to have the seed of a child, I shall also see you die when you attempt to discharge semen in your wife. In other words, whenever you attempt to sexually unite with your wife, you shall die.

TEXT 36

एवं मित्रसहं शप्त्वा पतिलोकपरायणा ।
तदस्थीनि समिद्धेऽग्नौ प्रास्य भर्तुर्गतिं गता ॥३६॥

evaṁ mitrasahaṁ śaptvā
pati-loka-parāyaṇā
tad-asthīni samiddhe 'gnau
prāsya bhartur gatiṁ gatā

evam—in this way; *mitrasaham*—King Saudāsa; *śaptvā*—after cursing; *pati-loka-parāyaṇā*—because of being inclined to go with her husband; *tat-asthīni*—her husband's bones; *samiddhe agnau*—in the burning fire; *prāsya*—after placing; *bhartuḥ*—of her husband; *gatim*—to the destination; *gatā*—she also went.

TRANSLATION

Thus the wife of the brāhmaṇa cursed King Saudāsa, known as Mitrasaha. Then, being inclined to go with her husband, she set fire to her husband's bones, fell into the fire herself, and went with him to the same destination.

TEXT 37

विशापो द्वादशाब्दान्ते मैथुनाय समुद्यतः ।
विज्ञाप्य ब्राह्मणीशापं महिष्या स निवारितः ॥३७॥

viśāpo dvādaśābdānte
maithunāya samudyataḥ
vijñāpya brāhmaṇī-śāpaṁ
mahiṣyā sa nivāritaḥ

viśāpaḥ—being released from the period of the curse; *dvādaśa-abda-ante*—after twelve years; *maithunāya*—for sexual intercourse with his wife; *samudyataḥ*—when Saudāsa was prepared to do it; *vijñāpya*—reminding him about; *brāhmaṇī-śāpam*—the curse given by the *brāhmaṇī; mahiṣyā*—by the Queen; *saḥ*—he (the King); *nivāritaḥ*—checked.

TRANSLATION

After twelve years, when King Saudāsa was released from the curse by Vasiṣṭha, he wanted to have sexual intercourse with his wife. But the Queen reminded him about the curse by the brāhmaṇī, and thus he was checked from sexual intercourse.

TEXT 38

अत ऊर्ध्वं स तत्याज स्त्रीसुखं कर्मणाप्रजाः ।
वसिष्ठस्तदनुज्ञातो मदयन्त्यां प्रजामधात् ॥३८॥

ata ūrdhvaṁ sa tatyāja
strī-sukhaṁ karmaṇāprajāḥ
vasiṣṭhas tad-anujñāto
madayantyāṁ prajām adhāt

ataḥ—in this way; *ūrdhvam*—in the near future; *saḥ*—he, the King; *tatyāja*—gave up; *strī-sukham*—the happiness of sexual intercourse; *karmaṇā*—by destiny; *aprajāḥ*—remained sonless; *vasiṣṭhaḥ*—the great saint Vasiṣṭha; *tat-anujñātaḥ*—being permitted by the King to beget a son; *madayantyām*—in the womb of Madayantī, King Saudāsa's wife; *prajām*—a child; *adhāt*—begot.

TRANSLATION

After being thus instructed, the King gave up the future happiness of sexual intercourse and by destiny remained sonless. Later,

with the King's permission, the great saint Vasiṣṭha begot a child in the womb of Madayantī.

TEXT 39

सा वै सप्त समा गर्भमबिभ्रन्न व्यजायत ।
जघ्नेऽश्मनोदरं तस्याः सोऽश्मकस्तेन कथ्यते ॥३९॥

sā vai sapta samā garbham
abibhran na vyajāyata
jaghne 'śmanodaraṁ tasyāḥ
so 'śmakas tena kathyate

sā—she, Queen Madayantī; *vai*—indeed; *sapta*—seven; *samāḥ*—years; *garbham*—the child within the womb; *abibhrat*—continued to bear; *na*—not; *vyajāyata*—gave delivery; *jaghne*—struck; *aśmanā*—by a stone; *udaram*—abdomen; *tasyāḥ*—of her; *saḥ*—a son; *aśmakaḥ*—by the name Aśmaka; *tena*—because of this; *kathyate*—was called.

TRANSLATION

Madayantī bore the child within the womb for seven years and did not give birth. Therefore Vasiṣṭha struck her abdomen with a stone, and then the child was born. Consequently, the child was known as Aśmaka ["the child born of a stone"].

TEXT 40

अश्मकाद्बालिको जज्ञे यः स्त्रीभिः परिरक्षितः ।
नारीकवच इत्युक्तो निःक्षत्रे मूलकोऽभवत् ॥४०॥

aśmakād bāliko jajñe
yaḥ strībhiḥ parirakṣitaḥ
nārī-kavaca ity ukto
niḥkṣatre mūlako 'bhavat

aśmakāt—from that son named Aśmaka; *bālikaḥ*—a son named Bālika; *jajñe*—was born; *yaḥ*—this child Bālika; *strībhiḥ*—by women;

parirakṣitaḥ—was protected; *nārī-kavacaḥ*—having a shield of women; *iti uktaḥ*—was known as such; *niḥkṣatre*—when there were no *kṣatriyas* (all *kṣatriyas* having been vanquished by Paraśurāma); *mūlakaḥ*—Mūlaka, the progenitor of the *kṣatriyas; abhavat*—he became.

TRANSLATION

From Aśmaka, Bālika took birth. Because Bālika was surrounded by women and was therefore saved from the anger of Paraśurāma, he was known as Nārīkavaca ["one who is protected by women"]. When Paraśurāma vanquished all the kṣatriyas, Bālika became the progenitor of more kṣatriyas. Therefore he was known as Mūlaka, the root of the kṣatriya dynasty.

TEXT 41

ततो दशरथस्तस्मात् पुत्र ऐडविडिस्ततः ।
राजा विश्वसहो यस्य खट्वाङ्गश्चक्रवर्त्यभूत् ॥४१॥

tato daśarathas tasmāt
putra aiḍaviḍis tataḥ
rājā viśvasaho yasya
khaṭvāṅgaś cakravarty abhūt

tataḥ—from Bālika; *daśarathaḥ*—a son named Daśaratha; *tasmāt*—from him; *putraḥ*—a son; *aiḍaviḍiḥ*—named Aiḍaviḍi; *tataḥ*—from him; *rājā viśvasahaḥ*—the famous King Viśvasaha was born; *yasya*—of whom; *khaṭvāṅgaḥ*—the king named Khaṭvāṅga; *cakravartī*—emperor; *abhūt*—became.

TRANSLATION

From Bālika came a son named Daśaratha, from Daśaratha came a son named Aiḍaviḍi, and from Aiḍaviḍi came King Viśvasaha. The son of King Viśvasaha was the famous Mahārāja Khaṭvāṅga.

TEXT 42

यो देवैरर्थितो दैत्यानवधीद् युधि दुर्जयः ।
मुहूर्तमायुर्ज्ञात्वैत्य स्वपुरं संदधे मनः ॥४२॥

yo devair arthito daityān
avadhīd yudhi durjayaḥ
muhūrtam āyur jñātvaitya
sva-puraṁ sandadhe manaḥ

yaḥ—King Khaṭvāṅga who; *devaiḥ*—by the demigods; *arthitaḥ*—being requested; *daityān*—the demons; *avadhīt*—killed; *yudhi*—in a fight; *durjayaḥ*—very fierce; *muhūrtam*—for a second only; *āyuḥ*—duration of life; *jñātvā*—knowing; *etya*—approached; *sva-puram*—his own abode; *sandadhe*—fixed; *manaḥ*—the mind.

TRANSLATION

King Khaṭvāṅga was unconquerable in any fight. Requested by the demigods to join them in fighting the demons, he won victory, and the demigods, being very pleased, wanted to give him a benediction. The King inquired from them about the duration of his life and was informed that he had only one moment more. Thus he immediately left his palace and went to his own residence, where he engaged his mind fully on the lotus feet of the Lord.

PURPORT

The example of Mahārāja Khaṭvāṅga in performing devotional service is brilliant. Mahārāja Khaṭvāṅga engaged himself for only a moment in devotional service to the Lord, but he was promoted back to Godhead. Therefore, if one practices devotional service from the beginning of his life, surely he will return home, back to Godhead, without a doubt (*asaṁśaya*).

In *Bhagavad-gītā* the word *asaṁśaya* is used to describe the devotee. There the Lord Himself gives this instruction:

mayy āsakta-manāḥ pārtha
yogaṁ yuñjan mad-āśrayaḥ
asaṁśayaṁ samagraṁ māṁ
yathā jñāsyasi tac chṛṇu

"Now hear, O son of Pṛthā [Arjuna], how by practicing *yoga* in full consciousness of Me, with mind attached to Me, you can know Me in full, free from doubt." (Bg. 7.1)

The Lord also instructs:

janma karma ca me divyam
evaṁ yo vetti tattvataḥ
tyaktvā dehaṁ punar janma
naiti mām eti so 'rjuna

"One who knows the transcendental nature of My appearance and activities does not, upon leaving the body, take his birth again in this material world, but attains My eternal abode, O Arjuna." (Bg. 4.9)

Therefore, from the very beginning of one's life one should practice *bhakti-yoga*, which increases one's attachment for Kṛṣṇa. If one daily sees the Deity in the temple, makes offerings by worshiping the Deity, chants the holy name of the Personality of Godhead, and preaches about the glorious activities of the Lord as much as possible, he thus becomes attached to Kṛṣṇa. This attachment is called *āsakti*. When one's mind is attached to Kṛṣṇa (*mayy āsakta-manāḥ*), one can fulfill the mission of life in one human birth. If one misses this opportunity, one does not know where he is going, how long he will remain in the cycle of birth and death, and when he will again achieve the human form of life and the chance to return home, back to Godhead. The most intelligent person, therefore, uses every moment of his life to render loving service to the Lord.

TEXT 43

न मे ब्रह्मकुलात् प्राणाः कुलदैवान्न चात्मजाः ।
न श्रियो न मही राज्यं न दाराश्चातिवल्लभाः ॥४३॥

na me brahma-kulāt prāṇāḥ
kula-daivān na cātmajāḥ
na śriyo na mahī rājyaṁ
na dārāś cātivallabhāḥ

na—not; *me*—my; *brahma-kulāt*—than the groups of *brāhmaṇas; prāṇāḥ*—life; *kula-daivāt*—than the personalities worshipable for my family; *na*—not; *ca*—also; *ātmajāḥ*—sons and daughters; *na*—nor;

śriyaḥ—opulence; *na*—nor; *mahī*—the earth; *rājyam*—kingdom; *na*—nor; *dārāḥ*—wife; *ca*—also; *ati-vallabhāḥ*—extremely dear.

TRANSLATION

Mahārāja Khaṭvāṅga thought: Not even my life is dearer to me than the brahminical culture and the brāhmaṇas, who are worshiped by my family. What then is to be said of my kingdom, land, wife, children and opulence? Nothing is dearer to me than the brāhmaṇas.

PURPORT

Mahārāja Khaṭvāṅga, being in favor of the brahminical culture, wanted to utilize one moment's time by fully surrendering unto the Supreme Personality of Godhead. The Lord is worshiped with this prayer:

namo brāhmaṇya-devāya
go brāhmaṇa-hitāya ca
jagad-dhitāya kṛṣṇāya
govindāya namo namaḥ

"I offer my respectful obeisances to the Supreme Absolute Truth, Kṛṣṇa, who is the well-wisher of the cows and the *brāhmaṇas* as well as the living entities in general. I offer my repeated obeisances to Govinda, who is the pleasure reservoir for all the senses." A devotee of Kṛṣṇa is very much attached to brahminical culture. Indeed, an expert personality who knows who Kṛṣṇa is and what He wants is a real *brāhmaṇa. Brahma jānātīti brāhmaṇaḥ.* Kṛṣṇa is the Parabrahman, and therefore all Kṛṣṇa conscious persons, or devotees of Kṛṣṇa, are exalted *brāhmaṇas.* Khaṭvāṅga Mahārāja regarded the devotees of Kṛṣṇa as the real *brāhmaṇas* and the real light for human society. One who desires to advance in Kṛṣṇa consciousness and spiritual understanding must give the utmost importance to brahminical culture and must understand Kṛṣṇa (*kṛṣṇāya govindāya*). Then his life will be successful.

TEXT 44

न बाल्येऽपि मतिर्मह्यमधर्मे रमते क्वचित् ।
नापश्यमुत्तमश्लोकादन्यत् किञ्चन वस्त्वहम् ।।४४।।

na bālye 'pi matir mahyam
adharme ramate kvacit
nāpaśyam uttamaślokād
anyat kiñcana vastv aham

na—not; *bālye*—in childhood; *api*—indeed; *matiḥ*—attraction; *mahyam*—of me; *adharme*—in irreligious principles; *ramate*—enjoys; *kvacit*—at any time; *na*—nor; *apaśyam*—I saw; *uttamaślokāt*—than the Personality of Godhead; *anyat*—anything else; *kiñcana*—anything; *vastu*—substance; *aham*—I.

TRANSLATION

I was never attracted, even in my childhood, by insignificant things or irreligious principles. I did not find anything more substantial than the Supreme Personality of Godhead.

PURPORT

Mahārāja Khaṭvāṅga provides a typical example of a Kṛṣṇa conscious person. A Kṛṣṇa conscious person does not see anything to be important but the Supreme Personality of Godhead, nor does he accept anything within this material world as being unconnected to the Supreme Lord. As stated in *Caitanya-caritāmṛta* (*Madhya* 8.274):

sthāvara-jaṅgama dekhe, nā dekhe tāra mūrti
sarvatra haya nija iṣṭa-deva-sphūrti

"The *mahā-bhāgavata*, the advanced devotee, certainly sees everything mobile and immobile, but he does not exactly see their forms. Rather, everywhere he immediately sees manifest the form of the Supreme Lord." Although a devotee is within the material world, he has no connection with it. *Nirbandhaḥ kṛṣṇa-sambandhe.* He accepts this material world in relationship with the Supreme Personality of Godhead. A devotee may be engaged in earning money, but he uses that money for propagating the Kṛṣṇa consciousness movement by constructing large temples and establishing worship of the Supreme Personality of Godhead. Khaṭvāṅga Mahārāja, therefore, was not a materialist. A materialist is always attached to wife, children, home, property and many other things for sense gratification, but, as stated above, Khaṭvāṅga Mahārāja was not attached to such things, nor could he think of anything existing without the purpose of the Supreme Lord. *Īśāvāsyam idaṁ sarvam:* everything is related to the Supreme Personality of Godhead. Of course, this consciousness is not for the ordinary person, but if one takes to the path of devotional service, as prescribed in *The Nectar of Devotion,* he can be trained in this consciousness and attain perfect understanding. For a Kṛṣṇa conscious person, nothing is palatable without a relationship with Kṛṣṇa.

TEXT 45

देवैः कामवरो दत्तो मह्यं त्रिभुवनेश्वरैः ।
न वृणे तमहं कामं भूतभावनभावनः ॥४५॥

devaiḥ kāma-varo datto
mahyaṁ tri-bhuvaneśvaraiḥ
na vṛṇe tam ahaṁ kāmaṁ
bhūtabhāvana-bhāvanaḥ

devaiḥ—by the demigods; *kāma-varaḥ*—the benediction to have whatever he wanted; *dattaḥ*—was given; *mahyam*—unto me; *tri-bhuvana-īśvaraiḥ*—by the demigods, the protectors of the three worlds (who can do whatever they like within this material world); *na vṛṇe*—did not accept; *tam*—that; *aham*—I; *kāmam*—everything desirable within this material world; *bhūtabhāvana-bhāvanaḥ*—being fully absorbed in the Supreme Personality of Godhead (and therefore not interested in anything material).

TRANSLATION

The demigods, the directors of the three worlds, wanted to give me whatever benediction I desired. I did not want their benedictions, however, because I am interested in the Supreme Personality of Godhead, who created everything in this material world. I am more interested in the Supreme Personality of Godhead than in all material benedictions.

PURPORT

A devotee is always transcendentally situated. *Paraṁ dṛṣṭvā nivartate:* one who has seen the Supreme Personality of Godhead is no longer interested in material sense enjoyment. Even such an exalted devotee as Dhruva Mahārāja went to the forest for the sake of material benefit, but when he actually saw the Supreme Personality of Godhead, he refused to accept any material benediction. He said, *svāmin kṛtārtho 'smi varaṁ na yāce:* "My dear Lord, I am fully satisfied with whatever You have given me or not given me. I have nothing to ask from You, for I am fully satisfied to be engaged in Your service." This is the mentality of a pure devotee, who does not want anything, material or spiritual, from the Personality of Godhead. Our Kṛṣṇa consciousness movement is therefore called *kṛṣṇa-bhāvanāmṛta-saṅgha,* the association of persons who are simply satisfied in thoughts of Kṛṣṇa. Being absorbed in thoughts of Kṛṣṇa is neither expensive nor troublesome. Kṛṣṇa says, *man-manā bhava mad-bhakto mad-yājī māṁ namaskuru:* "Engage your mind always in thinking of Me, offer obeisances and worship Me." (Bg. 9.34) Anyone can always think of Kṛṣṇa, without difficulties or obstacles. This is called *kṛṣṇa-bhāvanāmṛta.* One who is absorbed in *kṛṣṇa-bhāvanāmṛta* has no material benefits to ask from Kṛṣṇa. Instead, such a person prays to the Lord for the benediction of being able to spread His glories all over the world. *Mama janmani janmanīśvare bhavatād bhaktir ahaitukī tvayi.* A Kṛṣṇa conscious person does not even want to stop his cycle of birth and death. He simply prays, "I may take birth as You like, but my only prayer is that I may be engaged in Your service."

TEXT 46

ये विक्षिप्तेन्द्रियधियो देवास्ते स्वहृदि स्थितम् ।
न विन्दन्ति प्रियं शश्वदात्मानं किमुतापरे ॥४६॥

ye vikṣiptendriya-dhiyo
devās te sva-hṛdi sthitam
na vindanti priyaṁ śaśvad
ātmānaṁ kim utāpare

ye—which personalities; *vikṣipta-indriya-dhiyaḥ*—whose senses, mind and intelligence are always agitated because of material conditions;

devāḥ—like the demigods; *te*—such persons; *sva-hṛdi*—in the core of the heart; *sthitam*—situated; *na*—not; *vindanti*—know; *priyam*—the dearmost Personality of Godhead; *śaśvat*—constantly, eternally; *ātmānam*—the Supreme Personality of Godhead; *kim uta*—what to speak of; *apare*—others (like human beings).

TRANSLATION

Even though the demigods have the advantages of being situated in the higher planetary system, their minds, senses and intelligence are agitated by material conditions. Therefore, even such elevated persons fail to realize the Supreme Personality of Godhead, who is eternally situated in the core of the heart. What then is to be said of others, such as human beings, who have fewer advantages?

PURPORT

It is a fact that the Supreme Personality of Godhead is always situated in everyone's heart (*īśvaraḥ sarva-bhūtānāṁ hṛd-deśe 'rjuna tiṣṭhati*). But because of our material anxieties, which are inevitable in this material world, we cannot understand the Supreme Lord, although He is situated so near to us. For those always agitated by material conditions, the yogic process is recommended so that one may concentrate his mind upon the Supreme Personality of Godhead within the heart. *Dhyānāvasthita-tad-gatena manasā paśyanti yaṁ yoginaḥ.* Because in material conditions the mind and senses are always agitated, by the yogic procedures like *dhāraṇā, āsana* and *dhyāna* one must quiet the mind and concentrate it upon the Supreme Personality of Godhead. In other words, the yogic process is a material attempt to realize the Lord, whereas *bhakti,* devotional service, is the spiritual process by which to realize Him. Mahārāja Khaṭvāṅga accepted the spiritual path, and therefore he was no longer interested in anything material. Kṛṣṇa says in *Bhagavad-gītā* (18.55), *bhaktyā mām abhijānāti:* "Only by devotional service can I be understood." One can understand Kṛṣṇa, the Parabrahman, the Supreme Personality of Godhead, only through devotional service. The Lord never says that one can understand Him by performing mystic *yoga* or by philosophically speculating. *Bhakti* is above all such material attempts. *Anyābhilāṣitā-śūnyaṁ jñāna-karmādy-*

anāvṛtam. Bhakti is uncontaminated, being unalloyed even by *jñāna* or pious activities.

TEXT 47

अथेशमायारचितेषु सङ्गं
गुणेषु गन्धर्वपुरोपमेषु ।
रूढं प्रकृत्यात्मनि विश्वकर्तु-
र्भावेन हित्वा तमहं प्रपद्ये ॥४७॥

atheśa-māyā-raciteṣu saṅgaṁ
guṇeṣu gandharva-puropameṣu
rūḍhaṁ prakṛtyātmani viśva-kartur
bhāvena hitvā tam ahaṁ prapadye

atha—therefore; *īśa-māyā*—by the external potency of the Supreme Personality of Godhead; *raciteṣu*—in things manufactured; *saṅgam*—attachment; *guṇeṣu*—in the modes of material nature; *gandharva-pura-upameṣu*—which are compared to the illusion of a *gandharva-pura*, a town or houses seen in the forest or on a hill; *rūḍham*—very powerful; *prakṛtyā*—by material nature; *ātmani*—unto the Supersoul; *viśva-kartuḥ*—of the creator of the whole universe; *bhāvena*—by devotional service; *hitvā*—giving up; *tam*—unto Him (the Lord); *aham*—I; *prapadye*—surrender.

TRANSLATION

Therefore I should now give up my attachment for things created by the external energy of the Supreme Personality of Godhead. I should engage in thought of the Lord and should thus surrender unto Him. This material creation, having been created by the external energy of the Lord, is like an imaginary town visualized on a hill or in a forest. Every conditioned soul has a natural attraction and attachment for material things, but one must simply give up this attachment and surrender unto the Supreme Personality of Godhead.

PURPORT

When passing through a mountainous region in an airplane, one may sometimes see a city in the sky with towers and palaces, or one may see similar things in a big forest. This is called a *gandharva-pura,* a phantasmagoria. This entire world resembles such a phantasmagoria, and every materially situated person has attachment for it. But Khaṭvāṅga Mahārāja, because of his advanced Kṛṣṇa consciousness, was not interested in such things. Even though a devotee may engage in apparently materialistic activities, he knows his position very well. *Nirbandhaḥ kṛṣṇa-sambandhe yuktaṁ vairāgyam ucyate.* If one engages all material things in relation with the loving service of the Lord, one is situated in *yukta-vairāgya,* proper renunciation. In this material world, nothing should be accepted for one's sense gratification: everything should be accepted for the service of the Lord. This is the mentality of the spiritual world. Mahārāja Khaṭvāṅga advises that one give up material attachments and surrender unto the Supreme Personality of Godhead. Thus one achieves success in life. This is pure *bhakti-yoga,* which involves *vairāgya-vidyā*—renunciation and knowledge.

vairāgya-vidyā-nija-bhakti-yoga-
śikṣārtham ekaḥ puruṣaḥ purāṇaḥ
śrī-kṛṣṇa-caitanya-śarīra-dhārī
kṛpāmbudhir yas tam ahaṁ prapadye

"Let me surrender unto the Personality of Godhead who has appeared now as Lord Śrī Caitanya Mahāprabhu. He is the ocean of all mercy and has come down to teach us material detachment, learning and devotional service to Himself." (*Caitanya-candrodaya-nāṭaka* 6.74) Śrī Kṛṣṇa Caitanya Mahāprabhu inaugurated this movement of *vairāgya-vidyā,* by which one detaches himself from material existence and engages in loving devotional service. The Kṛṣṇa consciousness movement of devotional service is the only process by which to counteract our false prestige in this material world.

TEXT 48

इति व्यवसितो बुद्ध्या नारायणगृहीतया ।
हित्वान्यभावमज्ञानं ततः स्वं भावमास्थितः ॥४८॥

iti vyavasito buddhyā
nārāyaṇa-gṛhītayā
hitvānya-bhāvam ajñānaṁ
tataḥ svaṁ bhāvam āsthitaḥ

iti—thus; *vyavasitaḥ*—having firmly decided; *buddhyā*—by proper intelligence; *nārāyaṇa-gṛhītayā*—completely controlled by the mercy of Nārāyaṇa, the Supreme Personality of Godhead; *hitvā*—giving up; *anya-bhāvam*—consciousness other than Kṛṣṇa consciousness; *ajñānam*—which is nothing but constant ignorance and darkness; *tataḥ*—thereafter; *svam*—his original position as an eternal servant of Kṛṣṇa; *bhāvam*—devotional service; *āsthitaḥ*—situated.

TRANSLATION

Thus Mahārāja Khaṭvāṅga, by his advanced intelligence in rendering service to the Lord, gave up false identification with the body full of ignorance. In his original position of eternal servitorship, he engaged himself in rendering service to the Lord.

PURPORT

When one actually becomes purely Kṛṣṇa conscious, no one has any right to rule over him. When situated in Kṛṣṇa consciousness, one is no longer in the darkness of ignorance, and when freed from all such darkness, one is situated in his original position. *Jīvera 'svarūpa' haya—kṛṣṇera 'nitya-dāsa.'* The living entity is eternally the servant of the Lord, and thus when he engages himself in the service of the Lord in all respects, he enjoys the perfection of life.

TEXT 49

यत् तद् ब्रह्म परं सूक्ष्ममशून्यं शून्यकल्पितम् ।
भगवान् वासुदेवेति यं गृणन्ति हि सात्वताः ॥४९॥

yat tad brahma paraṁ sūkṣmam
aśūnyaṁ śūnya-kalpitam

bhagavān vāsudeveti
yaṁ gṛṇanti hi sātvatāḥ

yat—that which; *tat*—such; *brahma param*—Parabrahman, the Supreme Personality of Godhead, Kṛṣṇa; *sūkṣmam*—spiritual, beyond all material conceptions; *aśūnyam*—not impersonal or void; *śūnya-kalpitam*—imagined to be void by less intelligent men; *bhagavān*—the Supreme Personality of Godhead; *vāsudeva*—Kṛṣṇa; *iti*—thus; *yam*—whom; *gṛṇanti*—sing about; *hi*—indeed; *sātvatāḥ*—pure devotees.

TRANSLATION

The Supreme Personality of Godhead, Vāsudeva, Kṛṣṇa, is extremely difficult to understand for unintelligent men who accept Him as impersonal or void, which He is not. The Lord is therefore understood and sung about by pure devotees.

PURPORT

As stated in *Śrīmad-Bhāgavatam* (1.2.11):

vadanti tat tattva-vidas
tattvaṁ yaj jñānam advayam
brahmeti paramātmeti
bhagavān iti śabdyate

The Absolute Truth is realized in three phases—as Brahman, Paramātmā and Bhagavān. Bhagavān is the origin of everything. Brahman is a partial representation of Bhagavān, and Vāsudeva, the Supersoul living everywhere and in everyone's heart, is also an advanced realization of the Supreme Personality of Godhead. But when one comes to understand the Supreme Personality of Godhead (*vāsudevaḥ sarvam iti*), when one realizes that Vāsudeva is both Paramātmā and the impersonal Brahman, he is then in perfect knowledge. Kṛṣṇa is therefore described by Arjuna as *paraṁ brahma paraṁ dhāma pavitraṁ paramaṁ bhavān.* The words *paraṁ brahma* refer to the shelter of the impersonal Brahman and also of the all-pervading Supersoul. When Kṛṣṇa says *tyaktvā dehaṁ punar janma naiti mām eti,* this means that the perfect devotee, after perfect realization, returns home, back to Godhead. Mahārāja Khaṭvāṅga accepted the shelter of the Supreme Personality of Godhead, and because of his full surrender he achieved perfection.

Thus end the Bhaktivedanta purports of the Ninth Canto, Ninth Chapter, of the Śrīmad-Bhāgavatam, *entitled "The Dynasty of Aṁśumān."*

CHAPTER TEN

The Pastimes of the Supreme Lord, Rāmacandra

This Tenth Chapter describes how Lord Rāmacandra appeared in the dynasty of Mahārāja Khaṭvāṅga. It also describes the Lord's activities, telling how He killed Rāvaṇa and returned to Ayodhyā, the capital of His kingdom.

The son of Mahārāja Khaṭvāṅga was Dīrghabāhu, and his son was Raghu. The son of Raghu was Aja, the son of Aja was Daśaratha, and the son of Daśaratha was Lord Rāmacandra, the Supreme Personality of Godhead. When the Lord descended into this world in His full quadruple expansion—as Lord Rāmacandra, Lakṣmaṇa, Bharata and Śatrughna—great sages like Vālmīki who were actually in knowledge of the Absolute Truth described His transcendental pastimes. Śrīla Śukadeva Gosvāmī describes these pastimes in brief.

Lord Rāmacandra went with Viśvāmitra and killed Rākṣasas like Mārīca. After breaking the stout and strong bow known as Haradhanu, the Lord married mother Sītā and cut down the prestige of Paraśurāma. To obey the order of His father, He entered the forest, accompanied by Lakṣmaṇa and Sītā. There He cut off the nose of Śūrpaṇakhā and killed the associates of Rāvaṇa, headed by Khara and Dūṣaṇa. Rāvaṇa's kidnapping of Sītādevī was the beginning of this demon's misfortune. When Mārīca assumed the form of a golden deer, Lord Rāmacandra went to bring the deer to please Sītādevī, but in the meantime Rāvaṇa took advantage of the Lord's absence to kidnap her. When Sītādevī was kidnapped, Lord Rāmacandra, accompanied by Lakṣmaṇa, searched for her throughout the forest. In the course of this search, They met Jaṭāyu. Then the Lord killed the demon Kabandha and the commander Vāli and established a friendly relationship with Sugrīva. After organizing the military strength of the monkeys and going with them to the shore of the sea, the Lord awaited the arrival of Samudra, the ocean personified, but when Samudra did not come, the Lord, the master of Samudra, became angry. Then Samudra came to the Lord with great haste and surrendered to Him, wanting to help Him in every way. The Lord then attempted to bridge the ocean, and, with the help of advice from Vibhīṣaṇa, He attacked Rāvaṇa's capital, Laṅkā. Previously, Hanumān, the eternal servant of the Lord, had set fire to Laṅkā, and now, with the help of Lakṣmaṇa, the forces of Lord Rāmacandra killed all the Rākṣasa soldiers. Then Lord Rāmacandra personally killed Rāvaṇa. Mandodarī and other wives lamented for Rāvaṇa, and in accordance with Lord Rāmacandra's order, Vibhīṣaṇa performed the funeral ceremonies for all the dead in the family. Lord Rāmacandra then gave Vibhīṣaṇa the right to rule Laṅkā and also granted him a long duration of life. The Lord delivered Sītādevī from the Aśoka forest and carried her in a flower airplane to His capital Ayodhyā, where He was received by His brother Bharata. When Lord Rāmacandra entered Ayodhyā, Bharata brought His wooden shoes, Vibhīṣaṇa and Sugrīva held a whisk and fan, Hanumān carried an umbrella, Śatrughna carried the Lord's bow and two quivers, and Sītādevī carried a waterpot containing water from holy places. Aṅgada carried a sword, and Jāmbavān (Ṛkṣarāja) carried a shield. After Lord Rāmacandra, accompanied by Lord Lakṣmaṇa and mother Sītādevī, met all His relatives, the great sage Vasiṣṭha enthroned Him as King. The chapter ends with a short description of Lord Rāmacandra's rule in Ayodhyā.

TEXT 1

श्रीशुक उवाच
खट्वाङ्गाद् दीर्घबाहुश्च रघुस्तस्मात् पृथुश्रवाः ।
अजस्ततो महाराजस्तस्माद् दशरथोऽभवत् ॥ १ ॥

śrī-śuka uvāca
khaṭvāṅgād dīrghabāhuś ca
raghus tasmāt pṛthu-śravāḥ
ajas tato mahā-rājas
tasmād daśaratho 'bhavat

śrī-śukaḥ uvāca—Śrī Śukadeva Gosvāmī said; *khaṭvāṅgāt*—from Mahārāja Khaṭvāṅga; *dīrghabāhuḥ*—the son named Dīrghabāhu; *ca*—

and; *raghuḥ tasmāt*—from him Raghu was born; *pṛthu-śravāḥ*—saintly and celebrated; *ajaḥ*—the son named Aja; *tataḥ*—from him; *mahā-rājaḥ*—the great king called Mahārāja Daśaratha; *tasmāt*—from Aja; *daśarathaḥ*—by the name Daśaratha; *abhavat*—was born.

TRANSLATION

Śukadeva Gosvāmī said: The son of Mahārāja Khaṭvāṅga was Dīrghabāhu, and his son was the celebrated Mahārāja Raghu. From Mahārāja Raghu came Aja, and from Aja was born the great personality Mahārāja Daśaratha.

TEXT 2

तस्यापि भगवानेष साक्षाद् ब्रह्ममयो हरिः ।
अंशांशेन चतुर्धागात् पुत्रत्वं प्रार्थितः सुरैः ।
रामलक्ष्मणभरतशत्रुघ्ना इति संज्ञया ॥ २ ॥

tasyāpi bhagavān eṣa
sākṣād brahmamayo hariḥ
aṁśāṁśena caturdhāgāt
putratvaṁ prārthitaḥ suraiḥ
rāma-lakṣmaṇa-bharata-
śatrughnā iti saṁjñayā

tasya—of him, Mahārāja Daśaratha; *api*—also; *bhagavān*—the Supreme Personality of Godhead; *eṣaḥ*—all of them; *sākṣāt*—directly; *brahma-mayaḥ*—the Supreme Parabrahman, the Absolute Truth; *hariḥ*—the Supreme Personality of Godhead; *aṁśa-aṁśena*—by an expansion of a plenary portion; *caturdhā*—by fourfold expansions; *agāt*—accepted; *putratvam*—sonhood; *prārthitaḥ*—being prayed for; *suraiḥ*—by the demigods; *rāma*—Lord Rāmacandra; *lakṣmaṇa*—Lord Lakṣmaṇa; *bharata*—Lord Bharata; *śatrughnāḥ*—and Lord Śatrughna; *iti*—thus; *saṁjñayā*—by different names.

TRANSLATION

Being prayed for by the demigods, the Supreme Personality of Godhead, the Absolute Truth Himself, directly appeared with His

expansion and expansions of the expansion. Their holy names were Rāma, Lakṣmaṇa, Bharata and Śatrughna. These celebrated incarnations thus appeared in four forms as the sons of Mahārāja Daśaratha.

PURPORT

Lord Rāmacandra and His brothers, Lakṣmaṇa, Bharata and Śatrughna, are all *viṣṇu-tattva,* not *jīva-tattva.* The Supreme Personality of Godhead expands into many, many forms. *Advaitam acyutam anādim ananta-rūpam.* Although they are one and the same, *viṣṇu-tattva* has many forms and incarnations. As confirmed in the *Brahma-saṁhitā* (5.39), *rāmādi-mūrtiṣu kalā-niyamena tiṣṭhan.* The Lord is situated in many forms, such as Rāma, Lakṣmaṇa, Bharata and Śatrughna, and these forms may exist in any part of His creation. All these forms exist permanently, eternally, as individual Personalities of Godhead, and they resemble many candles, all equally powerful. Lord Rāmacandra, Lakṣmaṇa, Bharata and Śatrughna, who, being *viṣṇu-tattva,* are all equally powerful, became the sons of Mahārāja Daśaratha in response to prayers by the demigods.

TEXT 3

तस्यानुचरितं राजन्नृषिभिस्तत्त्वदर्शिभिः ।
श्रुतं हि वर्णितं भूरि त्वया सीतापतेर्मुहुः ॥ ३ ॥

tasyānucaritaṁ rājann
ṛṣibhis tattva-darśibhiḥ
śrutaṁ hi varṇitaṁ bhūri
tvayā sītā-pater muhuḥ

tasya—of Him, the Supreme Personality of Godhead Lord Rāmacandra and His brothers; *anucaritam*—transcendental activities; *rājan*—O King (Mahārāja Parīkṣit); *ṛṣibhiḥ*—by great sages or saintly persons; *tattva-darśibhiḥ*—by persons who know the Absolute Truth; *śrutam*—have all been heard; *hi*—indeed; *varṇitam*—as they have been so nicely described; *bhūri*—many; *tvayā*—by you; *sītā-pateḥ*—of Lord Rāmacandra, the husband of mother Sītā; *muhuḥ*—more than often.

TRANSLATION

O King Parīkṣit, the transcendental activities of Lord Rāmacandra have been described by great saintly persons who have seen the truth. Because you have heard again and again about Lord Rāmacandra, the husband of mother Sītā, I shall describe these activities only in brief. Please listen.

PURPORT

Modern Rākṣasas, posing as educationally advanced merely because they have doctorates, have tried to prove that Lord Rāmacandra is not the Supreme Personality of Godhead but an ordinary person. But those who are learned and spiritually advanced will never accept such notions; they will accept the descriptions of Lord Rāmacandra and His activities only as presented by *tattva-darśīs,* those who know the Absolute Truth. In *Bhagavad-gītā* (4.34) the Supreme Personality of Godhead advises:

tad viddhi praṇipātena
paripraśnena sevayā
upadekṣyanti te jñānaṁ
jñāninas tattva-darśinaḥ

"Just try to learn the truth by approaching a spiritual master. Inquire from him submissively and render service unto him. The self-realized soul can impart knowledge unto you because he has seen the truth." Unless one is *tattva-darśī,* in complete knowledge of the Absolute Truth, one cannot describe the activities of the Personality of Godhead. Therefore although there are many so-called *Rāmāyaṇas,* or histories of Lord Rāmacandra's activities, some of them are not actually authoritative. Sometimes Lord Rāmacandra's activities are described in terms of one's own imaginations, speculations or material sentiments. But the characteristics of Lord Rāmacandra should not be handled as something imaginary. While describing the history of Lord Rāmacandra, Śukadeva Gosvāmī told Mahārāja Parīkṣit, "You have already heard about the activities of Lord Rāmacandra." Apparently, therefore, five thousand years ago there were many *Rāmāyaṇas,* or histories of Lord Rāmacandra's activities, and there are many still. But we must select only those books written by *tattva-darśīs* (*jñāninas tattva-darśinaḥ*), not the books of so-called scholars who claim knowledge only on the basis of a doctorate. This is a warning by Śukadeva Gosvāmī. *Ṛṣibhis tattva-darśibhiḥ.* Although the *Rāmāyaṇa* composed by Vālmīki is a huge literature, the same activities are summarized here by Śukadeva Gosvāmī in a few verses.

TEXT 4

गुर्वर्थे त्यक्तराज्यो व्यचरदनुवनं
पद्मपद्भ्यां प्रियायाः
पाणिस्पर्शाक्षमाभ्यां मृजितपथरुजो
यो हरीन्द्रानुजाभ्याम् ।
वैरूप्याच्छूर्पणख्याः प्रियविरहरुषा-
रोपितभ्रूविजृम्भ-
त्रस्ताब्धिर्बद्धसेतुः खलदवदहनः
कोसलेन्द्रोऽवतान्नः ॥ ४ ॥

gurv-arthe tyakta-rājyo vyacarad anuvanaṁ padma-padbhyāṁ priyāyāḥ
pāṇi-sparśākṣamābhyāṁ mṛjita-patha-rujo yo harīndrānujābhyām
vairūpyāc chūrpaṇakhyāḥ priya-viraha-ruṣāropita-bhrū-vijṛmbha-
trastābdhir baddha-setuḥ khala-dava-dahanaḥ kosalendro 'vatān naḥ

guru-arthe—for the sake of keeping the promise of His father; *tyakta-rājyaḥ*—giving up the position of king; *vyacarat*—wandered; *anuvanam*—from one forest to another; *padma-padbhyām*—by His two lotus feet; *priyāyāḥ*—with His very dear wife, mother Sītā; *pāṇi-sparśa-akṣamābhyām*—which were so delicate that they were unable to bear even the touch of Sītā's palm; *mṛjita-patha-rujaḥ*—whose fatigue due to walking on the street was diminished; *yaḥ*—the Lord who; *harīndra-anujābhyām*—accompanied by the king of the monkeys, Hanumān, and His younger brother Lakṣmaṇa; *vairūpyāt*—because of being disfigured; *śūrpaṇakhyāḥ*—of the Rākṣasī (demoness) named Śūrpaṇakhā; *priya-viraha*—being aggrieved by separation from His very dear wife; *ruṣā āropita-bhrū-vijṛmbha*—by flickering of His raised eyebrows in anger; *trasta*—fearing; *abdhiḥ*—the ocean; *baddha-setuḥ*—one who constructed a bridge over the ocean; *khala-dava-dahanaḥ*—killer of envious persons like Rāvaṇa, like a fire devouring a forest; *kosala-indraḥ*—the King of Ayodhyā; *avatāt*—be pleased to protect; *naḥ*—us.

TRANSLATION

To keep the promise of His father intact, Lord Rāmacandra immediately gave up the position of king and, accompanied by His wife, mother Sītā, wandered from one forest to another on His lotus feet, which were so delicate that they were unable to bear even the touch of Sītā's palms. The Lord was also accompanied by Hanumān [or by another monkey, Sugrīva], king of the monkeys, and by His own younger brother Lord Lakṣmaṇa, both of whom gave Him relief from the fatigue of wandering in the forest. Having cut off the nose and ears of Śūrpaṇakhā, thus disfiguring her, the Lord was separated from mother Sītā. He therefore became angry, moving His eyebrows and thus frightening the ocean, who then allowed the Lord to construct a bridge to cross the ocean. Subsequently, the Lord entered the kingdom of Rāvaṇa to kill him, like a fire devouring a forest. May that Supreme Lord, Rāmacandra, give us all protection.

TEXT 5

विश्वामित्राध्वरे येन मारीचाद्या निशाचराः ।
पश्यतो लक्ष्मणस्यैव हता नैर्ऋतपुङ्गवाः ॥ ५ ॥

viśvāmitrādhvare yena
mārīcādyā niśā-carāḥ
paśyato lakṣmaṇasyaiva
hatā nairṛta-puṅgavāḥ

viśvāmitra-adhvare—in the sacrificial arena of the great sage Viśvāmitra; *yena*—by whom (Lord Rāmacandra); *mārīca-ādyāḥ*—headed by Mārīca; *niśā-carāḥ*—the uncivilized persons wandering at night in the darkness of ignorance; *paśyataḥ lakṣmaṇasya*—being seen by Lakṣmaṇa; *eva*—indeed; *hatāḥ*—were killed; *nairṛta-puṅgavāḥ*—the great chiefs of the Rākṣasas.

TRANSLATION

In the arena of the sacrifice performed by Viśvāmitra, Lord Rāmacandra, the King of Ayodhyā, killed many demons, Rākṣasas and uncivilized men who wandered at night in the mode of darkness. May Lord Rāmacandra, who killed these demons in the presence of Lakṣmaṇa, be kind enough to give us protection.

TEXTS 6–7

यो लोकवीरसमितौ धनुरैशमुग्रं
सीतास्वयंवरगृहे त्रिशतोपनीतम् ।
आदाय बालगजलील इवेक्षुयष्टिं
सज्जयीकृतं नृप विकृष्य बभञ्ज मध्ये ॥ ६ ॥
जित्वानुरूपगुणशीलवयोऽङ्गरूपां
सीताभिधां श्रियमुरस्यभिलब्धमानाम् ।
मार्गे व्रजन् भृगुपतेर्व्यनयत् प्ररूढं
दर्पं महीमकृत यस्त्रिरराजबीजाम् ॥ ७ ॥

yo loka-vīra-samitau dhanur aiśam ugraṁ
sītā-svayaṁvara-gṛhe triśatopanītam
ādāya bāla-gaja-līla ivekṣu-yaṣṭiṁ
sajjyī-kṛtaṁ nṛpa vikṛṣya babhañja madhye

jitvānurūpa-guṇa-śīla-vayo 'ṅga-rūpāṁ
sītābhidhāṁ śriyam urasy abhilabdhamānām
mārge vrajan bhṛgupater vyanayat prarūḍhaṁ
darpaṁ mahīm akṛta yas trir arāja-bījām

yaḥ—Lord Rāmacandra who; *loka-vīra-samitau*—in the society or in the midst of many heroes of this world; *dhanuḥ*—the bow; *aiśam*—of

Lord Śiva; *ugram*—very fierce; *sītā-svayaṁvara-gṛhe*—in the hall where mother Sītā stood to select her husband; *triśata-upanītam*—the bow carried by three hundred men; *ādāya*—taking (that bow); *bāla-gaja-līlaḥ*—acting like a baby elephant in a forest of sugarcane; *iva*—like that; *ikṣu-yaṣṭim*—a stick of sugarcane; *sajjyī-kṛtam*—fastened the string of the bow; *nṛpa*—O King; *vikṛṣya*—by bending; *babhañja*—broke it; *madhye*—in the middle; *jitvā*—gaining by victory; *anurūpa*—just befitting His position and beauty; *guṇa*—qualities; *śīla*—behavior; *vayaḥ*—age; *aṅga*—body; *rūpām*—beauty; *sītā-abhidhām*—the girl named Sītā; *śriyam*—the goddess of fortune; *urasi*—on the chest; *abhilabdhamānām*—had gotten her previously; *mārge*—on the way; *vrajan*—while walking; *bhṛgupateḥ*—of Bhṛgupati; *vyanayat*—destroyed; *prarūḍham*—rooted very deep; *darpam*—pride; *mahīm*—the earth; *akṛta*—finished; *yaḥ*—one who; *triḥ*—three times (seven); *arāja*—without a royal dynasty; *bījām*—seed.

TRANSLATION

O King, the pastimes of Lord Rāmacandra were wonderful, like those of a baby elephant. In the assembly where mother Sītā was to choose her husband, in the midst of the heroes of this world, He broke the bow belonging to Lord Śiva. This bow was so heavy that it was carried by three hundred men, but Lord Rāmacandra bent and strung it and broke it in the middle, just as a baby elephant breaks a stick of sugarcane. Thus the Lord achieved the hand of mother Sītā, who was equally as endowed with transcendental qualities of form, beauty, behavior, age and nature. Indeed, she was the goddess of fortune who constantly rests on the chest of the Lord. While returning from Sītā's home after gaining her at the assembly of competitors, Lord Rāmacandra met Paraśurāma. Although Paraśurāma was very proud, having rid the earth of the royal order twenty-one times, he was defeated by the Lord, who appeared to be a kṣatriya of the royal order.

TEXT 8

यः सत्यपाशपरिवीतपितुर्निदेशं
स्त्रैणस्य चापि शिरसा जगृहे सभार्यः ।

राज्यं श्रियं प्रणयिनः सुहृदो निवासं
त्यक्त्वा ययौ वनमसूनिव मुक्तसङ्गः ॥ ८ ॥

yaḥ satya-pāśa-parivīta-pitur nideśaṁ
straiṇasya cāpi śirasā jagṛhe sabhāryaḥ
rājyaṁ śriyaṁ praṇayinaḥ suhṛdo nivāsaṁ
tyaktvā yayau vanam asūn iva mukta-saṅgaḥ

yaḥ—Lord Rāmacandra who; *satya-pāśa-parivīta-pituḥ*—of His father, who was bound by the promise to his wife; *nideśam*—the order; *straiṇasya*—of the father who was very much attached to his wife; *ca*—also; *api*—indeed; *śirasā*—on His head; *jagṛhe*—accepted; *sa-bhāryaḥ*—with His wife; *rājyam*—the kingdom; *śriyam*—opulence; *praṇayinaḥ*—relatives; *suhṛdaḥ*—friends; *nivāsam*—residence; *tyaktvā*—giving up; *yayau*—went; *vanam*—to the forest; *asūn*—life; *iva*—like; *mukta-saṅgaḥ*—a liberated soul.

TRANSLATION

Carrying out the order of His father, who was bound by a promise to his wife, Lord Rāmacandra left behind His kingdom, opulence, friends, well-wishers, residence and everything else, just as a liberated soul gives up his life, and went to the forest with Sītā.

PURPORT

Mahārāja Daśaratha had three wives. One of them, Kaikeyī, served him very pleasingly, and he therefore wanted to give her a benediction. Kaikeyī, however, said that she would ask for the benediction when it was necessary. At the time of the coronation of Prince Rāmacandra, Kaikeyī requested her husband to enthrone her son Bharata and send Rāmacandra to the forest. Mahārāja Daśaratha, being bound by his promise, ordered Rāmacandra to go to the forest, according to the dictation of his beloved. And the Lord, as an obedient son, accepted the order immediately. He left everything without hesitation, just as a liberated soul or great *yogī* gives up his life without material attraction.

TEXT 9

रक्षःस्वसुर्व्यकृत रूपमशुद्धबुद्धे-
स्तस्याः खरत्रिशिरदूषणमुख्यबन्धून् ।
जघ्ने चतुर्दशसहस्रमपारणीय-
कोदण्डपाणिरटमान उवास कृच्छ्रम् ॥ ९ ॥

rakṣaḥ-svasur vyakṛta rūpam aśuddha-buddhes
tasyāḥ khara-triśira-dūṣaṇa-mukhya-bandhūn
jaghne caturdaśa-sahasram apāraṇīya-
kodaṇḍa-pāṇir aṭamāna uvāsa kṛcchram

rakṣaḥ-svasuḥ—of Śūrpaṇakhā, the sister of the Rākṣasa (Rāvaṇa); *vyakṛta*—(Lord Rāma) deformed; *rūpam*—the form; *aśuddha-buddheḥ*—because her intelligence was polluted by lusty desires; *tasyāḥ*—of her; *khara-triśira-dūṣaṇa-mukhya-bandhūn*—many friends, headed by Khara, Triśira and Dūṣaṇa; *jaghne*—He (Lord Rāmacandra) killed; *caturdaśa-sahasram*—fourteen thousand; *apāraṇīya*—invincible; *kodaṇḍa*—bows and arrows; *pāṇiḥ*—in His hand; *aṭamānaḥ*—wandering in the forest; *uvāsa*—lived there; *kṛcchram*—with great difficulties.

TRANSLATION

While wandering in the forest, where He accepted a life of hardship, carrying His invincible bow and arrows in His hand, Lord Rāmacandra deformed Rāvaṇa's sister, who was polluted with lusty desires, by cutting off her nose and ears. He also killed her fourteen thousand Rākṣasa friends, headed by Khara, Triśira and Dūṣaṇa.

TEXT 10

सीताकथाश्रवणदीपितहृच्छयेन
सृष्टं विलोक्य नृपते दशकन्धरेण ।
जघ्नेऽद्भुतैणवपुषाश्रमतोऽपकृष्टो
मारीचमाशु विशिखेन यथा कमुग्रः ॥१०॥

sītā-kathā-śravaṇa-dīpita-hṛc-chayena
sṛṣṭaṁ vilokya nṛpate daśa-kandhareṇa
jaghne 'dbhutaiṇa-vapuṣāśramato 'pakṛṣṭo
mārīcam āśu viśikhena yathā kam ugraḥ

sītā-kathā—topics about Sītādevī; *śravaṇa*—by hearing; *dīpita*—agitated; *hṛt-śayena*—lusty desires within the mind of Rāvaṇa; *sṛṣṭam*—created; *vilokya*—seeing that; *nṛpate*—O King Parīkṣit; *daśa-kandhareṇa*—by Rāvaṇa, who had ten heads; *jaghne*—the Lord killed; *adbhuta-eṇa-vapuṣā*—by a deer made of gold; *āśramataḥ*—from His residence; *apakṛṣṭaḥ*—distracted to a distance; *mārīcam*—the demon Mārīca, who assumed the form of a golden deer; *āśu*—immediately; *viśikhena*—by a sharp arrow; *yathā*—as; *kam*—Dakṣa; *ugraḥ*—Lord Śiva.

TRANSLATION

O King Parīkṣit, when Rāvaṇa, who had ten heads on his shoulders, heard about the beautiful and attractive features of Sītā, his mind was agitated by lusty desires, and he went to kidnap her. To distract Lord Rāmacandra from His āśrama, Rāvaṇa sent Mārīca in the form of a golden deer, and when Lord Rāmacandra saw that wonderful deer, He left His residence and followed it and finally killed it with a sharp arrow, just as Lord Śiva killed Dakṣa.

TEXT 11

रक्षोऽधमेन वृकवद् विपिनेऽसमक्षं
वैदेहराजदुहितर्यपयापितायाम् ।
भ्रात्रा वने कृपणवत् प्रियया वियुक्तः
स्त्रीसङ्गिनां गतिमिति प्रथयंश्चचार ॥११॥

rakṣo-'dhamena vṛkavad vipine 'samakṣaṁ
vaideha-rāja-duhitary apayāpitāyām
bhrātrā vane kṛpaṇavat priyayā viyuktaḥ
strī-saṅgināṁ gatim iti prathayaṁś cacāra

rakṣaḥ-adhamena—by the most wicked among Rākṣasas, Rāvaṇa; *vṛka-vat*—like a tiger; *vipine*—in the forest; *asamakṣam*—unprotected; *vaideha-rāja-duhitari*—by this condition of mother Sītā, the daughter of the King of Videha; *apayāpitāyām*—having been kidnapped; *bhrātrā*—with His brother; *vane*—in the forest; *kṛpaṇa-vat*—as if a very distressed person; *priyayā*—by his dear wife; *viyuktaḥ*—separated; *strī-saṅginām*—of persons attracted to or connected with women; *gatim*—destination; *iti*—thus; *prathayan*—giving an example; *cacāra*—wandered.

TRANSLATION

When Rāmacandra entered the forest and Lakṣmaṇa was also absent, the worst of the Rākṣasas, Rāvaṇa, kidnapped Sītādevī, the daughter of the King of Videha, just as a tiger seizes unprotected sheep when the shepherd is absent. Then Lord Rāmacandra wandered in the forest with His brother Lakṣmaṇa as if very much distressed due to separation from His wife. Thus He showed by His personal example the condition of a person attached to women.

PURPORT

In this verse the words *strī-saṅgināṁ gatim iti* indicate that the condition of a person attached to women was shown by the Lord Himself. According to moral instructions, *gṛhe nārīṁ vivarjayet:* when one goes on a tour, one should not bring his wife. Formerly men used to travel without conveyances, but still, as far as possible, when one leaves home one should not take his wife with him, especially if one is in such a condition as Lord Rāmacandra when banished by the order of His father. Whether in the forest or at home, if one is attached to women this attachment is always troublesome, as shown by the Supreme Personality of Godhead by His personal example.

Of course, this is the material side of *strī-saṅgī*, but the situation of Lord Rāmacandra is spiritual, for He does not belong to the material world. *Nārāyaṇaḥ paro 'vyaktāt:* Nārāyaṇa is beyond the material creation. Because He is the creator of the material world, He is not subject to the conditions of the material world. The separation of Lord Rāmacandra from Sītā is spiritually understood as *vipralambha*, which is an activity of the *hlādinī* potency of the Supreme Personality of Godhead belonging to the *śṛṅgāra-rasa*, the mellow of conjugal love in the spiritual world. In the spiritual world the Supreme Personality of Godhead has all the dealings of love, displaying the symptoms called *sāttvika, sañcārī, vilāpa, mūrcchā* and *unmāda*. Thus when Lord Rāmacandra was separated from Sītā, all these spiritual symptoms were manifested. The Lord is neither impersonal nor impotent. Rather, He is *sac-cid-ānanda-vigraha*, the eternal form of knowledge and bliss. Thus He has all the symptoms of spiritual bliss. Feeling separation from one's beloved is also an item of spiritual bliss. As explained by Śrīla Svarūpa Dāmodara Gosvāmī, *rādhā-kṛṣṇa-praṇaya-vikṛtir hlādinī-śaktiḥ:* the dealings of love between Rādhā and Kṛṣṇa are displayed as the pleasure potency of the Lord. The Lord is the original source of all pleasure, the reservoir of all pleasure. Lord Rāmacandra, therefore, manifested the truth both spiritually and materially. Materially those who are attached to women suffer, but spiritually when there are feelings of separation between the Lord and His pleasure potency the spiritual bliss of the Lord increases. This is further explained in *Bhagavad-gītā* (9.11):

avajānanti māṁ mūḍhā
mānuṣīṁ tanum āśritam
paraṁ bhāvam ajānanto
mama bhūta-maheśvaram

One who does not know the spiritual potency of the Supreme Personality of Godhead thinks of the Lord as an ordinary human being. But the Lord's mind, intelligence and senses can never be affected by material conditions. This fact is further explained in the *Skanda Purāṇa*, as quoted by Madhvācārya:

nitya-pūrṇa-sukha-jñāna-
svarūpo 'sau yato vibhuḥ
ato 'sya rāma ity ākhyā
tasya duḥkhaṁ kuto 'ṇv api

tathāpi loka-śikṣārtham
aduḥkho duḥkha-vartivat
antarhitāṁ loka-dṛṣṭyā
sītām āsīt smarann iva

jñāpanārthaṁ punar nitya-
sambandhaḥ svātmanaḥ śriyāḥ
ayodhyāyā vinirgacchan
sarva-lokasya ceśvaraḥ
pratyakṣaṁ tu śriyā sārdhaṁ
jagāmānādir avyayaḥ

nakṣatra-māsa-gaṇitaṁ
trayodaśa-sahasrakam
brahmaloka-samaṁ cakre
samastaṁ kṣiti-maṇḍalam

rāmo rāmo rāma iti
sarveṣām abhavat tadā
sarvoramamayo loko
yadā rāmas tv apālayat

It was actually impossible for Rāvaṇa to take away Sītā. The form of Sītā taken by Rāvaṇa was an illusory representation of mother Sītā—*māyā-sītā.* When Sītā was tested in the fire, this *māyā-sītā* was burnt, and the real Sītā came out of the fire.

A further understanding to be derived from this example is that a woman, however powerful she may be in the material world, must be given protection, for as soon as she is unprotected she will be exploited by Rākṣasas like Rāvaṇa. Here the words *vaideha-rāja-duhitari* indicate that before mother Sītā was married to Lord Rāmacandra she was protected by her father, Vaideha-rāja. And when she was married she was protected by her husband. Therefore the conclusion is that a woman should always be protected. According to the Vedic rule, there is no scope for a woman's being independent (*asamakṣam*), for a woman cannot protect herself independently.

TEXT 12

दग्ध्वात्मकृत्यहतकृत्यमहन् कबन्धं
सख्यं विधाय कपिभिर्दयितागतिं तैः ।

बुद्ध्वाथ वालिनि हते प्लवगेन्द्रसैन्यै-
र्वेलामगात् स मनुजोऽजभवार्चिताङ्घ्रिः ॥१२॥

dagdhvātma-kṛtya-hata-kṛtyam ahan kabandhaṁ
sakhyaṁ vidhāya kapibhir dayitā-gatiṁ taiḥ
buddhvātha vālini hate plavagendra-sainyair
velām agāt sa manujo 'ja-bhavārcitāṅghriḥ

dagdhvā—by burning; *ātma-kṛtya-hata-kṛtyam*—after performing religious rituals required after the death of Jaṭāyu, who died for the Lord's cause; *ahan*—killed; *kabandham*—the demon Kabandha; *sakhyam*—friendship; *vidhāya*—after creating; *kapibhiḥ*—with the monkey chiefs; *dayitā-gatim*—the arrangement for delivering Sītā; *taiḥ*—by them; *buddhvā*—knowing; *atha*—thereafter; *vālini hate*—when Vāli had been killed; *plavaga-indra-sainyaiḥ*—with the help of the soldiers of the monkeys; *velām*—to the beach of the ocean; *agāt*—went; *saḥ*—He, Lord Rāmacandra; *manu-jaḥ*—appearing as a human being; *aja*—by Lord Brahmā; *bhava*—and by Lord Śiva; *arcita-aṅghriḥ*—whose lotus feet are worshiped.

TRANSLATION

Lord Rāmacandra, whose lotus feet are worshiped by Lord Brahmā and Lord Śiva, had assumed the form of a human being. Thus He performed the funeral ceremony of Jaṭāyu, who was killed by Rāvaṇa. The Lord then killed the demon named Kabandha, and after making friends with the monkey chiefs, killing Vāli and arranging for the deliverance of mother Sītā, He went to the beach of the ocean.

PURPORT

When Rāvaṇa kidnapped Sītā, he was obstructed on the way by Jaṭāyu, a large bird. But the powerful Rāvaṇa defeated Jaṭāyu in the fight and cut his wing. When Rāmacandra was searching for Sītā, He found Jaṭāyu almost dead and was informed that Sītā has been carried off by Rāvaṇa. When Jaṭāyu died, Lord Rāmacandra did the duty of a son by performing the funeral ceremony, and then He made friends with the monkeys to deliver Sītādevī.

TEXT 13

यद्रोषविभ्रमविवृत्तकटाक्षपात-
संभ्रान्तनक्रमकरो भयगीर्णघोषः ।
सिन्धुः शिरस्यर्हणं परिगृह्य रूपी
पादारविन्दमुपगम्य बभाष एतत् ॥१३॥

yad-roṣa-vibhrama-vivṛtta-kaṭākṣa-pāta-
sambhrānta-nakra-makaro bhaya-gīrṇa-ghoṣaḥ
sindhuḥ śirasy arhaṇaṁ parigṛhya rūpī
pādāravindam upagamya babhāṣa etat

yat-roṣa—whose anger; *vibhrama*—induced by; *vivṛtta*—turned; *kaṭākṣa-pāta*—by the glance; *sambhrānta*—agitated; *nakra*—crocodiles; *makaraḥ*—and sharks; *bhaya-gīrṇa-ghoṣaḥ*—whose loud sound was silenced through fear; *sindhuḥ*—the ocean; *śirasi*—on his head; *arhaṇam*—all paraphernalia for worshiping the Lord; *parigṛhya*—carrying; *rūpī*—taking form; *pāda-aravindam*—the lotus feet of the Lord; *upagamya*—reaching; *babhāṣa*—said; *etat*—the following.

TRANSLATION

After reaching the beach, Lord Rāmacandra fasted for three days, awaiting the arrival of the ocean personified. When the ocean did not come, the Lord exhibited His pastimes of anger, and simply by His glancing over the ocean, all the living entities within it, including the crocodiles and sharks, were agitated by fear. Then the personified ocean fearfully approached Lord Rāmacandra, taking all paraphernalia to worship Him. Falling at the Lord's lotus feet, the personified ocean spoke as follows.

TEXT 14

न त्वां वयं जडधियो नु विदाम भूमन्
कूटस्थमादिपुरुषं जगतामधीशम् ।
यत्सत्त्वतः सुरगणा रजसः प्रजेशा
मन्योश्च भूतपतयः स भवान् गुणेशः ॥१४॥

na tvāṁ vayaṁ jaḍa-dhiyo nu vidāma bhūman
kūṭa-stham ādi-puruṣaṁ jagatām adhīśam
yat-sattvataḥ sura-gaṇā rajasaḥ prajeśā
manyoś ca bhūta-patayaḥ sa bhavān guṇeśaḥ

na—not; *tvām*—Your Lordship; *vayam*—we; *jaḍa-dhiyaḥ*—dull-minded, possessing blunt intelligence; *nu*—indeed; *vidāmaḥ*—can know; *bhūman*—O Supreme; *kūṭa-stham*—within the core of the heart; *ādi-puruṣam*—the original Personality of Godhead; *jagatām*—of the universes, which progressively go on; *adhīśam*—the supreme master; *yat*—fixed under Your direction; *sattvataḥ*—infatuated with *sattva-guṇa; sura-gaṇāḥ*—such demigods; *rajasaḥ*—infatuated with *rajo-guṇa; prajā-īśāḥ*—the Prajāpatis; *manyoḥ*—influenced by *tamo-guṇa; ca*—and; *bhūta-patayaḥ*—rulers of ghosts; *saḥ*—such a personality; *bhavān*—Your Lordship; *guṇa-īśaḥ*—the master of all three modes of material nature.

TRANSLATION

O all-pervading Supreme Person, we are dull-minded and did not understand who You are, but now we understand that You are the Supreme Person, the master of the entire universe, the unchanging and original Personality of Godhead. The demigods are infatuated with the mode of goodness, the Prajāpatis with the mode of passion, and the lord of ghosts with the mode of ignorance, but You are the master of all these qualities.

PURPORT

The word *jaḍa-dhiyaḥ* refers to intelligence like that of an animal. A person with such intelligence cannot understand the Supreme Personality of Godhead. Without being beaten, an animal cannot understand the purpose of a man. Similarly, those who are dull-minded cannot understand the Supreme Personality of Godhead, but when punished severely by the modes of material nature, they begin to understand Him. A Hindi poet has said:

duḥkha se saba hari bhaje
sukha se bhaje koī

sukha se agar hari bhaje
duḥkha kāthāṅ se haya

When one is distressed he goes to the church or temple to worship the Lord, but when opulent he forgets the Lord. Therefore, punishment by the Lord through material nature is necessary in human society, for without it men forget the supremacy of the Lord due to their dull, blunt intelligence.

TEXT 15

कामं प्रयाहि जहि विश्रवसोऽवमेहं
त्रैलोक्यरावणमवाप्नुहि वीर पत्नीम् ।
बध्नीहि सेतुमिह ते यशसो वितत्यै
गायन्ति दिग्विजयिनो यमुपेत्य भूपाः ॥१५॥

kāmaṁ prayāhi jahi viśravaso 'vamehaṁ
trailokya-rāvaṇam avāpnuhi vīra patnīm
badhnīhi setum iha te yaśaso vitatyai
gāyanti dig-vijayino yam upetya bhūpāḥ

kāmam—as You like; *prayāhi*—You may go over my water; *jahi*—just conquer; *viśravasaḥ*—of Viśravā Muni; *avameham*—pollution, like urine; *trailokya*—for the three worlds; *rāvaṇam*—the person known as Rāvaṇa, the cause of weeping; *avāpnuhi*—regain; *vīra*—O great hero; *patnīm*—Your wife; *badhnīhi*—just construct; *setum*—a bridge; *iha*—here (on this water); *te*—of Your good self; *yaśasaḥ*—fame; *vitatyai*—to expand; *gāyanti*—will glorify; *dik-vijayinaḥ*—great heroes who have conquered all directions; *yam*—which (bridge); *upetya*—coming near; *bhūpāḥ*—great kings.

TRANSLATION

My Lord, You may use my water as You like. Indeed, You may cross it and go to the abode of Rāvaṇa, who is the great source of disturbance and crying for the three worlds. He is the son of Viśravā, but is condemned like urine. Please go kill him and thus

regain Your wife, Sītādevī. O great hero, although my water presents no impediment to Your going to Laṅkā, please construct a bridge over it to spread Your transcendental fame. Upon seeing this wonderfully uncommon deed of Your Lordship, all the great heroes and kings in the future will glorify You.

PURPORT

It is said that a son and urine emanate from the same source—the genitals. When a son is a devotee or a great learned person, the seminal discharge for begetting a son is successful, but if the son is unqualified and brings no glory to his family, he is no better than urine. Here Rāvaṇa is compared to urine because he was a cause of disturbances to the three worlds. Thus the ocean personified wanted him killed by Lord Rāmacandra.

One feature of the Supreme Personality of Godhead Lord Rāmacandra is omnipotence. The Lord can act without regard to material impediments or inconveniences, but to prove that He is the Supreme Personality of Godhead and was not merely advertised as Godhead or elected by popular vote, He constructed a wonderful bridge over the ocean. Nowadays it has become fashionable to create some artificial God who performs no uncommon activities; a little magic will bewilder a foolish person into selecting an artificial God because he does not understand how powerful God is. Lord Rāmacandra, however, constructed a bridge over the water with stone by making the stone float. This is proof of God's uncommonly wonderful power. Why should someone be accepted as God without displaying extraordinary potency by doing something never to be done by any common man? We accept Lord Rāmacandra as the Supreme Personality of Godhead because He constructed this bridge, and we accept Lord Kṛṣṇa as the Supreme Personality of Godhead because He lifted Govardhana Hill when He was only seven years old. We should not accept any rascal as God or an incarnation of God, for God displays special features in His various activities. Therefore, the Lord Himself says in *Bhagavad-gītā* (4.9):

janma karma ca me divyam
evaṁ yo vetti tattvataḥ

tyaktvā dehaṁ punar janma
naiti mām eti so 'rjuna

"One who knows the transcendental nature of My appearance and activities does not, upon leaving the body, take his birth again in this material world, but attains My eternal abode, O Arjuna." The activities of the Lord are not common; they are all transcendentally wonderful and not able to be performed by any other living being. The symptoms of the Lord's activities are all mentioned in the *śāstras*, and after one understands them one can accept the Lord as He is.

TEXT 16

बद्ध्वोदधौ रघुपतिर्विविधाद्रिकूटैः
सेतुं कपीन्द्रकरकम्पितभूरुहाङ्गैः ।
सुग्रीवनीलहनुमत्प्रमुखैरनीकै-
र्लङ्कां विभीषणदृशाविशदग्रदग्धाम् ॥१६॥

baddhvodadhau raghu-patir vividhādri-kūṭaiḥ
setuṁ kapīndra-kara-kampita-bhūruhāṅgaiḥ
sugrīva-nīla-hanumat-pramukhair anīkair
laṅkāṁ vibhīṣaṇa-dṛśāviśad agra-dagdhām

baddhvā—after constructing; *udadhau*—in the water of the ocean; *raghu-patiḥ*—Lord Rāmacandra; *vividha*—varieties of; *adri-kūṭaiḥ*—with peaks of great mountains; *setum*—a bridge; *kapi-indra*—of powerful monkeys; *kara-kampita*—moved by the great hands; *bhūruha-aṅgaiḥ*—with the trees and plants; *sugrīva*—Sugrīva; *nīla*—Nīla; *hanumat*—Hanumān; *pramukhaiḥ*—led by; *anīkaiḥ*—with such soldiers; *laṅkām*—Laṅkā, the kingdom of Rāvaṇa; *vibhīṣaṇa-dṛśā*—by the direction of Vibhīṣaṇa, the brother of Rāvaṇa; *āviśat*—entered; *agra-dagdhām*—which was previously burnt (by the monkey soldier Hanumān).

TRANSLATION

Śukadeva Gosvāmī said: After constructing a bridge over the ocean by throwing into the water the peaks of mountains whose

trees and other vegetation had been shaken by the hands of great monkeys, Lord Rāmacandra went to Laṅkā to release Sītādevī from the clutches of Rāvaṇa. With the direction and help of Vibhīṣaṇa, Rāvaṇa's brother, the Lord, along with the monkey soldiers, headed by Sugrīva, Nīla and Hanumān, entered Rāvaṇa's kingdom, Laṅkā, which had previously been burnt by Hanumān.

PURPORT

Great mountain peaks covered with trees and plants were thrown into the sea by the monkey soldiers and began to float by the supreme will of the Lord. By the supreme will of the Lord, many great planets float weightlessly in space like swabs of cotton. If this is possible, why should great mountain peaks not be able to float on water? This is the omnipotence of the Supreme Personality of Godhead. He can do anything and everything He likes, because He is not under the control of the material nature; indeed, material nature is controlled by Him. *Mayādhyakṣeṇa prakṛtiḥ sūyate sacarācaram:* only under His direction does *prakṛti,* or material nature, work. Similar information is given in the *Brahma-saṁhitā* (5.52):

yasyājñayā bhramati sambhṛta-kāla-cakro
govindam ādi-puruṣaṁ tam ahaṁ bhajāmi

Describing how material nature works, the *Brahma-saṁhitā* says that the sun moves as desired by the Supreme Personality of Godhead. Consequently, for Lord Rāmacandra to construct a bridge over the Indian Ocean with the help of monkey soldiers who threw great mountain peaks into the water is not at all wonderful; it is wonderful only in the sense that it has kept the name and fame of Lord Rāmacandra eternally celebrated.

TEXT 17

सा वानरेन्द्रबलरुद्धविहारकोष्ठ-
श्रीद्वारगोपुरसदोवलभीविटङ्का ।
निर्भज्यमानधिषणध्वजहेमकुम्भ-
शृङ्गाटका गजकुलैर्ह्रदिनीव घूर्णा ॥१७॥

sā vānarendra-bala-ruddha-vihāra-koṣṭha-
śrī-dvāra-gopura-sado-valabhī-viṭaṅkā
nirbhajyamāna-dhiṣaṇa-dhvaja-hema-kumbha-
śṛṅgāṭakā gaja-kulair hradinīva ghūrṇā

sā—the place known as Laṅkā; *vānara-indra*—of the great chiefs of the monkeys; *bala*—by the strength; *ruddha*—stopped, encircled; *vihāra*—pleasure houses; *koṣṭha*—the places where food grains were stocked; *śrī*—the treasury houses; *dvāra*—the doors of palaces; *gopura*—the gates of the city; *sadaḥ*—the assembly houses; *valabhī*—the frontage of great palaces; *viṭaṅkā*—the rest houses for the pigeons; *nirbhajyamāna*—in the process of being dismantled; *dhiṣaṇa*—platforms; *dhvaja*—the flags; *hema-kumbha*—golden waterpots on the domes; *śṛṅgāṭakā*—and the crossroads; *gaja-kulaiḥ*—by herds of elephants; *hradinī*—a river; *iva*—like; *ghūrṇā*—agitated.

TRANSLATION

After entering Laṅkā, the monkey soldiers, led by chiefs like Sugrīva, Nīla and Hanumān, occupied all the sporting houses, granaries, treasuries, palace doorways, city gates, assembly houses, palace frontages and even the resting houses of the pigeons. When the city's crossroads, platforms, flags and golden waterpots on its domes were all destroyed, the entire city of Laṅkā appeared like a river disturbed by a herd of elephants.

TEXT 18

रक्षःपतिस्तदवलोक्य निकुम्भकुम्भ-
धूम्राक्षदुर्मुखसुरान्तकनरान्तकादीन् ।
पुत्रं प्रहस्तमतिकायविकम्पनादीन्
सर्वानुगान् समहिनोदथ कुम्भकर्णम् ॥१८॥

rakṣaḥ-patis tad avalokya nikumbha-kumbha-
dhūmrākṣa-durmukha-surāntaka-narāntakādīn
putraṁ prahastam atikāya-vikampanādīn
sarvānugān samahinod atha kumbhakarṇam

rakṣaḥ-patiḥ—the master of the Rākṣasas (Rāvaṇa); *tat*—such disturbances; *avalokya*—after seeing; *nikumbha*—Nikumbha; *kumbha*—Kumbha; *dhūmrākṣa*—Dhūmrākṣa; *durmukha*—Durmukha; *surāntaka*—Surāntaka; *narāntaka*—Narāntaka; *ādīn*—all of them together; *putram*—his son, Indrajit; *prahastam*—Prahasta; *atikāya*—Atikāya; *vikampana*—Vikampana; *ādīn*—all of them together; *sarva-anugān*—all followers of Rāvaṇa; *samahinot*—ordered (to fight with the enemies); *atha*—at last; *kumbhakarṇam*—Kumbhakarṇa, the most important brother.

TRANSLATION

When Rāvaṇa, the master of the Rākṣasas, saw the disturbances created by the monkey soldiers, he called for Nikumbha, Kumbha, Dhūmrākṣa, Durmukha, Surāntaka, Narāntaka and other Rākṣasas and also his son Indrajit. Thereafter he called for Prahasta, Atikāya, Vikampana and finally Kumbhakarṇa. Then he induced all his followers to fight against the enemies.

TEXT 19

तां यातुधानपृतनामसिशूलचाप-
प्रासर्ष्टिशक्तिशरतोमरखड्गदुर्गाम् ।
सुग्रीवलक्ष्मणमरुत्सुतगन्धमाद-
नीलाङ्गदर्क्षपनसादिभिरन्वितोऽगात् ॥१९॥

tāṁ yātudhāna-pṛtanām asi-śūla-cāpa-
prāsarṣṭi-śaktiśara-tomara-khaḍga-durgām
sugrīva-lakṣmaṇa-marutsuta-gandhamāda-
nīlāṅgadarkṣa-panasādibhir anvito 'gāt

tām—all of them; *yātudhāna-pṛtanām*—the soldiers of the Rākṣasas; *asi*—by swords; *śūla*—by lances; *cāpa*—by bows; *prāsa-ṛṣṭi*—*prāsa* weapons and *ṛṣṭi* weapons; *śakti-śara*—*śakti* arrows; *tomara*—*tomara* weapons; *khaḍga*—by a type of sword; *durgām*—all invincible; *sugrīva*—by the monkey named Sugrīva; *lakṣmaṇa*—by Lord Rāmacandra's younger brother; *marut-suta*—by Hanumān; *gandhamāda*—

by Gandhamāda, another monkey; *nīla*—by the monkey named Nīla; *aṅgada*—Aṅgada; *ṛkṣa*—Ṛkṣa; *panasa*—Panasa; *ādibhiḥ*—and by other soldiers; *anvitaḥ*—being surrounded, Lord Rāmacandra; *agāt*—came in front of (for the sake of fighting).

TRANSLATION

Lord Rāmacandra, surrounded by Lakṣmaṇa and monkey soldiers like Sugrīva, Hanumān, Gandhamāda, Nīla, Aṅgada, Jāmbavān and Panasa, attacked the soldiers of the Rākṣasas, who were fully equipped with various invincible weapons like swords, lances, bows, prāsas, ṛṣṭis, śakti arrows, khaḍgas and tomaras.

TEXT 20

तेऽनीकपा रघुपतेरभिपत्य सर्वे
द्वन्द्वं वरूथमिभपत्तिरथाश्वयोधैः ।
जघ्नुर्द्रुमैर्गिरिगदेषुभिरङ्गदाद्याः
सीताभिमर्षहतमङ्गलरावणेशान् ॥२०॥

te 'nīkapā raghupater abhipatya sarve
dvandvaṁ varūtham ibha-patti-rathāśva-yodhaiḥ
jaghnur drumair giri-gadeṣubhir aṅgadādyāḥ
sītābhimarṣa-hata-maṅgala-rāvaṇeśān

te—all of them; *anīka-pāḥ*—the commanders of the soldiers; *raghu-pateḥ*—of Lord Śrī Rāmacandra; *abhipatya*—chasing the enemy; *sarve*—all of them; *dvandvam*—fighting; *varūtham*—the soldiers of Rāvaṇa; *ibha*—by elephants; *patti*—by infantry; *ratha*—by chariots; *aśva*—by horses; *yodhaiḥ*—by such warriors; *jaghnuḥ*—killed them; *drumaiḥ*—by throwing big trees; *giri*—by peaks of mountains; *gadā*—by clubs; *iṣubhiḥ*—by arrows; *aṅgada-ādyāḥ*—all the soldiers of Lord Rāmacandra, headed by Aṅgada and others; *sītā*—of mother Sītā; *abhimarṣa*—by the anger; *hata*—had been condemned; *maṅgala*—whose auspiciousness; *rāvaṇa-īśān*—the followers or dependents of Rāvaṇa.

TRANSLATION

Aṅgada and the other commanders of the soldiers of Rāmacandra faced the elephants, infantry, horses and chariots of the enemy and hurled against them big trees, mountain peaks, clubs and arrows. Thus the soldiers of Lord Rāmacandra killed Rāvaṇa's soldiers, who had lost all good fortune because Rāvaṇa had been condemned by the anger of mother Sītā.

PURPORT

The soldiers Lord Rāmacandra recruited in the jungle were all monkeys and did not have proper equipment with which to fight the soldiers of Rāvaṇa, for Rāvaṇa's soldiers were equipped with weapons of modern warfare whereas the monkeys could only throw stones, mountain peaks and trees. It was only Lord Rāmacandra and Lakṣmaṇa who shot some arrows. But because the soldiers of Rāvaṇa were condemned by the curse of mother Sītā, the monkeys were able to kill them simply by throwing stones and trees. There are two kinds of strength—*daiva* and *puruṣākāra*. *Daiva* refers to the strength achieved from the Transcendence, and *puruṣākāra* refers to the strength organized by one's own intelligence and power. Transcendental power is always superior to the power of the materialist. Depending on the mercy of the Supreme Lord, one must fight one's enemies even though one may not be equipped with modern weapons. Therefore Kṛṣṇa instructed Arjuna, *mām anusmara yudhya ca:* "Think of Me and fight." We should fight our enemy to the best of our ability, but for victory we must depend on the mercy of the Supreme Personality of Godhead.

TEXT 21

रक्षःपतिः स्वबलनष्टिमवेक्ष्य रुष्ट
आरुह्य यानकमथाभिससार रामम् ।
स्वःस्यन्दने द्युमति मातलिनोपनीते
विभ्राजमानमहनन्निशितैः क्षुरप्रैः ॥२१॥

rakṣaḥ-patiḥ sva-bala-naṣṭim avekṣya ruṣṭa
āruhya yānakam athābhisasāra rāmam

svaḥ-syandane dyumati mātalinopanīte
vibhrājamānam ahanan niśitaiḥ kṣurapraiḥ

rakṣaḥ-patiḥ—the leader of the Rākṣasas, Rāvaṇa; *sva-bala-naṣṭim*—the destruction of his own soldiers; *avekṣya*—after observing; *ruṣṭaḥ*—became very angry; *āruhya*—riding on; *yānakam*—his beautiful airplane decorated with flowers; *atha*—thereafter; *abhisasāra*—proceeded toward; *rāmam*—Lord Rāmacandra; *svaḥ-syandane*—in the celestial chariot of Indra; *dyumati*—glittering; *mātalinā*—by Mātali, the chariot driver of Indra; *upanīte*—having been brought; *vibhrājamānam*—Lord Rāmacandra, as if brilliantly illuminating; *ahanat*—Rāvaṇa struck Him; *niśitaiḥ*—very sharp; *kṣurapraiḥ*—with arrows.

TRANSLATION

Thereafter, when Rāvaṇa, the King of the Rākṣasas, observed that his soldiers had been lost, he was extremely angry. Thus he mounted his airplane, which was decorated with flowers, and proceeded toward Lord Rāmacandra, who sat on the effulgent chariot brought by Mātali, the chariot driver of Indra. Then Rāvaṇa struck Lord Rāmacandra with sharp arrows.

TEXT 22

रामस्तमाह पुरुषादपुरीष यन्नः
कान्तासमक्षमसतापहृता श्ववत् ते ।
त्यक्तत्रपस्य फलमद्य जुगुप्सितस्य
यच्छामि काल इव कर्तुरलङ्घ्यवीर्यः ॥२२॥

rāmas tam āha puruṣāda-purīṣa yan naḥ
kāntāsamakṣam asatāpahṛtā śvavat te
tyakta-trapasya phalam adya jugupsitasya
yacchāmi kāla iva kartur alaṅghya-vīryaḥ

rāmaḥ—Lord Rāmancadra; *tam*—unto him, Rāvaṇa; *āha*—said; *puruṣa-ada-purīṣa*—you are the stool of the man-eaters (Rākṣasas);

yat—because; *naḥ*—My; *kāntā*—wife; *asamakṣam*—helpless because of My absence; *asatā*—by you, the most sinful; *apahṛtā*—was kidnapped; *śva-vat*—like a dog who takes food from the kitchen in the absence of the proprietor; *te*—of you; *tyakta-trapasya*—because you are shameless; *phalam adya*—I shall give you the result today; *jugupsitasya*—of you, the most abominable; *yacchāmi*—I shall punish you; *kālaḥ iva*—like death; *kartuḥ*—of you, who are the performer of all sinful activities; *alaṅghya-vīryaḥ*—but I, being omnipotent, never fail in My attempt.

TRANSLATION

Lord Rāmacandra said to Rāvaṇa: You are the most abominable of the man-eaters. Indeed, you are like their stool. You resemble a dog, for as a dog steals eatables from the kitchen in the absence of the householder, in My absence you kidnapped My wife, Sītādevī. Therefore as Yamarāja punishes sinful men, I shall also punish you. You are most abominable, sinful and shameless. Today, therefore, I, whose attempt never fails, shall punish you.

PURPORT

Na ca daivāt paraṁ balam: no one can surpass the strengh of the Transcendence. Rāvaṇa was so sinful and shameless that he did not know what the result would be of kidnapping mother Sītā, the pleasure potency of Rāmacandra. This is the disqualification of the Rākṣasas. *Asatyam apratiṣṭhaṁ te jagad āhur anīśvaram.* The Rākṣasas are unaware that the Supreme Lord is the ruler of the creation. They think that everything has come about by chance or accident and that there is no ruler, king or controller. Therefore the Rākṣasas act independently, as they like, going even so far as to kidnap the goddess of fortune. This policy of Rāvaṇa's is extremely dangerous for the materialist; indeed, it brings ruin to the materialistic civilization. Nonetheless, because atheists are Rākṣasas, they dare to do things that are most abominable, and thus they are punished without fail. Religion consists of the orders of the Supreme Lord, and one who carries out these orders is religious. One who fails to carry out the Lord's orders is irreligious, and he is to be punished.

TEXT 23

एवं क्षिपन् धनुषि संधितमुत्ससर्ज
बाणं स वज्रमिव तद्धृदयं बिभेद ।
सोऽसृग् वमन् दशमुखैर्न्यपतद् विमाना-
द्धाहेति जल्पति जने सुकृतीव रिक्तः ॥२३॥

evaṁ kṣipan dhanuṣi sandhitam utsasarja
bāṇaṁ sa vajram iva tad-dhṛdayaṁ bibheda
so 'sṛg vaman daśa-mukhair nyapatad vimānād
dhāheti jalpati jane sukṛtīva riktaḥ

evam—in this way; *kṣipan*—chastising (Rāvaṇa); *dhanuṣi*—on the bow; *sandhitam*—fixed an arrow; *utsasarja*—released (toward him); *bāṇam*—the arrow; *saḥ*—that arrow; *vajram iva*—like a thunderbolt; *tat-hṛdayam*—the heart of Rāvaṇa; *bibheda*—pierced; *saḥ*—he, Rāvaṇa; *asṛk*—blood; *vaman*—vomiting; *daśa-mukhaiḥ*—through the ten mouths; *nyapatat*—fell down; *vimānāt*—from his airplane; *hāhā*—alas, what happened; *iti*—thus; *jalpati*—roaring; *jane*—when all the people present there; *sukṛtī iva*—like a pious man; *riktaḥ*—when the results of his pious activities are finished.

TRANSLATION

After thus rebuking Rāvaṇa, Lord Rāmacandra fixed an arrow to His bow, aimed at Rāvaṇa, and released the arrow, which pierced Rāvaṇa's heart like a thunderbolt. Upon seeing this, Rāvaṇa's followers raised a tumultuous sound, crying, "Alas! Alas! What has happened? What has happened?" as Rāvaṇa, vomiting blood from his ten mouths, fell from his airplane, just as a pious man falls to earth from the heavenly planets when the results of his pious activities are exhausted.

PURPORT

In *Bhagavad-gītā* (9.21) it is said, *kṣīṇe puṇye martya-lokaṁ viśanti:* "When the results of their pious activities are exhausted, those who have enjoyed in the heavenly planets fall again to earth." The fruitive activities of this material world are such that whether one acts piously or impiously one must remain within the material world according to different conditions, for neither pious nor impious actions can relieve one from *māyā's* clutches of repeated birth and death. Somehow or other, Rāvaṇa was raised to an exalted position as the king of a great kingdom with all material opulences, but because of his sinful act of kidnapping mother Sītā, all the results of his pious activities were destroyed. If one offends an exalted personality, especially the Supreme Personality of Godhead, one certainly becomes most abominable; bereft of the results of pious activities, one must fall down like Rāvaṇa and other demons. It is therefore advised that one transcend both pious and impious activities and remain in the pure state of freedom from all designations (*sarvopādhi-vinirmuktaṁ tat-paratvena nirmalam*). When one is fixed in devotional service, he is above the material platform. On the material platform there are higher and lower positions, but when one is above the material platform he is always fixed in a spiritual position (*sa guṇān samatītyaitān brahma-bhūyāya kalpate*). Rāvaṇa or those like him may be very powerful and opulent in this material world, but theirs is not a secure position, because, after all, they are bound by the results of their *karma* (*karmaṇā daiva-netreṇa*). We should not forget that we are completely dependent on the laws of nature.

prakṛteḥ kriyamāṇāni
guṇaiḥ karmāṇi sarvaśaḥ
ahaṅkāra-vimūḍhātmā
kartāham iti manyate

"The bewildered spirit soul, under the influence of the three modes of material nature, thinks himself the doer of activities that are in actuality carried out by nature." (Bg. 3.27) One should not be proud of one's exalted position and act like Rāvaṇa, thinking oneself independent of material nature's laws.

TEXT 24

ततो निष्क्रम्य लङ्काया यातुधान्यः सहस्रशः ।
मन्दोदर्या समं तत्र प्ररुदन्त्य उपाद्रवन् ॥२४॥

tato niṣkramya laṅkāyā
yātudhānyaḥ sahasraśaḥ
mandodaryā samaṁ tatra
prarudantya upādravan

tataḥ—thereafter; *niṣkramya*—coming out; *laṅkāyāḥ*—from Laṅkā; *yātudhānyaḥ*—the wives of the Rākṣasas; *sahasraśaḥ*—by thousands and thousands; *mandodaryā*—headed by Mandodarī, the wife of Rāvaṇa; *samam*—with; *tatra*—there; *prarudantyaḥ*—crying in lamentation; *upādravan*—came near (their dead husbands).

TRANSLATION

Thereafter, all the women whose husbands had fallen in the battle, headed by Mandodarī, the wife of Rāvaṇa, came out of Laṅkā. Continuously crying, they approached the dead bodies of Rāvaṇa and the other Rākṣasas.

TEXT 25

स्वान् स्वान् बन्धून् परिष्वज्य लक्ष्मणेषुभिरर्दितान् ।
रुरुदुः सुस्वरं दीना घ्नन्त्य आत्मानमात्मना ॥२५॥

svān svān bandhūn pariṣvajya
lakṣmaṇeṣubhir arditān
ruruduḥ susvaraṁ dīnā
ghnantya ātmānam ātmanā

svān svān—their own respective husbands; *bandhūn*—friends; *pariṣvajya*—embracing; *lakṣmaṇa-iṣubhiḥ*—by the arrows of Lakṣmaṇa; *arditān*—who were killed; *ruruduḥ*—all the wives cried piteously; *su-svaram*—it was very sweet to hear; *dīnāḥ*—very poor; *ghnantyaḥ*—striking; *ātmānam*—their breasts; *ātmanā*—by themselves.

TRANSLATION

Striking their breasts in affliction because their husbands had been killed by the arrows of Lakṣmaṇa, the women embraced their

respective husbands and cried piteously in voices appealing to everyone.

TEXT 26

हा हताः स्म वयं नाथ लोकरावण रावण ।
कं यायाच्छरणं लङ्का त्वद्विहीना परार्दिता ॥२६॥

hā hatāḥ sma vayaṁ nātha
loka-rāvaṇa rāvaṇa
kaṁ yāyāc charaṇaṁ laṅkā
tvad-vihīnā parārditā

hā—alas; *hatāḥ*—killed; *sma*—in the past; *vayam*—all of us; *nātha*—O protector; *loka-rāvaṇa*—O husband, who created the crying of so many other people; *rāvaṇa*—O Rāvaṇa, one who can cause crying of others; *kam*—unto whom; *yāyāt*—will go; *śaraṇam*—shelter; *laṅkā*—the state of Laṅkā; *tvat-vihīnā*—being bereft of your good self; *para-arditā*—being defeated by the enemies.

TRANSLATION

O my lord, O master! You epitomized trouble for others, and therefore you were called Rāvaṇa. But now that you have been defeated, we also are defeated, for without you the state of Laṅkā has been conquered by the enemy. To whom will it go for shelter?

PURPORT

Rāvaṇa's wife Mandodarī and the other wives knew very well how cruel a person Rāvaṇa was. The very word "Rāvaṇa" means "one who causes crying for others." Rāvaṇa continuously caused trouble for others, but when his sinful activities culminated in giving trouble to Sītādevī, he was killed by Lord Rāmacandra.

TEXT 27

न वै वेद महाभाग भवान् कामवशं गतः ।
तेजोऽनुभावं सीताया येन नीतो दशामिमाम् ॥२७॥

na vai veda mahā-bhāga
bhavān kāma-vaśaṁ gataḥ
tejo 'nubhāvaṁ sītāyā
yena nīto daśām imām

na—not; *vai*—indeed; *veda*—did know; *mahā-bhāga*—O greatly fortunate one; *bhavān*—yourself; *kāma-vaśam*—influenced by lusty desires; *gataḥ*—having become; *tejaḥ*—by influence; *anubhāvam*—as a result of such influence; *sītāyāḥ*—of mother Sītā; *yena*—by which; *nītaḥ*—brought into; *daśām*—condition; *imām*—like this (destruction).

TRANSLATION

O greatly fortunate one, you came under the influence of lusty desires, and therefore you could not understand the influence of mother Sītā. Now, because of her curse, you have been reduced to this state, having been killed by Lord Rāmacandra.

PURPORT

Not only was mother Sītā powerful, but any woman who follows in the footsteps of mother Sītā can also become similarly powerful. There are many instances of this in the history of Vedic literature. Whenever we find a description of ideal chaste women, mother Sītā is among them. Mandodarī, the wife of Rāvaṇa, was also very chaste. Similarly, Draupadī was one of five exalted chaste women. As a man must follow great personalities like Brahmā and Nārada, a woman must follow the path of such ideal women as Sītā, Mandodarī and Draupadī. By staying chaste and faithful to her husband, a woman enriches herself with supernatural power. It is a moral principle that one should not be influenced by lusty desires for another's wife. *Mātṛvat para-dāreṣu:* an intelligent person must look upon another's wife as being like his mother. This is a moral injunction from *Cāṇakya-śloka* (10).

mātṛvat para-dāreṣu
para-dravyeṣu loṣṭravat
ātmavat sarva-bhūteṣu
yaḥ paśyati sa paṇḍitaḥ

"One who considers another's wife as his mother, another's possessions as a lump of dirt and treats all other living beings as he would himself, is considered to be learned." Thus Rāvaṇa was condemned not only by Lord Rāmacandra but even by his own wife, Mandodarī. Because she was a chaste woman, she knew the power of another chaste woman, especially such a wife as mother Sītādevī.

TEXT 28

कृतैषा विधवा लङ्का वयं च कुलनन्दन ।
देहः कृतोऽन्नं गृध्राणामात्मा नरकहेतवे ॥२८॥

kṛtaiṣā vidhavā laṅkā
vayaṁ ca kula-nandana
dehaḥ kṛto 'nnaṁ gṛdhrāṇām
ātmā naraka-hetave

kṛtā—made by you; *eṣā*—all of this; *vidhavā*—without a protector; *laṅkā*—the state of Laṅkā; *vayam ca*—and us; *kula-nandana*—O pleasure of the Rākṣasas; *dehaḥ*—the body; *kṛtaḥ*—made by you; *annam*—eatable; *gṛdhrāṇām*—of the vultures; *ātmā*—and your soul; *naraka-hetave*—for going to hell.

TRANSLATION

O pleasure of the Rākṣasa dynasty, because of you the state of Laṅkā and also we ourselves now have no protector. By your deeds you have made your body fit to be eaten by vultures and your soul fit to go to hell.

PURPORT

One who follows the path of Rāvaṇa is condemned in two ways: his body is fit to be eaten by dogs and vultures, and the soul goes to hell. As stated by the Lord Himself in *Bhagavad-gītā* (16.19):

tān ahaṁ dviṣataḥ krūrān
saṁsāreṣu narādhamān
kṣipāmy ajasram aśubhān
āsurīṣv eva yoniṣu

"Those who are envious and mischievous, who are the lowest among men, are cast by Me into the ocean of material existence, into various demoniac species of life." Thus the destination of godless atheists such as Rāvaṇa, Hiraṇyakaśipu, Kaṁsa and Dantavakra is a hellish condition of life. Mandodarī, the wife of Rāvaṇa, could understand all this because she was a chaste woman. Although lamenting for the death of her husband, she knew what would happen to his body and soul, for although one cannot see directly with one's material eyes, one can see with eyes of knowledge (*paśyanti jñāna-cakṣuṣaḥ*). In Vedic history there are many instances of how one becomes godless and is condemned by the laws of nature.

TEXT 29

श्रीशुक उवाच
स्वानां विभीषणश्चक्रे कोसलेन्द्रानुमोदितः ।
पितृमेधविधानेन यदुक्तं साम्परायिकम् ॥२९॥

śrī-śuka uvāca
svānāṁ vibhīṣaṇaś cakre
kosalendrānumoditaḥ
pitṛ-medha-vidhānena
yad uktaṁ sāmparāyikam

śrī-śukaḥ uvāca—Śrī Śukadeva Gosvāmī said; *svānām*—of his own family members; *vibhīṣaṇaḥ*—Vibhīṣaṇa, the brother of Rāvaṇa and devotee of Lord Rāmacandra; *cakre*—executed; *kosala-indra-anumoditaḥ*—approved by the King of Kosala, Lord Rāmacandra; *pitṛ-medha-vidhānena*—by the funeral ceremony performed by the son after the death of his father or some family member; *yat uktam*—which have been prescribed; *sāmparāyikam*—duties to be performed after a person's death to save him from the path to hell.

TRANSLATION

Śrī Śukadeva Gosvāmī said: Vibhīṣaṇa, the pious brother of Rāvaṇa and devotee of Lord Rāmacandra, received approval from Lord Rāmacandra, the King of Kosala. Then he performed the

prescribed funeral ceremonies for his family members to save them from the path to hell.

PURPORT

After giving up the body, one is transferred to another body, but sometimes, if one is too sinful, he is checked from transmigrating to another body, and thus he becomes a ghost. To save a diseased person from ghostly life, the funeral ceremony, or *śrāddha* ceremony, as prescribed in authorized *śāstra,* must be performed. Rāvaṇa was killed by Lord Rāmacandra and was destined for hellish life, but by Lord Rāmacandra's advice, Vibhīṣaṇa, Rāvaṇa's brother, performed all the duties prescribed in relation to the dead. Thus Lord Rāmacandra was kind to Rāvaṇa even after Rāvaṇa's death.

TEXT 30

ततो ददर्श भगवानशोकवनिकाश्रमे ।
क्षामां स्वविरहव्याधिं शिंशपामूलमाश्रिताम् ॥३०॥

tato dadarśa bhagavān
aśoka-vanikāśrame
kṣāmāṁ sva-viraha-vyādhiṁ
śiṁśapā-mūlam-āśritām

tataḥ—thereafter; *dadarśa*—saw; *bhagavān*—the Supreme Personality of Godhead; *aśoka-vanika-āśrame*—in a small cottage in the forest of Aśoka trees; *kṣāmām*—very lean and thin; *sva-viraha-vyādhim*—suffering from the disease of separation from Lord Rāmacandra; *śiṁśapā*—of the tree known as Śiṁśapā; *mūlam*—the root; *āśritām*—taking shelter of.

TRANSLATION

Thereafter, Lord Rāmacandra found Sītādevī sitting in a small cottage beneath the tree named Śiṁśapā in a forest of Aśoka trees. She was lean and thin, being aggrieved because of separation from Him.

TEXT 31

रामः प्रियतमां भार्यां दीनां वीक्ष्यान्वकम्पत ।
आत्मसंदर्शनाह्लादविकसन्मुखपङ्कजाम् ॥३१॥

rāmaḥ priyatamāṁ bhāryāṁ
dīnāṁ vīkṣyānvakampata
ātma-sandarśanāhlāda-
vikasan-mukha-paṅkajām

rāmaḥ—Lord Rāmacandra; *priya-tamām*—upon His dearmost; *bhāryām*—wife; *dīnām*—so poorly situated; *vīkṣya*—looking; *anvakampata*—became very compassionate; *ātma-sandarśana*—when one sees his beloved; *āhlāda*—an ecstasy of joyful life; *vikasat*—manifesting; *mukha*—mouth; *paṅkajām*—like a lotus.

TRANSLATION

Seeing His wife in that condition, Lord Rāmacandra was very compassionate. When Rāmacandra came before her, she was exceedingly happy to see her beloved, and her lotuslike mouth showed her joy.

TEXT 32

आरोप्यारुरुहे यानं भ्रातृभ्यां हनुमद्युतः ।
विभीषणाय भगवान् दत्त्वा रक्षोगणेशताम् ।
लङ्कामायुश्च कल्पान्तं ययौ चीर्णव्रतः पुरीम् ॥३२॥

āropyāruruhe yānaṁ
bhrātṛbhyāṁ hanumad-yutaḥ
vibhīṣaṇāya bhagavān
dattvā rakṣo-gaṇeśatām
laṅkām āyuś ca kalpāntaṁ
yayau cīrṇa-vrataḥ purīm

āropya—keeping or placing; *āruruhe*—got up; *yānam*—on the airplane; *bhrātṛbhyām*—with His brother Lakṣmaṇa and the commander Sugrīva; *hanumat-yutaḥ*—accompanied by Hanumān;

vibhīṣaṇāya—unto Vibhīṣaṇa, the brother of Rāvaṇa; *bhagavān*—the Lord; *dattvā*—gave charge; *rakṣaḥ-gaṇa-īśatām*—the power to rule over the Rākṣasa population of Laṅkā; *laṅkām*—the state of Laṅkā; *āyuḥ ca*—and the duration of life; *kalpa-antam*—for many, many years, until the end of one *kalpa; yayau*—returned home; *cīrṇa-vrataḥ*—finishing the duration of time living in the forest; *purīm*—to Ayodhyā-purī.

TRANSLATION

After giving Vibhīṣaṇa the power to rule the Rākṣasa population of Laṅkā for the duration of one kalpa, Lord Rāmacandra, the Supreme Personality of Godhead [Bhagavān], placed Sītādevī on an airplane decorated with flowers and then got on the plane Himself. The period for His living in the forest having ended, the Lord returned to Ayodhyā, accompanied by Hanumān, Sugrīva and His brother Lakṣmaṇa.

TEXT 33

अवकीर्यमाणः सुकुसुमैर्लोकपालार्पितैः पथि ।
उपगीयमानचरितः शतधृत्यादिभिर्मुदा ॥३३॥

avakīryamāṇaḥ sukusumair
lokapālārpitaiḥ pathi
upagīyamāna-caritaḥ
śatadhṛty-ādibhir mudā

avakīryamāṇaḥ—being overflooded; *su-kusumaiḥ*—by fragrant and beautiful flowers; *loka-pāla-arpitaiḥ*—offered by the princely order; *pathi*—on the road; *upagīyamāna-caritaḥ*—being glorified for His uncommon activities; *śatadhṛti-ādibhiḥ*—by personalities like Lord Brahmā and other demigods; *mudā*—with great jubilation.

TRANSLATION

When Lord Rāmacandra returned to His capital, Ayodhyā, He was greeted on the road by the princely order, who showered His body with beautiful, fragrant flowers, while great personalities

like Lord Brahmā and other demigods glorified the activities of the Lord in great jubilation.

TEXT 34

गोमूत्रयावकं श्रुत्वा भ्रातरं वल्कलाम्बरम् ।
महाकारुणिकोऽतप्यज्जटिलं स्थण्डिलेशयम् ॥३४॥

go-mūtra-yāvakaṁ śrutvā
bhrātaraṁ valkalāmbaram
mahā-kāruṇiko 'tapyaj
jaṭilaṁ sthaṇḍile-śayam

go-mūtra-yāvakam—eating barley boiled in the urine of a cow; *śrutvā*—hearing; *bhrātaram*—His brother Bharata; *valkala-ambaram*—covered with the bark of trees; *mahā-kāruṇikaḥ*—the supremely merciful Lord Rāmacandra; *atapyat*—lamented very much; *jaṭilam*—wearing matted locks of hair; *sthaṇḍile-śayam*—lying down on a grass mattress, or *kuśāsana.*

TRANSLATION

Upon reaching Ayodhyā, Lord Rāmacandra heard that in His absence His brother Bharata was eating barley cooked in the urine of a cow, covering His body with the bark of trees, wearing matted locks of hair, and lying on a mattress of kuśa. The most merciful Lord very much lamented this.

TEXTS 35–38

भरतः प्राप्तमाकर्ण्य पौरामात्यपुरोहितैः ।
पादुके शिरसि न्यस्य रामं प्रत्युद्यतोऽग्रजम् ॥३५॥
नन्दिग्रामात् स्वशिबिराद् गीतवादित्रनिःस्वनैः ।
ब्रह्मघोषेण च मुहुः पठद्भिर्ब्रह्मवादिभिः ॥३६॥
स्वर्णकक्षपताकाभिर्हैमैश्चित्रध्वजै रथैः ।
सदश्वै रुक्मसन्नाहैर्भटैः पुरटवर्मभिः ॥३७॥

श्रेणीभिर्वारमुख्याभिर्भृत्यैश्चैव पदानुगैः ।
पारमेष्ठ्यान्युपादाय पण्यान्युच्चावचानि च ।
पादयोर्न्यपतत् प्रेम्णा प्रक्लिन्नहृदयेक्षणः ॥३८॥

bharataḥ prāptam ākarṇya
paurāmātya-purohitaiḥ
pāduke śirasi nyasya
rāmaṁ pratyudyato 'grajam

nandigrāmāt sva-śibirād
gīta-vāditra-niḥsvanaiḥ
brahma-ghoṣeṇa ca muhuḥ
paṭhadbhir brahmavādibhiḥ

svarṇa-kakṣa-patākābhir
haimaiś citra-dhvajai rathaiḥ
sad-aśvai rukma-sannāhair
bhaṭaiḥ puraṭa-varmabhiḥ

śreṇībhir vāra-mukhyābhir
bhṛtyaiś caiva padānugaiḥ
pārameṣṭhyāny upādāya
paṇyāny uccāvacāni ca
pādayor nyapatat premṇā
praklinna-hṛdayekṣaṇaḥ

bharataḥ—Lord Bharata; *prāptam*—coming back home; *ākarṇya*—hearing; *paura*—all kinds of citizens; *amātya*—all the ministers; *purohitaiḥ*—accompanied by all the priests; *pāduke*—the two wooden shoes; *śirasi*—on the head; *nyasya*—keeping; *rāmam*—unto Lord Rāmacandra; *pratyudyataḥ*—going forward to receive; *agrajam*—His eldest brother; *nandigrāmāt*—from His residence, known as Nandigrāma; *sva-śibirāt*—from His own camp; *gīta-vāditra*—songs and vibrations of drums and other musical instruments; *niḥsvanaiḥ*—accompanied by such sounds; *brahma-ghoṣeṇa*—by the sound of chanting of Vedic *mantras; ca*—and; *muhuḥ*—always; *paṭhadbhiḥ*—reciting from the *Vedas; brahma-vādibhiḥ*—by first-class *brāhmaṇas; svarṇa-kakṣa-patākābhiḥ*—decorated with flags with golden embroidery; *haimaiḥ*—golden; *citra-dhvajaiḥ*—with decorated flags; *rathaiḥ*—with chariots; *sat-aśvaiḥ*—having very beautiful horses; *rukma*—golden; *sannāhaiḥ*—with harnesses; *bhaṭaiḥ*—by soldiers; *puraṭa-varmabhiḥ*—covered with armor made of gold; *śreṇībhiḥ*—by such a line or procession; *vāra-mukhyābhiḥ*—accompanied by beautiful, well-dressed prostitutes; *bhṛtyaiḥ*—by servants; *ca*—also; *eva*—indeed; *pada-anugaiḥ*—by infantry; *pārameṣṭhyāni*—other paraphernalia befitting a royal reception; *upādāya*—taking all together; *paṇyāni*—valuable jewels, etc.; *ucca-avacāni*—of different values; *ca*—also; *pādayoḥ*—at the lotus feet of the Lord; *nyapatat*—fell down; *premṇā*—in ecstatic love; *praklinna*—softened, moistened; *hṛdaya*—the core of the heart; *īkṣaṇaḥ*—whose eyes.

TRANSLATION

When Lord Bharata understood that Lord Rāmacandra was returning to the capital, Ayodhyā, He immediately took upon His own head Lord Rāmacandra's wooden shoes and came out from His camp at Nandigrāma. Lord Bharata was accompanied by ministers, priests and other respectable citizens, by professional musicians vibrating pleasing musical sounds, and by learned brāhmaṇas loudly chanting Vedic hymns. Following in the procession were chariots drawn by beautiful horses with harnesses of golden rope. These chariots were decorated by flags with golden embroidery and by other flags of various sizes and patterns. There were soldiers bedecked with golden armor, servants bearing betel nut, and many well-known and beautiful prostitutes. Many servants followed on foot, bearing an umbrella, whisks, different grades of precious jewels, and other paraphernalia befitting a royal reception. Accompanied in this way, Lord Bharata, His heart softened in ecstasy and His eyes full of tears, approached Lord Rāmacandra and fell at His lotus feet with great ecstatic love.

TEXTS 39–40

पादुके न्यस्य पुरतः प्राञ्जलिर्बाष्पलोचनः ।
तमाश्लिष्य चिरं दोर्भ्यां स्नापयन् नेत्रजैर्जलैः ॥३९॥

रामो लक्ष्मणसीताभ्यां विप्रेभ्यो येऽर्हसत्तमाः ।
तेभ्यः स्वयं नमश्चक्रे प्रजाभिश्च नमस्कृतः ॥४०॥

pāduke nyasya purataḥ
prāñjalir bāṣpa-locanaḥ
tam āśliṣya ciraṁ dorbhyāṁ
snāpayan netrajair jalaiḥ

rāmo lakṣmaṇa-sītābhyāṁ
viprebhyo ye 'rha-sattamāḥ
tebhyaḥ svayaṁ namaścakre
prajābhiś ca namaskṛtaḥ

pāduke—the two wooden shoes; *nyasya*—after placing; *purataḥ*—before Lord Rāmacandra; *prāñjaliḥ*—with folded hands; *bāṣpa-locanaḥ*—with tears in the eyes; *tam*—unto Him, Bharata; *āśliṣya*—embracing; *ciram*—for a long time; *dorbhyām*—with His two arms; *snāpayan*—bathing; *netra-jaiḥ*—coming from His eyes; *jalaiḥ*—with the water; *rāmaḥ*—Lord Rāmacandra; *lakṣmaṇa-sītābhyām*—with Lakṣmaṇa and mother Sītā; *viprebhyaḥ*—unto the learned *brāhmaṇas; ye*—also others who; *arha-sattamāḥ*—worthy of being worshiped; *tebhyaḥ*—unto them; *svayam*—personally; *namaḥ-cakre*—offered respectful obeisances; *prajābhiḥ*—by the citizens; *ca*—and; *namaḥ-kṛtaḥ*—was offered obeisances.

TRANSLATION

After offering the wooden shoes before Lord Rāmacandra, Lord Bharata stood with folded hands, His eyes full of tears, and Lord Rāmacandra bathed Bharata with tears while embracing Him with both arms for a long time. Accompanied by mother Sītā and Lakṣmaṇa, Lord Rāmacandra then offered His respectful obeisances unto the learned brāhmaṇas and the elderly persons in the family, and all the citizens of Ayodhyā offered their respectful obeisances unto the Lord.

TEXT 41

धुन्वन्त उत्तरासङ्गान् पतिं वीक्ष्य चिरागतम् ।
उत्तराः कोसला माल्यैः किरन्तो ननृतुर्मुदा ॥४१॥

dhunvanta uttarāsaṅgān
patiṁ vīkṣya cirāgatam
uttarāḥ kosalā mālyaiḥ
kiranto nanṛtur mudā

dhunvantaḥ—waving; *uttara-āsaṅgān*—the upper cloths covering the body; *patim*—the Lord; *vīkṣya*—seeing; *cira-āgatam*—returned after many years of banishment; *uttarāḥ kosalāḥ*—the citizens of Ayodhyā; *mālyaiḥ kirantaḥ*—offering Him garlands; *nanṛtuḥ*—began to dance; *mudā*—in great jubilation.

TRANSLATION

The citizens of Ayodhyā, upon seeing their King return after a long absence, offered Him flower garlands, waved their upper cloths, and danced in great jubilation.

TEXTS 42–43

पादुके भरतोऽगृह्णाच्चामरव्यजनोत्तमे ।
विभीषणः ससुग्रीवः श्वेतच्छत्रं मरुत्सुतः ॥४२॥
धनुर्निषङ्गाञ्छत्रुघ्नः सीता तीर्थकमण्डलुम् ।
अबिभ्रदङ्गदः खड्गं हैमं चर्मर्क्षराण् नृप ॥४३॥

pāduke bharato 'gṛhṇāc
cāmara-vyajanottame
vibhīṣaṇaḥ sasugrīvaḥ
śveta-cchatraṁ marut-sutaḥ

dhanur-niṣaṅgāñ chatrughnaḥ
sītā tīrtha-kamaṇḍalum

abibhrad aṅgadaḥ khaḍgaṁ
haimaṁ carmarkṣa-rāṇ nṛpa

pāduke—the two wooden shoes; *bharataḥ*—Lord Bharata; *agṛhṇāt*—carried; *cāmara*—whisk; *vyajana*—fan; *uttame*—very opulent; *vibhīṣaṇaḥ*—the brother of Rāvaṇa; *sa-sugrīvaḥ*—with Sugrīva; *śveta-chatram*—a white umbrella; *marut-sutaḥ*—Hanumān, the son of the wind-god; *dhanuḥ*—the bow; *niṣaṅgān*—with two quivers; *śatrughnaḥ*—one of the brothers of Lord Rāmacandra; *sītā*—mother Sītā; *tīrtha-kamaṇḍalum*—the waterpot filled with water from holy places; *abibhrat*—carried; *aṅgadaḥ*—the monkey commander named Aṅgada; *khaḍgam*—the sword; *haimam*—made of gold; *carma*—shield; *ṛkṣa-rāṭ*—the King of the Ṛkṣas, Jāmbavān; *nṛpa*—O King.

TRANSLATION

O King, Lord Bharata carried Lord Rāmacandra's wooden shoes, Sugrīva and Vibhīṣaṇa carried a whisk and an excellent fan, Hanumān carried a white umbrella, Śatrughna carried a bow and two quivers, and Sītādevī carried a waterpot filled with water from holy places. Aṅgada carried a sword, and Jāmbavān, King of the Ṛkṣas, carried a golden shield.

TEXT 44

पुष्पकस्थोनुतः स्त्रीभिः स्तूयमानश्च वन्दिभिः ।
विरेजे भगवान् राजन् ग्रहैश्चन्द्र इवोदितः ॥४४॥

puṣpaka-stho nutaḥ strībhiḥ
stūyamānaś ca vandibhiḥ
vireje bhagavān rājan
grahaiś candra ivoditaḥ

puṣpaka-sthaḥ—seated on the airplane made of flowers; *nutaḥ*—worshiped; *strībhiḥ*—by the women; *stūyamānaḥ*—being offered prayers; *ca*—and; *vandibhiḥ*—by the reciters; *vireje*—beautified; *bhagavān*—the Supreme Personality of Godhead, Lord Rāmacandra;

rājan—O King Parīkṣit; *grahaiḥ*—among the planets; *candraḥ*—the moon; *iva*—like; *uditaḥ*—risen.

TRANSLATION

O King Parīkṣit, as the Lord sat on His airplane of flowers, with women offering Him prayers and reciters chanting about His characteristics, He appeared like the moon with the stars and planets.

TEXTS 45–46

भ्रात्राभिनन्दितः सोऽथ सोत्सवां प्राविशत् पुरीम् ।
प्रविश्य राजभवनं गुरुपत्नीः स्वमातरम् ॥४५॥
गुरून् वयस्यावरजान् पूजितः प्रत्यपूजयत् ।
वैदेही लक्ष्मणश्चैव यथावत् समुपेयतुः ॥४६॥

bhrātrābhinanditaḥ so 'tha
sotsavāṁ prāviśat purīm
praviśya rāja-bhavanaṁ
guru-patnīḥ sva-mātaram

gurūn vayasyāvarajān
pūjitaḥ pratyapūjayat
vaidehī lakṣmaṇaś caiva
yathāvat samupeyatuḥ

bhrātrā—by His brother (Bharata); *abhinanditaḥ*—being welcomed properly; *saḥ*—He, Lord Rāmacandra; *atha*—thereafter; *sa-utsavām*—in the midst of a festival; *prāviśat*—entered; *purīm*—the city of Ayodhyā; *praviśya*—after entering; *rāja-bhavanam*—the royal palace; *guru-patnīḥ*—Kaikeyī and other stepmothers; *sva-mātaram*—His own mother (Kauśalyā); *gurūn*—the spiritual masters (Śrī Vasiṣṭha and others); *vayasya*—unto friends of the same age; *avara-jān*—and those who were younger than He; *pūjitaḥ*—being worshiped by them; *pratyapūjayat*—He returned the obeisances; *vaidehī*—mother Sītā;

lakṣmaṇaḥ—Lakṣmaṇa; *ca eva*—and; *yathā-vat*—in a befitting way; *samupeyatuḥ*—being welcomed, entered the palace.

TRANSLATION

Thereafter, having been welcomed by His brother Bharata, Lord Rāmacandra entered the city of Ayodhyā in the midst of a festival. When He entered the palace, He offered obeisances to all the mothers, including Kaikeyī and the other wives of Mahārāja Daśaratha, and especially His own mother, Kauśalyā. He also offered obeisances to the spiritual preceptors, such as Vasiṣṭha. Friends of His own age and younger friends worshiped Him, and He returned their respectful obeisances, as did Lakṣmaṇa and mother Sītā. In this way they all entered the palace.

TEXT 47

पुत्रान् स्वमातरस्तास्तु प्राणांस्तन्व इवोत्थिताः ।
आरोप्याङ्केऽभिषिञ्चन्त्यो बाष्पौघैर्विजहुः शुचः ॥४७॥

putrān sva-mātaras tās tu
prāṇāṁs tanva ivotthitāḥ
āropyāṅke 'bhiṣiñcantyo
bāṣpaughair vijahuḥ śucaḥ

putrān—the sons; *sva-mātaraḥ*—Their mothers; *tāḥ*—they, headed by Kauśalyā and Kaikeyī; *tu*—but; *prāṇān*—life; *tanvaḥ*—bodies; *iva*—like; *utthitāḥ*—arisen; *āropya*—keeping; *aṅke*—on the lap; *abhiṣiñcantyaḥ*—moistening (the bodies of their sons); *bāṣpa*—by tears; *oghaiḥ*—continuously pouring; *vijahuḥ*—gave up; *śucaḥ*—lamentation due to separation from their sons.

TRANSLATION

Upon seeing their sons, the mothers of Rāma, Lakṣmaṇa, Bharata and Śatrughna immediately arose, like unconscious bodies returning to consciousness. The mothers placed their sons on their laps and bathed Them with tears, thus relieving themselves of the grief of long separation.

TEXT 48

जटा निर्मुच्य विधिवत् कुलवृद्धैः समं गुरुः ।
अभ्यषिञ्चद् यथैवेन्द्रं चतुःसिन्धुजलादिभिः ॥४८॥

jaṭā nirmucya vidhivat
kula-vṛddhaiḥ samaṁ guruḥ
abhyaṣiñcad yathaivendraṁ
catuḥ-sindhu-jalādibhiḥ

jaṭāḥ—the matted locks of hair on the head; *nirmucya*—shaving clean; *vidhi-vat*—according to regulative principles; *kula-vṛddhaiḥ*—the elderly persons in the family; *samam*—with; *guruḥ*—the family priest or spiritual master, Vasiṣṭha; *abhyaṣiñcat*—performed the *abhiṣeka* ceremony of Lord Rāmacandra; *yathā*—as; *eva*—like; *indram*—unto King Indra; *catuḥ-sindhu-jala*—with the water of the four oceans; *ādibhiḥ*—and with other paraphernalia for bathing.

TRANSLATION

The family priest or spiritual master, Vasiṣṭha, had Lord Rāmacandra cleanly shaved, freeing Him from His matted locks of hair. Then, with the cooperation of the elderly members of the family, he performed the bathing ceremony [abhiṣeka] for Lord Rāmacandra with the water of the four seas and with other substances, just as it was performed for King Indra.

TEXT 49

एवं कृतशिरःस्नानः सुवासाः स्रग्व्यलङ्कृतः ।
स्वलङ्कृतैः सुवासोभिर्भ्रातृभिर्भार्यया बभौ ॥४९॥

evaṁ kṛta-śiraḥ-snānaḥ
suvāsāḥ sragvy-alaṅkṛtaḥ
svalaṅkṛtaiḥ suvāsobhir
bhrātṛbhir bhāryayā babhau

evam—thus; *kṛta-śiraḥ-snānaḥ*—having completely bathed, washing the head; *su-vāsāḥ*—being nicely dressed; *sragvi-alaṅkṛtaḥ*—being decorated with a garland; *su-alaṅkṛtaiḥ*—decorated nicely; *su-vāsobhiḥ*—dressed nicely; *bhrātṛbhiḥ*—with His brothers; *bhāryayā*—and with His wife, Sītā; *babhau*—the Lord became very brilliant.

TRANSLATION

Lord Rāmacandra, fully bathed and His head clean-shaven, dressed Himself very nicely and was decorated with a garland and ornaments. Thus He shone brightly, surrounded by His brothers and wife, who were similarly dressed and ornamented.

TEXT 50

अग्रहीदासनं भ्रात्रा प्रणिपत्य प्रसादितः ।
प्रजाः स्वधर्मनिरता वर्णाश्रमगुणान्विताः ।
जुगोप पितृवद् रामो मेनिरे पितरं च तम् ॥५०॥

agrahīd āsanaṁ bhrātrā
praṇipatya prasāditaḥ
prajāḥ sva-dharma-niratā
varṇāśrama-guṇānvitāḥ
jugopa pitṛvad rāmo
menire pitaraṁ ca tam

agrahīt—accepted; *āsanam*—the throne of the state; *bhrātrā*—by His brother (Bharata); *praṇipatya*—after fully surrendering unto Him; *prasāditaḥ*—having been pleased; *prajāḥ*—and the citizens; *sva-dharma-niratāḥ*—fully engaged in their respective occupational duties; *varṇāśrama*—according to the system of *varṇa* and *āśrama; guṇa-anvitāḥ*—all of them being qualified in that process; *jugopa*—the Lord protected them; *pitṛ-vat*—exactly like a father; *rāmaḥ*—Lord Rāmacandra; *menire*—they considered; *pitaram*—exactly like a father; *ca*—also; *tam*—Him, Lord Rāmacandra.

TRANSLATION

Being pleased by the full surrender and submission of Lord Bharata, Lord Rāmacandra then accepted the throne of the state.

He cared for the citizens exactly like a father, and the citizens, being fully engaged in their occupational duties of varṇa and āśrama, accepted Him as their father.

PURPORT

People are very fond of the pattern of Rāma-rājya, and even today politicians sometimes form a party called Rāma-rājya, but unfortunately they have no obedience to Lord Rāma. It is sometimes said that people want the kingdom of God without God. Such an aspiration, however, is never to be fulfilled. Good government can exist when the relationship between the citizens and the government is like that exemplified by Lord Rāmacandra and His citizens. Lord Rāmacandra ruled His kingdom exactly as a father takes care of his children, and the citizens, being obliged to the good government of Lord Rāmacandra, accepted the Lord as their father. Thus the relationship between the citizens and the government should be exactly like that between father and son. When the sons in a family are well trained, they are obedient to the father and mother, and when the father is well qualified, he takes good care of the children. As indicated here by the words *sva-dharma-niratā varṇāśrama-guṇān-vitāḥ*, the people were good citizens because they accepted the institution of *varṇa* and *āśrama*, which arranges society in the *varṇa* divisions of *brāhmaṇa, kṣatriya, vaiśya* and *śūdra* and the *āśrama* divisions of *brahmacarya, gṛhastha, vānaprastha* and *sannyāsa.* This is actual human civilization. People must be trained according to the different *varṇāśrama* occupational duties. As confirmed in *Bhagavad-gītā* (4.13), *cātur-varṇyaṁ mayā sṛṣṭaṁ guṇa-karma-vibhāgaśaḥ:* the four *varṇas* must be established according to varying qualities and work. The first principle for good government is that it must institute this *varṇāśrama* system. The purpose of *varṇāśrama* is to enable people to become God conscious. *Varṇāśramācāravatā puruṣeṇa paraḥ pumān viṣṇur ārādhyate.* The entire *varṇāśrama* scheme is intended to enable people to become Vaiṣṇavas. *Viṣṇur asya devatā.* When people worship Lord Viṣṇu as the Supreme Lord, they become Vaiṣṇavas. Thus people should be trained to become Vaiṣṇavas through the system of *varṇa* and *āśrama,* as they were during the reign of Lord Rāmacandra, when everyone was fully trained to follow the *varṇāśrama* principles.

Simply enforcing laws and ordinances cannot make the citizens obedient and lawful. That is impossible. Throughout the entire world there are so many states, legislative assemblies and parliaments, but still the citizens are rogues and thieves. Good citizenship, therefore, cannot be enforced; the citizens must be trained. As there are schools and colleges to train students to become chemical engineers, lawyers or specialists in many other departments of knowledge, there must be schools and colleges to train students to become *brāhmaṇas, kṣatriyas, vaiśyas, śūdras, brahmacārīs, gṛhasthas, vānaprasthas* and *sannyāsīs.* This will provide the preliminary condition for good citizenship (*varṇāśrama-guṇānvitāḥ*). Generally speaking, if the king or president is a *rājarṣi,* the relationship between the citizens and the chief executive will be clear, and there will be no possibility of disruption in the state, because the number of thieves and rogues will decrease. In Kali-yuga, however, because the *varṇāśrama* system is neglected, people are generally thieves and rogues. In the system of democracy, such thieves and rogues naturally collect money from other thieves and rogues, and thus there is chaos in every government, and no one is happy. But here the example of good government is to be found in the reign of Lord Rāmacandra. If people follow this example, there will be good government all over the world.

TEXT 51

त्रेतायां वर्तमानायां कालः कृतसमोऽभवत् ।
रामे राजनि धर्मज्ञे सर्वभूतसुखावहे ॥५१॥

tretāyāṁ vartamānāyāṁ
kālaḥ kṛta-samo 'bhavat
rāme rājani dharma-jñe
sarva-bhūta-sukhāvahe

tretāyām—in the Tretā-yuga; *vartamānāyām*—although situated in that period; *kālaḥ*—the period; *kṛta*—with Satya-yuga; *samaḥ*—equal; *abhavat*—it so became; *rāme*—because of Lord Rāmacandra's being present; *rājani*—as the ruling king; *dharma-jñe*—because He was fully religious; *sarva-bhūta*—of all living entities; *sukha-āvahe*—giving full happiness.

TRANSLATION

Lord Rāmacandra became King during Tretā-yuga, but because of His good government, the age was like Satya-yuga. Everyone was religious and completely happy.

PURPORT

Among the four *yugas*—Satya, Tretā, Dvāpara and Kali—the Kali-yuga is the worst, but if the process of *varṇāśrama-dharma* is introduced, even in this age of Kali, the situation of Satya-yuga can be invoked. The Hare Kṛṣṇa movement, or Kṛṣṇa consciousness movement, is meant for this purpose.

kaler doṣa-nidhe rājann
asti hy eko mahān guṇaḥ
kīrtanād eva kṛṣṇasya
mukta-saṅgaḥ paraṁ vrajet

"My dear King, although Kali-yuga is full of faults, there is still one good quality about this age: simply by chanting the Hare Kṛṣṇa *mahā-mantra*, one can become free from material bondage and be promoted to the transcendental kingdom." (*Bhāg.* 12.3.51) If people take to this *saṅkīrtana* movement of chanting Hare Kṛṣṇa, Hare Rāma, they will certainly be freed from the contamination of Kali-yuga, and the people of this age will be happy, as people were in Satya-yuga, the golden age. Anyone, anywhere, can easily take to this Hare Kṛṣṇa movement; one need only chant the Hare Kṛṣṇa *mahā-mantra*, observe the rules and regulations, and stay free from the contamination of sinful life. Even if one is sinful and cannot give up sinful life immediately, if he chants the Hare Kṛṣṇa *mahā-mantra* with devotion and faith he will certainly be freed from all sinful activities, and his life will be successful. *Paraṁ vijayate śrī-kṛṣṇa-saṅkīrtanam.* This is the blessing of Lord Rāmacandra, who has appeared in this age of Kali as Lord Gaurasundara.

TEXT 52

वनानि नद्यो गिरयो वर्षाणि द्वीपसिन्धवः ।
सर्वे कामदुघा आसन् प्रजानां भरतर्षभ ॥५२॥

vanāni nadyo girayo
varṣāṇi dvīpa-sindhavaḥ
sarve kāma-dughā āsan
prajānāṁ bharatarṣabha

vanāni—the forests; *nadyaḥ*—the rivers; *girayaḥ*—the hills and mountains; *varṣāṇi*—various parts of the states or divisions on the surface of the earth; *dvīpa*—islands; *sindhavaḥ*—the oceans and seas; *sarve*—all of them; *kāma-dughāḥ*—full of their respective opulences; *āsan*—existed like that; *prajānām*—of all the living beings; *bharata-ṛṣabha*—O Mahārāja Parīkṣit, best of the Bharata dynasty.

TRANSLATION

O Mahārāja Parīkṣit, best of the Bharata dynasty, during the reign of Lord Rāmacandra the forests, the rivers, the hills and mountains, the states, the seven islands and the seven seas were all favorable in supplying the necessities of life for all living beings.

TEXT 53

नाधिव्याधिजराग्लानिदुःखशोकभयक्लमाः ।
मृत्युश्चानिच्छतां नासीद् रामे राजन्यधोक्षजे ॥५३॥

nādhi-vyādhi-jarā-glāni-
duḥkha-śoka-bhaya-klamāḥ
mṛtyuś cānicchatāṁ nāsīd
rāme rājany adhokṣaje

na—not; *ādhi*—*adhyātmika, adhibhautika* and *adhidaivika* sufferings (that is, sufferings from the body and mind, from other living entities and from nature); *vyādhi*—diseases; *jarā*—old age; *glāni*—bereavement; *duḥkha*—grief; *śoka*—lamentation; *bhaya*—fear; *klamāḥ*—and fatigue; *mṛtyuḥ*—death; *ca*—also; *anicchatām*—of those who did not like it; *na āsīt*—there was not; *rāme*—during the rule of Lord Rāmacandra; *rājani*—because of His being the king; *adhokṣaje*—the Supreme Personality of Godhead, who is beyond this material world.

TRANSLATION

When Lord Rāmacandra, the Supreme Personality of Godhead, was the King of this world, all bodily and mental suffering, disease, old age, bereavement, lamentation, distress, fear and fatigue were completely absent. There was even no death for those who did not want it.

PURPORT

All these facilities existed because of Lord Rāmacandra's presence as the King of the entire world. A similar situation could be introduced immediately, even in this age called Kali, the worst of all ages. It is said, *kali-kāle nāma-rūpe kṛṣṇa-avatāra:* Kṛṣṇa descends in this Kali-yuga in the form of His holy name—Hare Kṛṣṇa, Hare Rāma. If we chant offenselessly, Rāma and Kṛṣṇa are still present in this age. The kingdom of Rāma was immensely popular and beneficial, and the spreading of this Hare Kṛṣṇa movement can immediately introduce a similar situation, even in this Kali-yuga.

TEXT 54

एकपत्नीव्रतधरो राजर्षिचरितः शुचिः ।
स्वधर्मं गृहमेधीयं शिक्षयन् स्वयमाचरत् ॥५४॥

eka-patnī-vrata-dharo
rājarṣi-caritaḥ śuciḥ
sva-dharmaṁ gṛha-medhīyaṁ
śikṣayan svayam ācarat

eka-patnī-vrata-dharaḥ—taking a vow not to accept a second wife or to have any connection with any other woman; *rāja-ṛṣi*—like a saintly king; *caritaḥ*—whose character; *śuciḥ*—pure; *sva-dharmam*—one's own occupational duty; *gṛha-medhīyam*—especially of persons situated in household life; *śikṣayan*—teaching (by personal behavior); *svayam*—personally; *ācarat*—executed His duty.

TRANSLATION

Lord Rāmacandra took a vow to accept only one wife and have no connection with any other women. He was a saintly king, and

everything in His character was good, untinged by qualities like anger. He taught good behavior for everyone, especially for householders, in terms of varṇāśrama-dharma. Thus He taught the general public by His personal activities.

PURPORT

Eka-patnī-vrata, accepting only one wife, was the glorious example set by Lord Rāmacandra. One should not accept more than one wife. In those days, of course, people did marry more than one wife. Even Lord Rāmacandra's father accepted more wives than one. But Lord Rāmacandra, as an ideal king, accepted only one wife, mother Sītā. When mother Sītā was kidnapped by Rāvaṇa and the Rākṣasas, Lord Rāmacandra, as the Supreme Personality of Godhead, could have married hundreds and thousands of Sītās, but to teach us how faithful He was to His wife, He fought with Rāvaṇa and finally killed him. The Lord punished Rāvaṇa and rescued His wife to instruct men to have only one wife. Lord Rāmacandra accepted only one wife and manifested sublime character, thus setting an example for householders. A householder should live according to the ideal of Lord Rāmacandra, who showed how to be a perfect person. Being a householder or living with a wife and children is never condemned, provided one lives according to the regulative principles of *varṇāśrama-dharma.* Those who live in accordance with these principles, whether as householders, *brahmacārīs* or *vānaprasthas*, are all equally important.

TEXT 55

प्रेम्णानुवृत्त्या शीलेन प्रश्रयावनता सती ।
भिया ह्रिया च भावज्ञा भर्तुः सीताहरन्मनः ॥५५॥

premṇānuvṛttyā śīlena
praśrayāvanatā satī
bhiyā hriyā ca bhāva-jñā
bhartuḥ sītāharan manaḥ

premṇā anuvṛttyā—because of service rendered to the husband with love and faith; *śīlena*—by such good character; *praśraya-avanatā*—always very submissive and ready to satisfy the husband; *satī*—chaste; *bhiyā*—by being afraid; *hriyā*—by shyness; *ca*—also; *bhāva-jñā*—understanding the attitude (of the husband); *bhartuḥ*—of her husband, Lord Rāmacandra; *sītā*—mother Sītā; *aharat*—simply captivated; *manaḥ*—the mind.

TRANSLATION

Mother Sītā was very submissive, faithful, shy and chaste, always understanding the attitude of her husband. Thus by her character and her love and service she completely attracted the mind of the Lord.

PURPORT

As Lord Rāmacandra is the ideal husband (*eka-patnī-vrata*), mother Sītā is the ideal wife. Such a combination makes family life very happy. *Yad yad ācarati śreṣṭhas tat tad evetaro janaḥ:* whatever example a great man sets, common people follow. If the kings, the leaders, and the *brāhmaṇas*, the teachers, would set forth the examples we receive from Vedic literature, the entire world would be heaven; indeed, there would no longer be hellish conditions within this material world.

Thus end the Bhaktivedanta purports of the Ninth Canto, Tenth Chapter, of the Śrīmad-Bhāgavatam, *entitled "The Pastimes of the Supreme Lord, Rāmacandra."*

CHAPTER ELEVEN

Lord Rāmacandra Rules the World

This chapter describes how Lord Rāmacandra resided in Ayodhyā with His younger brothers and performed various sacrifices.

Lord Rāmacandra, the Supreme Personality of Godhead, performed various sacrifices by which to worship Himself, and at the end of these sacrifices He gave land to the *hotā, adhvaryu, udgātā* and *brahmā* priests. He gave them the eastern, western, northern and southern directions respectively, and the balance He gave to the *ācārya.* Lord Rāmacandra's faith in the *brāhmaṇas* and affection for His servants was observed by all the *brāhmaṇas,* who then offered their prayers to the Lord and returned whatever they had taken from Him. They regarded the enlightenment given to them by the Lord within the core of their hearts as a sufficient contribution. Lord Rāmacandra subsequently dressed Himself like an ordinary person and began wandering within the capital to understand what impression the citizens had of Him. By chance, one night He heard a man talking to his wife, who had gone to another man's house. In the course of rebuking his wife, the man spoke suspiciously of the character of Sītādevī. The Lord immediately returned home, and, fearing such rumors, He superficially decided to give up Sītādevī's company. Thus He banished Sītādevī, who was pregnant, to the shelter of Vālmīki Muni, where she gave birth to twin sons, named Lava and Kuśa. In Ayodhyā, Lakṣmaṇa begot two sons named Aṅgada and Citraketu, Bharata begot two sons named Takṣa and Puṣkala, and Śatrughna begot two sons named Subāhu and Śrutasena. When Bharata went out to conquer various lands on behalf of the emperor, Lord Rāmacandra, He fought many millions of Gandharvas. By killing them in the fight, He acquired immense wealth, which He then brought home. Śatrughna killed a demon named Lavaṇa at Madhuvana and thus established the capital of Mathurā. Meanwhile, Sītādevī placed her two sons in the care of Vālmīki Muni and then entered into the earth. Upon hearing of this, Lord Rāmacandra was very much aggrieved, and thus He performed sacrifices for thirteen thousand years. After describing the pastimes of Lord Rāmacandra's disappearance and establishing that the Lord appears for His pastimes only, Śukadeva Gosvāmī ends this chapter by describing the results of hearing about the activities of Lord Rāmacandra and by describing how the Lord protected His citizens and displayed affection for His brothers.

TEXT 1

श्रीशुक उवाच
भगवानात्मनात्मानं राम उत्तमकल्पकैः ।
सर्वदेवमयं देवमीजेऽथाचार्यवान् मखैः ॥ १ ॥

śrī-śuka uvāca
bhagavān ātmanātmānaṁ
rāma uttama-kalpakaiḥ
sarva-devamayaṁ devam
īje 'thācāryavān makhaiḥ

śrī-śukaḥ uvāca—Śrī Śukadeva Gosvāmī said; *bhagavān*—the Supreme Personality of Godhead; *ātmanā*—by Himself; *ātmānam*—Himself; *rāmaḥ*—Lord Rāmacandra; *uttama-kalpakaiḥ*—with very opulent paraphernalia; *sarva-deva-mayam*—the heart and soul of all the demigods; *devam*—the Supreme Lord Himself; *īje*—worshiped; *atha*—thus; *ācāryavān*—under the guidance of an *ācārya; makhaiḥ*—by performing sacrifices.

TRANSLATION

Śukadeva Gosvāmī said: Thereafter, the Supreme Personality of Godhead, Lord Rāmacandra, accepted an ācārya and performed sacrifices [yajñas] with opulent paraphernalia. Thus He Himself worshiped Himself, for He is the Supreme Lord of all demigods.

PURPORT

Sarvārhaṇam acyutejyā. If Acyuta, the Supreme Personality of Godhead, is worshiped, then everyone is worshiped. As stated in *Śrīmad-Bhāgavatam* (4.31.14):

yathā taror mūla-niṣecanena
tṛpyanti tat-skandha-bhujopaśākhāḥ
prāṇopahārāc ca yathendriyāṇāṁ
tathaiva sarvārhaṇam acyutejyā

"As pouring water on the root of a tree nourishes the trunk, branches, twigs and leaves, and as supplying food to the stomach enlivens the senses and limbs of the body, worshiping the Supreme Personality of Godhead satisfies the demigods, who are part of that Supreme Personality." Performing *yajña* involves worshiping the Supreme Lord. Here the Supreme Lord worshiped the Supreme Lord. Therefore it is said, *bhagavān ātmanātmānam īje:* the Lord worshiped Himself by Himself. This does not, of course, justify the Māyāvāda philosophy, by which one thinks himself the Supreme Personality of Godhead. The *jīva*, the living entity, is always different from the Supreme Lord. The living entities (*vibhinnāṁśa*) never become one with the Lord, although Māyāvādīs sometimes imitate the Lord's worship of Himself. Lord Kṛṣṇa meditated upon Himself every morning as a *gṛhastha*, and similarly Lord Rāmacandra performed *yajñas* to satisfy Himself, but this does not mean that an ordinary living being should imitate the Lord by accepting the process of *ahaṅgraha-upāsanā*. Such unauthorized worship is not recommended herein.

TEXT 2

होत्रेऽददाद् दिशं प्राचीं ब्रह्मणे दक्षिणां प्रभुः ।
अध्वर्यवे प्रतीचीं वा उत्तरां सामगाय सः ॥ २ ॥

hotre 'dadād diśaṁ prācīṁ
brahmaṇe dakṣiṇāṁ prabhuḥ
adhvaryave pratīcīṁ vā
uttarāṁ sāmagāya saḥ

hotre—unto the *hotā* priest, who offers oblations; *adadāt*—gave; *diśam*—direction; *prācīm*—the whole eastern side; *brahmaṇe*—unto the *brahmā* priest, who supervises what is done in the sacrificial arena; *dakṣiṇām*—the southern side; *prabhuḥ*—Lord Rāmacandra;

adhvaryave—unto the *adhvaryu* priest; *pratīcīm*—the whole western side; *vā*—also; *uttarām*—the northern side; *sāma-gāya*—unto the *udgātā* priest, who sings the *Sāma Veda; saḥ*—He (Lord Rāmacandra).

TRANSLATION

Lord Rāmacandra gave the entire east to the hotā priest, the entire south to the brahmā priest, the west to the adhvaryu priest, and the north to the udgātā priest, the reciter of the Sāma Veda. In this way, He donated His kingdom.

TEXT 3

आचार्याय ददौ शेषां यावती भूस्तदन्तरा ।
मन्यमान इदं कृत्स्नं ब्राह्मणोऽर्हति निःस्पृहः ॥ ३ ॥

ācāryāya dadau śeṣāṁ
yāvatī bhūs tad-antarā
manyamāna idaṁ kṛtsnaṁ
brāhmaṇo 'rhati niḥspṛhaḥ

ācāryāya—unto the *ācārya,* the spiritual master; *dadau*—gave; *śeṣām*—the balance; *yāvatī*—whatever; *bhūḥ*—land; *tat-antarā*—existing between the east, west, north and south; *manyamānaḥ*—thinking; *idam*—all this; *kṛtsnam*—wholly; *brāhmaṇaḥ*—the *brāhmaṇas; arhati*—deserve to possess; *niḥspṛhaḥ*—having no desire.

TRANSLATION

Thereafter, thinking that because the brāhmaṇas have no material desires they should possess the entire world, Lord Rāmacandra delivered the land between the east, west, north and south to the ācārya.

TEXT 4

इत्ययं तदलङ्कारवासोभ्यामवशेषितः ।
तथा राज्ञ्यपि वैदेही सौमङ्गल्यावशेषिता ॥ ४ ॥

ity ayaṁ tad-alaṅkāra-
vāsobhyām avaśeṣitaḥ
tathā rājñy api vaidehī
saumaṅgalyāvaśeṣitā

iti—in this way (after giving everything to the *brāhmaṇas*); *ayam*—Lord Rāmacandra; *tat*—His; *alaṅkāra-vāsobhyām*—with personal ornaments and garments; *avaśeṣitaḥ*—remained; *tathā*—as well as; *rājñī*—the Queen (mother Sītā); *api*—also; *vaidehī*—the daughter of the King of Videha; *saumaṅgalyā*—with only the nose ring; *avaśeṣitā*—remained.

TRANSLATION

After thus giving everything in charity to the brāhmaṇas, Lord Rāmacandra retained only His personal garments and ornaments, and similarly the Queen, mother Sītā, was left with only her nose ring, and nothing else.

TEXT 5

ते तु ब्राह्मणदेवस्य वात्सल्यं वीक्ष्य संस्तुतम् ।
प्रीताः क्लिन्नधियस्तस्मै प्रत्यर्प्येदं बभाषिरे ॥ ५ ॥

te tu brāhmaṇa-devasya
vātsalyaṁ vīkṣya saṁstutam
prītāḥ klinna-dhiyas tasmai
pratyarpyedaṁ babhāṣire

te—the *hotā, brahmā* and other priests; *tu*—but; *brāhmaṇa-devasya*—of Lord Rāmacandra, who loved the *brāhmaṇas* so much; *vātsalyam*—the paternal affection; *vīkṣya*—after seeing; *saṁstutam*—worshiped with prayers; *prītāḥ*—being very pleased; *klinna-dhiyaḥ*—with melted hearts; *tasmai*—unto Him (Lord Rāmacandra); *pratyarpya*—returning; *idam*—this (all the land given to them); *babhāṣire*—spoke.

TRANSLATION

All the brāhmaṇas who were engaged in the various activities of the sacrifice were very pleased with Lord Rāmacandra, who was

greatly affectionate and favorable to the brāhmaṇas. Thus with melted hearts they returned all the property received from Him and spoke as follows.

PURPORT

In the previous chapter it was said that the *prajās*, the citizens, strictly followed the system of *varṇāśrama-dharma*. The *brāhmaṇas* acted exactly like *brāhmaṇas*, the *kṣatriyas* exactly like *kṣatriyas*, and so on. Therefore, when Lord Rāmacandra gave everything in charity to the *brāhmaṇas*, the *brāhmaṇas*, being qualified, wisely considered that *brāhmaṇas* are not meant to possess property to make a profit from it. The qualifications of a *brāhmaṇa* are given in *Bhagavad-gītā* (18.42):

śamo damas tapaḥ śaucaṁ
kṣāntir ārjavam eva ca
jñānaṁ vijñānam āstikyaṁ
brahma-karma svabhāvajam

"Peacefulness, self-control, austerity, purity, tolerance, honesty, wisdom, knowledge, and religiousness—these are the qualities by which the *brāhmaṇas* work." The brahminical character offers no scope for possessing land and ruling citizens; these are the duties of a *kṣatriya*. Therefore, although the *brāhmaṇas* did not refuse Lord Rāmacandra's gift, after accepting it they returned it to the King. The *brāhmaṇas* were so pleased with Lord Rāmacandra's affection toward them that their hearts melted. They saw that Lord Rāmacandra, aside from being the Supreme Personality of Godhead, was fully qualified as a *kṣatriya* and was exemplary in character. One of the qualifications of a *kṣatriya* is to be charitable. A *kṣatriya*, or ruler, levies taxes upon the citizens not for his personal sense gratification but to give charity in suitable cases. *Dānam īśvara-bhāvaḥ*. On one hand, *kṣatriyas* have the propensity to rule, but on the other they are very liberal with charity. When Mahārāja Yudhiṣṭhira gave charity, he engaged Karṇa to take charge of distributing it. Karṇa was very famous as Dātā Karṇa. The word *dātā* refers to one who gives charity very liberally. The kings always kept a large quantity of food grains in stock, and whenever there was any scarcity of grains, they would distribute grains in charity. A *kṣatriya's* duty is to give charity, and a *brāhmaṇa's* duty is to accept charity, but not more than needed to maintain body and soul together. Therefore, when the *brāhmaṇas* were given so much land by Lord Rāmacandra, they returned it to Him and were not greedy.

TEXT 6

अप्रत्तं नस्त्वया किं नु भगवन् भुवनेश्वर ।
यन्नोऽन्तर्हृदयं विश्य तमो हंसि स्वरोचिषा ॥ ६ ॥

aprattaṁ nas tvayā kiṁ nu
bhagavan bhuvaneśvara
yan no 'ntar-hṛdayaṁ viśya
tamo haṁsi sva-rociṣā

aprattam—not given; *naḥ*—unto us; *tvayā*—by Your Lordship; *kim*—what; *nu*—indeed; *bhagavan*—O Supreme Lord; *bhuvana-īśvara*—O master of the whole universe; *yat*—because; *naḥ*—our; *antaḥ-hṛdayam*—within the core of the heart; *viśya*—entering; *tamaḥ*—the darkness of ignorance; *haṁsi*—You annihilate; *sva-rociṣā*—by Your own effulgence.

TRANSLATION

O Lord, You are the master of the entire universe. What have You not given to us? You have entered the core of our hearts and dissipated the darkness of our ignorance by Your effulgence. This is the supreme gift. We do not need a material donation.

PURPORT

When Dhruva Mahārāja was offered a benediction by the Supreme Personality of Godhead, he replied, "O my Lord, I am fully satisfied. I do not need any material benediction." Similarly, when Prahlāda Mahārāja was offered a benediction by Lord Nṛsiṁhadeva, he also refused to accept it and instead declared that a devotee should not be like a *vaṇik*, a mercantile man who gives something in exchange for some profit. One who becomes a devotee for some material profit is not a pure devotee.

Brāhmaṇas are always enlightened by the Supreme Personality of Godhead within the heart (*sarvasya cāhaṁ hṛdi sanniviṣṭo mattaḥ smṛtir jñānam apohanaṁ ca*). And because the *brāhmaṇas* and Vaiṣṇavas are always directed by the Supreme Personality of Godhead, they are not greedy for material wealth. What is absolutely necessary they possess, but they do not want an expanded kingdom. An example of this was given by Vāmanadeva. Acting as a *brahmacārī,* Lord Vāmanadeva wanted only three paces of land. Aspiring to possess more and more for personal sense gratification is simply ignorance, and this ignorance is conspicuous by its absence from the heart of a *brāhmaṇa* or Vaiṣṇava.

TEXT 7

नमो ब्रह्मण्यदेवाय रामायाकुण्ठमेधसे ।
उत्तमश्लोकधुर्याय न्यस्तदण्डार्पिताङ्घ्रये ॥ ७ ॥

namo brahmaṇya-devāya
rāmāyākuṇṭha-medhase
uttamaśloka-dhuryāya
nyasta-daṇḍārpitāṅghraye

namaḥ—we offer our respectful obeisances; *brahmaṇya-devāya*—unto the Supreme Personality of Godhead, who accepts the *brāhmaṇas* as His worshipable deity; *rāmāya*—unto Lord Rāmacandra; *akuṇṭha-medhase*—whose memory and knowledge are never disturbed by anxiety; *uttamaśloka-dhuryāya*—the best of very famous persons; *nyasta-daṇḍa-arpita-aṅghraye*—whose lotus feet are worshiped by sages beyond the jurisdiction of punishment.

TRANSLATION

O Lord, You are the Supreme Personality of Godhead, who have accepted the brāhmaṇas as Your worshipable deity. Your knowledge and memory are never disturbed by anxiety. You are the chief of all famous persons within this world, and Your lotus feet are worshiped by sages who are beyond the jurisdiction of punishment. O Lord Rāmacandra, let us offer our respectful obeisances unto You.

TEXT 8

कदाचिल्लोकजिज्ञासुर्गूढो रात्र्यामलक्षितः ।
चरन् वाचोऽश‍ृणोद् रामो भार्यामुद्दिश्य कस्यचित् ॥८॥

kadācil loka-jijñāsur
gūḍho rātryām alakṣitaḥ
caran vāco 'śṛṇod rāmo
bhāryām uddiśya kasyacit

kadācit—once upon a time; *loka-jijñāsuḥ*—desiring to know about the public; *gūḍhaḥ*—hiding Himself by a disguise; *rātryām*—at night; *alakṣitaḥ*—without being identified by anyone else; *caran*—walking; *vācaḥ*—speaking; *aśṛṇot*—heard; *rāmaḥ*—Lord Rāmacandra; *bhāryām*—unto His wife; *uddiśya*—indicating; *kasyacit*—of someone.

TRANSLATION

Śukadeva Gosvāmī continued: Once while Lord Rāmacandra was walking at night incognito, hiding Himself by a disguise to find out the people's opinion of Himself, He heard a man speaking unfavorably about His wife, Sītādevī.

TEXT 9

नाहं बिभर्मि त्वां दुष्टामसतीं परवेश्मगाम् ।
स्त्रैणो हि बिभृयात् सीतां रामो नाहं भजे पुनः ॥ ९ ॥

nāhaṁ bibharmi tvāṁ duṣṭām
asatīṁ para-veśma-gām
straiṇo hi bibhṛyāt sītāṁ
rāmo nāhaṁ bhaje punaḥ

na—not; *aham*—I; *bibharmi*—can maintain; *tvām*—you; *duṣṭām*—because you are polluted; *asatīm*—unchaste; *para-veśma-gām*—one who has gone to another man's house and committed adultery; *straiṇaḥ*—a person who is henpecked; *hi*—indeed; *bibhṛyāt*—can accept; *sītām*—even Sītā; *rāmaḥ*—like Lord Rāmacandra; *na*—not; *aham*—I; *bhaje*—shall accept; *punaḥ*—again.

TRANSLATION

[Speaking to his unchaste wife, the man said] You go to another man's house, and therefore you are unchaste and polluted. I shall not maintain you any more. A henpecked husband like Lord Rāma may accept a wife like Sītā, who went to another man's house, but I am not henpecked like Him, and therefore I shall not accept you again.

TEXT 10

इति लोकाद् बहुमुखाद् दुराराध्यादसंविदः ।
पत्या भीतेन सा त्यक्ता प्राप्ता प्राचेतसाश्रमम् ॥१०॥

iti lokād bahu-mukhād
durārādhyād asaṁvidaḥ
patyā bhītena sā tyaktā
prāptā prācetasāśramam

iti—thus; *lokāt*—from persons; *bahu-mukhāt*—who can talk nonsensically in various ways; *durārādhyāt*—whom it is very difficult to stop; *asaṁvidaḥ*—who are without full knowledge; *patyā*—by the husband; *bhītena*—being afraid; *sā*—mother Sītā; *tyaktā*—was abandoned; *prāptā*—went; *prācetasa-āśramam*—to the hermitage of Prācetasa (Vālmīki Muni).

TRANSLATION

Śukadeva Gosvāmī said: Men with a poor fund of knowledge and a heinous character speak nonsensically. Fearing such rascals, Lord Rāmacandra abandoned His wife, Sītādevī, although she was pregnant. Thus Sītādevī went to the āśrama of Vālmīki Muni.

TEXT 11

अन्तर्वत्न्यागते काले यमौ सा सुषुवे सुतौ ।
कुशो लव इति ख्यातौ तयोश्चक्रे क्रिया मुनिः ॥११॥

antarvatny āgate kāle
yamau sā suṣuve sutau

kuśo lava iti khyātau
tayoś cakre kriyā muniḥ

antarvatnī—the pregnant wife; *āgate*—arrived; *kāle*—in due course of time; *yamau*—twins; *sā*—Sītādevī; *suṣuve*—gave birth to; *sutau*—two sons; *kuśaḥ*—Kuśa; *lavaḥ*—Lava; *iti*—thus; *khyātau*—celebrated; *tayoḥ*—of them; *cakre*—performed; *kriyāḥ*—the ritualistic ceremonies of birth; *muniḥ*—the great sage Vālmīki.

TRANSLATION

When the time came, the pregnant mother Sītādevī gave birth to twin sons, later celebrated as Lava and Kuśa. The ritualistic ceremonies for their birth were performed by Vālmīki Muni.

TEXT 12

अङ्गदश्चित्रकेतुश्च लक्ष्मणस्यात्मजौ स्मृतौ ।
तक्षः पुष्कल इत्यास्तां भरतस्य महीपते ॥१२॥

aṅgadaś citraketuś ca
lakṣmaṇasyātmajau smṛtau
takṣaḥ puṣkala ity āstāṁ
bharatasya mahīpate

aṅgadaḥ—Aṅgada; *citraketuḥ*—Citraketu; *ca*—also; *lakṣmaṇasya*—of Lord Lakṣmaṇa; *ātmajau*—two sons; *smṛtau*—were said to be; *takṣaḥ*—Takṣa; *puṣkalaḥ*—Puṣkala; *iti*—thus; *āstām*—were; *bharatasya*—of Lord Bharata; *mahīpate*—O King Parīkṣit.

TRANSLATION

O Mahārāja Parīkṣit, Lord Lakṣmaṇa had two sons, named Aṅgada and Citraketu, and Lord Bharata also had two sons, named Takṣa and Puṣkala.

TEXTS 13–14

सुबाहुः श्रुतसेनश्च शत्रुघ्नस्य बभूवतुः ।
गन्धर्वान् कोटिशो जघ्ने भरतो विजये दिशाम् ॥१३॥

तदीयं धनमानीय सर्वं राज्ञे न्यवेदयत् ।
शत्रुघ्नश्च मधोः पुत्रं लवणं नाम राक्षसम् ।
हत्वा मधुवने चक्रे मथुरां नाम वै पुरीम् ॥१४॥

subāhuḥ śrutasenaś ca
śatrughnasya babhūvatuḥ
gandharvān koṭiśo jaghne
bharato vijaye diśām

tadīyaṁ dhanam ānīya
sarvaṁ rājñe nyavedayat
śatrughnaś ca madhoḥ putraṁ
lavaṇaṁ nāma rākṣasam
hatvā madhuvane cakre
mathurāṁ nāma vai purīm

subāhuḥ—Subāhu; *śrutasenaḥ*—Śrutasena; *ca*—also; *śatrughnasya*—of Lord Śatrughna; *babhūvatuḥ*—were born; *gandharvān*—persons related with the Gandharvas, who are mostly pretenders; *koṭiśaḥ*—by the tens of millions; *jaghne*—killed; *bharataḥ*—Lord Bharata; *vijaye*—while conquering; *diśām*—all directions; *tadīyam*—of the Gandharvas; *dhanam*—riches; *ānīya*—bringing; *sarvam*—everything; *rājñe*—unto the King (Lord Rāmacandra); *nyavedayat*—offered; *śatrughnaḥ*—Śatrughna; *ca*—and; *madhoḥ*—of Madhu; *putram*—the son; *lavaṇam*—Lavaṇa; *nāma*—by the name; *rākṣasam*—a man-eater; *hatvā*—by killing; *madhuvane*—in the great forest known as Madhuvana; *cakre*—constructed; *mathurām*—Mathurā; *nāma*—by the name; *vai*—indeed; *purīm*—a great town.

TRANSLATION

Śatrughna had two sons, named Subāhu and Śrutasena. When Lord Bharata went to conquer all directions, He had to kill many millions of Gandharvas, who are generally pretenders. Taking all their wealth, He offered it to Lord Rāmacandra. Śatrughna also killed a Rākṣasa named Lavaṇa, who was the son of Madhu Rākṣasa.

Thus He established in the great forest known as Madhuvana the town known as Mathurā.

TEXT 15

मुनौ निक्षिप्य तनयौ सीता भर्त्रा विवासिता ।
ध्यायन्ती रामचरणौ विवरं प्रविवेश ह ॥१५॥

munau nikṣipya tanayau
sītā bhartrā vivāsitā
dhyāyantī rāma-caraṇau
vivaraṁ praviveśa ha

munau—unto the great sage Vālmīki; *nikṣipya*—giving in charge; *tanayau*—the two sons Lava and Kuśa; *sītā*—mother Sītādevī; *bhartrā*—by her husband; *vivāsitā*—banished; *dhyāyantī*—meditating upon; *rāma-caraṇau*—the lotus feet of Lord Rāmacandra; *vivaram*—within the earth; *praviveśa*—she entered; *ha*—indeed.

TRANSLATION

Being forsaken by her husband, Sītādevī entrusted her two sons to the care of Vālmīki Muni. Then, meditating upon the lotus feet of Lord Rāmacandra, she entered into the earth.

PURPORT

It was impossible for Sītādevī to live in separation from Lord Rāmacandra. Therefore, after entrusting her two sons to the care of Vālmīki Muni, she entered into the earth.

TEXT 16

तच्छ्रुत्वा भगवान् रामो रुन्धन्नपि धिया शुचः ।
स्मरंस्तस्या गुणांस्तांस्तान्नाशक्नोद् रोद्धुमीश्वरः॥१६॥

tac chrutvā bhagavān rāmo
rundhann api dhiyā śucaḥ

smaraṁs tasyā guṇāṁs tāṁs tān
nāśaknod roddhum īśvaraḥ

tat—this (the news of Sītādevī's entering the earth); *śrutvā*—hearing; *bhagavān*—the Supreme Personality of Godhead; *rāmaḥ*—Lord Rāmacandra; *rundhan*—trying to reject; *api*—although; *dhiyā*—by intelligence; *śucaḥ*—grief; *smaran*—remembering; *tasyāḥ*—of her; *guṇān*—qualities; *tān tān*—under different circumstances; *na*—not; *aśaknot*—was able; *roddhum*—to check; *īśvaraḥ*—although the supreme controller.

TRANSLATION

After hearing the news of mother Sītā's entering the earth, the Supreme Personality of Godhead was certainly aggrieved. Although He is the Supreme Personality of Godhead, upon remembering the exalted qualities of mother Sītā, He could not check His grief in transcendental love.

PURPORT

Lord Rāmacandra's grief at the news of Sītādevī's entering the earth is not to be considered material. In the spiritual world also there are feelings of separation, but such feelings are considered spiritual bliss. Grief in separation exists even in the Absolute, but such feelings of separation in the spiritual world are transcendentally blissful. Such feelings are a sign of *tasya prema-vaśyatva-svabhāva*, being under the influence of *hlādinī-śakti* and being controlled by love. In the material world such feelings of separation are only a perverted reflection.

TEXT 17

स्त्रीपुंप्रसङ्ग एतादृक्सर्वत्र त्रासमावहः ।
अपीश्वराणां किमुत ग्राम्यस्य गृहचेतसः ॥१७॥

strī-puṁ-prasaṅga etādṛk
sarvatra trāsam-āvahaḥ
apīśvarāṇāṁ kim uta
grāmyasya gṛha-cetasaḥ

strī-pum-prasaṅgaḥ—attraction between husband and wife, or man and woman; *etādṛk*—like this; *sarvatra*—everywhere; *trāsam-āvahaḥ*—the cause of fear; *api*—even; *īśvarāṇām*—of controllers; *kim uta*—and what to speak of; *grāmyasya*—of ordinary men of this material world; *gṛha-cetasaḥ*—who are attached to materialistic household life.

TRANSLATION

The attraction between man and woman, or male and female, always exists everywhere, making everyone always fearful. Such feelings are present even among the controllers like Brahmā and Lord Śiva and is the cause of fear for them, what to speak of others who are attached to household life in this material world.

PURPORT

As explained above, when the feelings of love and transcendental bliss from the spiritual world are pervertedly reflected in this material world, they are certainly the cause of bondage. As long as men feel attracted to women in this material world and women feel attracted to men, the bondage of repeated birth and death will continue. But in the spiritual world, where there is no fear of birth and death, such feelings of separation are the cause of transcendental bliss. In the absolute reality there are varieties of feeling, but all of them are of the same quality of transcendental bliss.

TEXT 18

तत ऊर्ध्वं ब्रह्मचर्यं धार्यन्नजुहोत् प्रभुः ।
त्रयोदशाब्दसाहस्रमग्निहोत्रमखण्डितम् ॥१८॥

tata ūrdhvaṁ brahmacaryaṁ
dhāryann ajuhot prabhuḥ
trayodaśābda-sāhasram
agnihotram akhaṇḍitam

tataḥ—thereafter; *ūrdhvam*—after mother Sītā's going into the earth; *brahmacaryam*—complete celibacy; *dhārayan*—observing; *ajuhot*—performed a ritualistic ceremony and sacrifice; *prabhuḥ*—Lord

Rāmacandra; *trayodaśa-abda-sāhasram*—for thirteen thousand years; *agnihotram*—the sacrifice known as Agnihotra-yajña; *akhaṇḍitam*—without ceasing.

TRANSLATION

After mother Sītā entered the earth, Lord Rāmacandra observed complete celibacy and performed an uninterrupted Agnihotra-yajña for thirteen thousand years.

TEXT 19

स्मरतां हृदि विन्यस्य विद्धं दण्डककण्टकैः ।
स्वपादपल्लवं राम आत्मज्योतिरगात् ततः ॥१९॥

smaratāṁ hṛdi vinyasya
viddhaṁ daṇḍaka-kaṇṭakaiḥ
sva-pāda-pallavaṁ rāma
ātma-jyotir agāt tataḥ

smaratām—of persons who always think of Him; *hṛdi*—in the core of the heart; *vinyasya*—placing; *viddham*—pierced; *daṇḍaka-kaṇṭakaiḥ*—by thorns in the forest of Daṇḍakāraṇya (while Lord Rāmacandra was living there); *sva-pāda-pallavam*—the petals of His lotus feet; *rāmaḥ*—Lord Rāmacandra; *ātma-jyotiḥ*—the rays of His bodily luster, known as the *brahmajyoti; agāt*—entered; *tataḥ*—beyond the *brahmajyoti*, or in His own Vaikuṇṭha planet.

TRANSLATION

After completing the sacrifice, Lord Rāmacandra, whose lotus feet were sometimes pierced by thorns when He lived in Daṇḍakāraṇya, placed those lotus feet in the hearts of those who always think of Him. Then He entered His own abode, the Vaikuṇṭha planet beyond the brahmajyoti.

PURPORT

The lotus feet of the Lord are always a subject matter for meditation for devotees. Sometimes when Lord Rāmacandra wandered in the forest of Daṇḍakāraṇya, thorns pricked His lotus feet. The devotees, upon thinking of this, would faint. The Lord does not feel pain or pleasure from any action or reaction of this material world, but the devotees cannot tolerate even the pricking of the Lord's lotus feet by a thorn. This was the attitude of the *gopīs* when they thought of Kṛṣṇa wandering in the forest, with pebbles and grains of sand pricking His lotus feet. This tribulation in the heart of a devotee cannot be understood by *karmīs, jñānīs* or *yogīs.* The devotees, who could not tolerate even thinking of the Lord's lotus feet being pricked by a thorn, were again put into tribulation by thinking of the Lord's disappearance, for the Lord had to return to His abode after finishing His pastimes in this material world.

The word *ātma-jyotiḥ* is significant. The *brahmajyoti,* which is greatly appreciated by *jñānīs,* or monistic philosophers who desire to enter it for liberation, is nothing but the rays of the Lord's body.

yasya prabhā prabhavato jagad-aṇḍa-koṭi-
koṭiṣv aśeṣa-vasudhādi-vibhūti-bhinnam
tad brahma niṣkalam anantam aśeṣa-bhūtaṁ
govindam ādi-puruṣaṁ tam ahaṁ bhajāmi

"I worship Govinda, the primeval Lord, who is endowed with great power. The glowing effulgence of His transcendental form is the impersonal Brahman, which is absolute, complete and unlimited and which displays the varieties of countless planets, with their different opulences, in millions and millions of universes." (*Brahma-saṁhitā* 5.40) The *brahmajyoti* is the beginning of the spiritual world, and beyond the *brahmajyoti* are the Vaikuṇṭha planets. In other words, the *brahmajyoti* stays outside the Vaikuṇṭha planets, just as the sunshine stays outside the sun. To enter the sun planet, one must go through the sunshine. Similarly, when the Lord or His devotees enter the Vaikuṇṭha planets, they go through the *brahmajyoti.* The *jñānīs,* or monistic philosophers, because of their impersonal conception of the Lord, cannot enter the Vaikuṇṭha planets, but they also cannot stay eternally in the *brahmajyoti.* Thus after some time they fall again to this material world. *Āruhya kṛcchreṇa paraṁ padaṁ tataḥ patanty adho 'nādṛta-yuṣmad-aṅghrayaḥ* (*Bhāg.* 10.2.32). The Vaikuṇṭha planets are covered by the *brahmajyoti,* and therefore one cannot properly understand what those Vaikuṇṭha planets are unless one is a pure devotee.

TEXT 20

नेदं यशो रघुपतेः सुरयाच्ञयात्त-
लीलातनोरधिकसाम्यविमुक्तधाम्नः ।
रक्षोवधो जलधिबन्धनमस्त्रपूगैः
किं तस्य शत्रुहनने कपयः सहायाः ॥२०॥

nedaṁ yaśo raghupateḥ sura-yācñayātta-
līlā-tanor adhika-sāmya-vimukta-dhāmnaḥ
rakṣo-vadho jaladhi-bandhanam astra-pūgaiḥ
kiṁ tasya śatru-hanane kapayaḥ sahāyāḥ

na—not; *idam*—all these; *yaśaḥ*—fame; *raghu-pateḥ*—of Lord Rāmacandra; *sura-yācñayā*—by the prayers of the demigods; *ātta-līlā-tanoḥ*—whose spiritual body is always engaged in various pastimes; *adhika-sāmya-vimukta-dhāmnaḥ*—no one is greater than or equal to Him; *rakṣaḥ-vadhaḥ*—killing the Rākṣasa (Rāvaṇa); *jaladhi-bandhanam*—bridging the ocean; *astra-pūgaiḥ*—with bow and arrows; *kim*—whether; *tasya*—His; *śatru-hanane*—in killing the enemies; *kapayaḥ*—the monkeys; *sahāyāḥ*—assistants.

TRANSLATION

Lord Rāmacandra's reputation for having killed Rāvaṇa with showers of arrows at the request of the demigods and for having built a bridge over the ocean does not constitute the factual glory of the Supreme Personality of Godhead Lord Rāmacandra, whose spiritual body is always engaged in various pastimes. Lord Rāmacandra has no equal or superior, and therefore He had no need to take help from the monkeys to gain victory over Rāvaṇa.

PURPORT

As stated in the *Vedas* (*Śvetāśvatara Upaniṣad* 6.8):

na tasya kāryaṁ karaṇaṁ ca vidyate
na tat-samaś cābhyadhikaś ca dṛśyate
parāsya śaktir vividhaiva śrūyate
svābhāvikī jñāna-bala-kriyā ca

"The Supreme Lord has nothing to do, and no one is found to be equal to or greater than Him, for everything is done naturally and systematically by His multifarious energies." The Lord has nothing to do (*na tasya kāryaṁ karaṇaṁ ca vidyate*); whatever He does is His pastime. The Lord has no duty to perform to oblige anyone. Nonetheless, He appears to act to protect His devotees or kill His enemies. Of course, no one can be the Lord's enemy, since who could be more powerful than the Lord? There is actually no question of anyone's being His enemy, but when the Lord wants to take pleasure in pastimes, He comes down to this material world and acts like a human being, thus showing His wonderful, glorious activities to please the devotees. His devotees always want to see the Lord victorious in varied activities, and therefore, to please Himself and them, the Lord sometimes agrees to act as a human being and perform wonderful, uncommon pastimes for the satisfaction of the devotees.

TEXT 21

यस्यामलं नृपसदःसु यशोऽधुनापि
गायन्त्यघघ्नमृषयो दिगिभेन्द्रपट्टम् ।
तं नाकपालवसुपालकिरीटजुष्ट-
पादाम्बुजं रघुपतिं शरणं प्रपद्ये ॥२१॥

yasyāmalaṁ nṛpa-sadaḥsu yaśo 'dhunāpi
gāyanty agha-ghnam ṛṣayo dig-ibhendra-paṭṭam
taṁ nākapāla-vasupāla-kirīṭa-juṣṭa-
pādāmbujaṁ raghupatiṁ śaraṇaṁ prapadye

yasya—whose (Lord Rāmacandra's); *amalam*—spotless, free from material qualities; *nṛpa-sadaḥsu*—in the assembly of great emperors like Mahārāja Yudhiṣṭhira; *yaśaḥ*—famous glories; *adhunā api*—even today; *gāyanti*—glorify; *agha-ghnam*—which vanquish all sinful reactions; *ṛṣayaḥ*—great saintly persons like Mārkaṇḍeya; *dik-ibha-indra-paṭṭam*—as the ornamental cloth covering the elephant that conquers the directions; *tam*—that; *nāka-pāla*—of heavenly demigods; *vasu-pāla*—of earthly kings; *kirīṭa*—by the helmets; *juṣṭa*—are worshiped; *pāda-ambujam*—whose lotus feet; *raghu-patim*—unto Lord Rāmacandra; *śaraṇam*—surrender; *prapadye*—I offer.

TRANSLATION

Lord Rāmacandra's spotless name and fame, which vanquish all sinful reactions, are celebrated in all directions, like the ornamental cloth of the victorious elephant that conquers all directions. Great saintly persons like Mārkaṇḍeya Ṛṣi still glorify His characteristics in the assemblies of great emperors like Mahārāja Yudhiṣṭhira. Similarly, all the saintly kings and all the demigods, including Lord Śiva and Lord Brahmā, worship the Lord by bowing down with their helmets. Let me offer my obeisances unto His lotus feet.

TEXT 22

स यैः स्पृष्टोऽभिदृष्टो वा संविष्टोऽनुगतोऽपि वा ।
कोसलास्ते ययुः स्थानं यत्र गच्छन्ति योगिनः ॥२२॥

sa yaiḥ spṛṣṭo 'bhidṛṣṭo vā
saṁviṣṭo 'nugato 'pi vā
kosalās te yayuḥ sthānaṁ
yatra gacchanti yoginaḥ

saḥ—He, Lord Rāmacandra; *yaiḥ*—by which persons; *spṛṣṭaḥ*—touched; *abhidṛṣṭaḥ*—seen; *vā*—either; *saṁviṣṭaḥ*—eating together, lying together; *anugataḥ*—followed as servants; *api vā*—even; *kosalāḥ*—all those inhabitants of Kosala; *te*—they; *yayuḥ*—departed; *sthānam*—to the place; *yatra*—wherein; *gacchanti*—they go; *yoginaḥ*—all the *bhakti-yogīs*.

TRANSLATION

Lord Rāmacandra returned to His abode, to which bhakti-yogīs are promoted. This is the place to which all the inhabitants of Ayodhyā went after they served the Lord in His manifest pastimes by offering Him obeisances, touching His lotus feet, fully observing Him as a fatherlike King, sitting or lying down with Him like equals, or even just accompanying Him.

PURPORT

The Lord says in *Bhagavad-gītā* (4.9):

janma karma ca me divyam
evaṁ yo vetti tattvataḥ
tyaktvā dehaṁ punar janma
naiti mām eti so 'rjuna

"One who knows the transcendental nature of My appearance and activities does not, upon leaving the body, take his birth again in this material world, but attains My eternal abode, O Arjuna." Here this is confirmed. All the inhabitants of Ayodhyā who saw Lord Rāmacandra as citizens, served Him as servants, sat and talked with Him as friends or were somehow or other present during His reign went back home, back to Godhead. After giving up the body, the devotee who becomes perfect in devotional service enters that particular universe where Lord Rāmacandra or Lord Kṛṣṇa is engaged in His pastimes. Then, after being trained to serve the Lord in various capacities in that *prakaṭa-līlā*, the devotee is finally promoted to *sanātana-dhāma*, the supreme abode in the spiritual world. This *sanātana-dhāma* is also mentioned in *Bhagavad-gītā* (*paras tasmāt tu bhāvo 'nyo 'vyakto 'vyaktāt sanātanaḥ*). One who enters the transcendental pastimes of the Lord is called *nitya-līlā-praviṣṭa*. To understand clearly why Lord Rāmacandra returned, it is mentioned herewith that the Lord went to that particular place where the *bhakti-yogīs* go. The impersonalists misunderstand the statements of *Śrīmad-Bhāgavatam* to mean that the Lord entered His own effulgence and therefore become impersonal. But the Lord is a person, and His devotees are persons. Indeed, the living entities, like the Lord, were persons in the past, they are persons in the present, and they will continue to be persons even after giving up the body. This is also confirmed in *Bhagavad-gītā.*

TEXT 23

पुरुषो रामचरितं श्रवणैरुपधारयन् ।
आनृशंस्यपरो राजन् कर्मबन्धैर्विमुच्यते ॥२३॥

puruṣo rāma-caritaṁ
śravaṇair upadhārayan
ānṛśaṁsya-paro rājan
karma-bandhair vimucyate

puruṣaḥ—any person; *rāma-caritam*—the narration concerning the activities of the Supreme Personality of Godhead Lord Rāmacandra; *śravaṇaiḥ*—by aural reception; *upadhārayan*—simply by this process of hearing; *ānṛśaṁsya-paraḥ*—becomes completely free from envy; *rājan*—O King Parīkṣit; *karma-bandhaiḥ*—by the bondage of fruitive activities; *vimucyate*—one becomes liberated.

TRANSLATION

O King Parīkṣit, anyone who aurally receives the narrations concerning the characteristics of Lord Rāmacandra's pastimes will ultimately be freed from the disease of envy and thus be liberated from the bondage of fruitive activities.

PURPORT

Here in this material world, everyone is envious of someone else. Even in religious life, it is sometimes found that if one devotee has advanced in spiritual activities, other devotees are envious of him. Such envious devotees are not completely freed from the bondage of birth and death. As long as one is not completely free from the cause of birth and death, one cannot enter the *sanātana-dhāma* or the eternal pastimes of the Lord. One becomes envious because of being influenced by the designations of the body, but the liberated devotee has nothing to do with the body, and therefore he is completely on the transcendental platform. A devotee is never envious of anyone, even his enemy. Because the devotee knows that the Lord is his supreme protector, he thinks, "What harm can the so-called enemy do?" Thus a devotee is confident about his protection. The Lord says, *ye yathā māṁ prapadyante tāṁs tathaiva bhajāmy aham:* "According to the proportion of one's surrender unto Me, I respond accordingly." A devotee must therefore be completely free from envy, especially of other devotees. To envy other devotees is a great offense, a *vaiṣṇava-aparādha.* A devotee who constantly engages in hearing and chanting (*śravaṇa-kīrtana*) is certainly freed from the disease of envy, and thus he becomes eligible to go back home, back to Godhead.

TEXT 24

श्रीराजोवाच

कथं स भगवान् रामो भ्रातॄन् वा स्वयमात्मनः ।
तस्मिन् वा तेऽन्ववर्तन्त प्रजाः पौराश्च ईश्वरे ॥२४॥

śrī-rājovāca
kathaṁ sa bhagavān rāmo
bhrātṝn vā svayam ātmanaḥ
tasmin vā te 'nvavartanta
prajāḥ paurāś ca īśvare

śrī-rājā uvāca—Mahārāja Parīkṣit inquired; *katham*—how; *saḥ*—He, the Lord; *bhagavān*—the Supreme Personality of Godhead; *rāmaḥ*—Lord Rāmacandra; *bhrātṝn*—unto the brothers (Lakṣmaṇa, Bharata and Śatrughna); *vā*—either; *svayam*—personally; *ātmanaḥ*—expansions of His person; *tasmin*—unto the Lord; *vā*—either; *te*—they (all the inhabitants and the brothers); *anvavartanta*—behaved; *prajāḥ*—all the inhabitants; *paurāḥ*—the citizens; *ca*—and; *īśvare*—unto the Supreme Lord.

TRANSLATION

Mahārāja Parīkṣit inquired from Śukadeva Gosvāmī: How did the Lord conduct Himself, and how did He behave in relationship

with His brothers, who were expansions of His own self? And how did His brothers and the inhabitants of Ayodhyā treat Him?

TEXT 25

श्रीबादरायणिरुवाच
अथादिशद् दिग्विजये भ्रातृंस्त्रिभुवनेश्वरः ।
आत्मानं दर्शयन् स्वानां पुरीमैक्षत सानुगः ॥२५॥

śrī-bādarāyaṇir uvāca
athādiśad dig-vijaye
bhrātṝṁs tri-bhuvaneśvaraḥ
ātmānaṁ darśayan svānāṁ
purīm aikṣata sānugaḥ

śrī-bādarāyaṇiḥ uvāca—Śrī Śukadeva Gosvāmī said; *atha*—hereafter (when the Lord accepted the throne on the request of Bharata); *ādiśat*—ordered; *dik-vijaye*—to conquer all the world; *bhrātṝn*—His younger brothers; *tri-bhuvana-īśvaraḥ*—the Lord of the universe; *ātmānam*—personally, Himself; *darśayan*—giving audience; *svānām*—to the family members and the citizens; *purīm*—the city; *aikṣata*—supervised; *sa-anugaḥ*—with other assistants.

TRANSLATION

Śukadeva Gosvāmī replied: After accepting the throne of the government by the fervent request of His younger brother Bharata, Lord Rāmacandra ordered His younger brothers to go out and conquer the entire world, while He personally remained in the capital to give audience to all the citizens and residents of the palace and supervise the governmental affairs with His other assistants.

PURPORT

The Supreme Personality of Godhead does not allow any of His devotees or assistants to be engaged in sense gratification. The younger brothers of Lord Rāmacandra were at home enjoying the personal presence of the Supreme Personality of Godhead, but the Lord ordered Them to go out and achieve victory all over the world. It was the custom (and this custom, in some places, is still current) that all other kings would have to accept the supremacy of the emperor. If the king of a small state did not accept the emperor's supremacy, there would be a fight, and the king of the small state would be obliged to accept the emperor as supreme; otherwise, it would not be possible for the emperor to rule the country.

Lord Rāmacandra showed His favor to His brothers by ordering Them to go out. Many of the Lord's devotees residing in Vṛndāvana have taken the vow not to leave Vṛndāvana to preach Kṛṣṇa consciousness. But the Lord says that Kṛṣṇa consciousness should be spread all over the world, in every village and every town. This is the open order of Lord Caitanya Mahāprabhu.

pṛthivīte āche yata nagarādi grāma
sarvatra pracāra haibe mora nāma

A pure devotee, therefore, must execute the order of the Lord and must not gratify his senses by remaining stagnant in one place, falsely proud, thinking that because he does not leave Vṛndāvana but chants in a solitary place he has become a great devotee. A devotee must carry out the order of the Supreme Personality of Godhead. Caitanya Mahāprabhu said, *yāre dekha, tāre kaha 'kṛṣṇa'-upadeśa.* Every devotee, therefore, should spread Kṛṣṇa consciousness by preaching, asking whomever he meets to accept the order of the Supreme Personality of Godhead. The Lord says, *sarva-dharmān parityajya mām ekaṁ śaraṇaṁ vraja:* "Abandon all varieties of religion and just surrender unto Me." This is the order of the Lord, who speaks as the supreme emperor. Everyone should be induced to accept this order, for this is victory (*dig-vijaya*). And it is the duty of the soldier, the devotee, to impress upon everyone this philosophy of life.

Of course, those who are *kaniṣṭha-adhikārīs* do not preach, but the Lord shows mercy to them also, as He did by staying personally in Ayodhyā to give audience to the people in general. One should not mistakenly think that the Lord asked His younger brothers to leave Ayodhyā because He especially favored the citizens. The Lord is merciful to everyone, and He knows how to show His favor to each individual person according to his capacity. One who abides by the order of the Lord is a pure devotee.

TEXT 26

आसिक्तमार्गां गन्धोदैः करिणां मदशीकरैः ।
स्वामिनं प्राप्तमालोक्य मत्तां वा सुतरामिव ॥२६॥

āsikta-mārgāṁ gandhodaiḥ
kariṇāṁ mada-śīkaraiḥ
svāminaṁ prāptam ālokya
mattāṁ vā sutarām iva

āsikta-mārgām—the streets were sprinkled; *gandha-udaiḥ*—with perfumed water; *kariṇām*—of elephants; *mada-śīkaraiḥ*—with particles of perfumed liquor; *svāminam*—the master or proprietor; *prāptam*—present; *ālokya*—seeing personally; *mattām*—very opulent; *vā*—either; *sutarām*—highly; *iva*—as if.

TRANSLATION

During the reign of Lord Rāmacandra, the streets of the capital, Ayodhyā, were sprinkled with perfumed water and drops of perfumed liquor, thrown about by elephants from their trunks. When the citizens saw the Lord personally supervising the affairs of the city in such opulence, they appreciated this opulence very much.

PURPORT

We have simply heard about the opulence of Rāma-rājya during the reign of Lord Rāmacandra. Now, here is one example of the opulence of the Lord's kingdom. The streets of Ayodhyā were not only cleaned but also sprinkled with perfumed water and drops of perfumed liquor, which were distributed by elephants through their trunks. There was no need of sprinkling machines, for the elephant has a natural ability to suck water through its trunk and again throw it out in a shower. We can understand the opulence of the city from this one example: it was actually sprinkled with perfumed water. Moreover, the citizens had the opportunity to see the Lord personally supervising the affairs of the state.

He was not a sleeping monarch, as we can understand from His activities in sending His brothers to see to affairs outside the capital and punish anyone who did not obey the emperor's orders. This is called *dig-vijaya.* The citizens were all given facilities for peaceful life, and they were also qualified with appropriate attributes according to *varṇāśrama.* As we have seen from the previous chapter, *varṇāśrama-guṇānvitāḥ:* the citizens were trained according to the *varṇāśrama* system. A class of men were *brāhmaṇas*, a class of men were *kṣatriyas*, a class were *vaiśyas*, and a class were *śūdras.* Without this scientific division, there can be no question of good citizenship. The King, being magnanimous and perfect in His duty, performed many sacrifices and treated the citizens as His sons, and the citizens, being trained in the *varṇāśrama* system, were obedient and perfectly ordered. The entire monarchy was so opulent and peaceful that the government was even able to sprinkle the street with perfumed water, what to speak of other management. Since the city was sprinkled with perfumed water, we can simply imagine how opulent it was in other respects. Why should the citizens not have felt happy during the reign of Lord Rāmacandra?

TEXT 27

प्रासादगोपुरसभाचैत्यदेवगृहादिषु ।
विन्यस्तहेमकलशैः पताकाभिश्च मण्डिताम् ॥२७॥

prāsāda-gopura-sabhā-
caitya-deva-gṛhādiṣu
vinyasta-hema-kalaśaiḥ
patākābhiś ca maṇḍitām

prāsāda—in palaces; *gopura*—palace gates; *sabhā*—assembly houses; *caitya*—raised platforms; *deva-gṛha*—temples wherein deities are worshiped; *ādiṣu*—and so on; *vinyasta*—placed; *hema-kalaśaiḥ*—with golden waterpots; *patākābhiḥ*—by flags; *ca*—also; *maṇḍitām*—bedecked.

TRANSLATION

The palaces, the palace gates, the assembly houses, the platforms for meeting places, the temples and all such places were decorated with golden waterpots and bedecked with various types of flags.

TEXT 28

पूगैः सवृन्तै रम्भाभिः पट्टिकाभिः सुवाससाम् ।
आदर्शैरंशुकैः स्रग्भिः कृतकौतुकतोरणाम् ॥२८॥

pūgaiḥ savṛntai rambhābhiḥ
paṭṭikābhiḥ suvāsasām
ādarśair aṁśukaiḥ sragbhiḥ
kṛta-kautuka-toraṇām

pūgaiḥ—by trees of betel nut; *sa-vṛntaiḥ*—with bunches of flowers and fruits; *rambhābhiḥ*—with banana trees; *paṭṭikābhiḥ*—with flags; *su-vāsasām*—decorated with colorful cloth; *ādarśaiḥ*—with mirrors; *aṁśukaiḥ*—with cloths; *sragbhiḥ*—with garlands; *kṛta-kautuka*—made auspicious; *toraṇām*—possessing reception gates.

TRANSLATION

Wherever Lord Rāmacandra visited, auspicious welcome gates were constructed, with banana trees and betel nut trees, full of flowers and fruits. The gates were decorated with various flags made of colorful cloth and with tapestries, mirrors and garlands.

TEXT 29

तमुपेयुस्तत्र तत्र पौरा अर्हणपाणयः ।
आशिषो युयुजुर्देव पाहीमां प्राक् त्वयोद्धृताम् ॥२९॥

tam upeyus tatra tatra
paurā arhaṇa-pāṇayaḥ
āśiṣo yuyujur deva
pāhīmāṁ prāk tvayoddhṛtām

tam—unto Him, Lord Rāmacandra; *upeyuḥ*—approached; *tatra tatra*—wherever He visited; *paurāḥ*—the inhabitants of the neighborhood; *arhaṇa-pāṇayaḥ*—carrying paraphernalia to worship the Lord; *āśiṣaḥ*—blessings from the Lord; *yuyujuḥ*—came down; *deva*—O my Lord; *pāhi*—just maintain; *imām*—this land; *prāk*—as before; *tvayā*—

by You; *uddhṛtām*—rescued (from the bottom of the sea in Your incarnation as Varāha).

TRANSLATION

Wherever Lord Rāmacandra visited, the people approached Him with paraphernalia of worship and begged the Lord's blessings. "O Lord," they said, "as You rescued the earth from the bottom of the sea in Your incarnation as a boar, may You now maintain it. Thus we beg Your blessings."

TEXT 30

ततः प्रजा वीक्ष्य पतिं चिरागतं
दिदृक्षयोत्सृष्टगृहाः स्त्रियो नराः ।
आरुह्य हर्म्याण्यरविन्दलोचन-
मतृप्तनेत्राः कुसुमैरवाकिरन् ॥३०॥

tataḥ prajā vīkṣya patiṁ cirāgataṁ
didṛkṣayotsṛṣṭa-gṛhāḥ striyo narāḥ
āruhya harmyāṇy aravinda-locanam
atṛpta-netrāḥ kusumair avākiran

tataḥ—thereafter; *prajāḥ*—the citizens; *vīkṣya*—by seeing; *patim*—the King; *cira-āgatam*—returned after a long time; *didṛkṣayā*—desiring to see; *utsṛṣṭa-gṛhāḥ*—vacating their respective residences; *striyaḥ*—the women; *narāḥ*—the men; *āruhya*—getting on top of; *harmyāṇi*—great palaces; *aravinda-locanam*—Lord Rāmacandra, whose eyes are like the petals of a lotus; *atṛpta-netrāḥ*—whose eyes were not fully satisfied; *kusumaiḥ*—by flowers; *avākiran*—showered the Lord.

TRANSLATION

Thereafter, not having seen the Lord for a long time, the citizens, both men and women, being very eager to see Him, left their homes and got up on the roofs of the palaces. Being incompletely satiated with seeing the face of the lotus-eyed Lord Rāmacandra, they showered flowers upon Him.

TEXTS 31–34

अथ प्रविष्टः स्वगृहं जुष्टं स्वैः पूर्वराजभिः ।
अनन्ताखिलकोशाढ्यमनर्घ्योरुपरिच्छदम् ॥३१॥
विद्रुमोदुम्बरद्वारैर्वैदूर्यस्तम्भपङ्क्तिभिः ।
स्थलैर्मारकतैः स्वच्छैर्भ्राजत्स्फटिकभित्तिभिः ॥३२॥
चित्रस्रग्भिः पट्टिकाभिर्वासोमणिगणांशुकैः ।
मुक्ताफलैश्चिदुल्लासैः कान्तकामोपपत्तिभिः ॥३३॥
धूपदीपैः सुरभिभिर्मण्डितं पुष्पमण्डनैः ।
स्त्रीपुम्भिः सुरसंकाशैर्जुष्टं भूषणभूषणैः ॥३४॥

atha praviṣṭaḥ sva-gṛhaṁ
juṣṭaṁ svaiḥ pūrva-rājabhiḥ
anantākhila-koṣāḍhyam
anarghyoruparicchadam

vidrumodumbara-dvārair
vaidūrya-stambha-paṅktibhiḥ
sthalair mārakataiḥ svacchair
bhrājat-sphaṭika-bhittibhiḥ

citra-sragbhiḥ paṭṭikābhir
vāso-maṇi-gaṇāṁśukaiḥ
muktā-phalaiś cid-ullāsaiḥ
kānta-kāmopapattibhiḥ

dhūpa-dīpaiḥ surabhibhir
maṇḍitaṁ puṣpa-maṇḍanaiḥ
strī-pumbhiḥ sura-saṅkāśair
juṣṭaṁ bhūṣaṇa-bhūṣaṇaiḥ

atha—thereafter; *praviṣṭaḥ*—He entered; *sva-gṛham*—His own palace; *juṣṭam*—occupied; *svaiḥ*—by His own family members; *pūrva-rājabhiḥ*—by the previous members of the royal family; *ananta*—unlimited; *akhila*—everywhere; *koṣa*—treasury; *āḍhyam*—prosperous; *anarghya*—priceless; *uru*—high; *paricchadam*—paraphernalia; *vidruma*—of coral; *udumbara-dvāraiḥ*—with the two sides of the doors; *vaidūrya-stambha*—with pillars of *vaidūrya-maṇi; paṅktibhiḥ*—in a line; *sthalaiḥ*—with floors; *mārakataiḥ*—made of *marakata* stone; *svacchaiḥ*—very cleanly polished; *bhrājat*—dazzling; *sphaṭika*—marble; *bhittibhiḥ*—foundations; *citra-sragbhiḥ*—with varieties of flower garlands; *paṭṭikābhiḥ*—with flags; *vāsaḥ*—clothing; *maṇi-gaṇa-aṁśukaiḥ*—by various effulgent and valuable stones; *muktā-phalaiḥ*—with pearls; *cit-ullāsaiḥ*—increasing celestial pleasure; *kānta-kāma*—fulfilling one's desires; *upapattibhiḥ*—by such paraphernalia; *dhūpa-dīpaiḥ*—with incense and lamps; *surabhibhiḥ*—very fragrant; *maṇḍitam*—decorated; *puṣpa-maṇḍanaiḥ*—by bunches of various flowers; *strī-pumbhiḥ*—by men and women; *sura-saṅkāśaiḥ*—appearing like the demigods; *juṣṭam*—full of; *bhūṣaṇa-bhūṣaṇaiḥ*—whose bodies beautified their ornaments.

TRANSLATION

Thereafter, Lord Rāmacandra entered the palace of His forefathers. Within the palace were various treasures and valuable wardrobes. The sitting places on the two sides of the entrance door were made of coral, the yards were surrounded by pillars of vaidūrya-maṇi, the floor was made of highly polished marakata-maṇi, and the foundation was made of marble. The entire palace was decorated with flags and garlands and bedecked with valuable stones, shining with a celestial effulgence. The palace was fully decorated with pearls and surrounded by lamps and incense. The men and women within the palace all resembled demigods and were decorated with various ornaments, which seemed beautiful because of being placed on their bodies.

TEXT 35

तस्मिन् स भगवान् रामः स्निग्धया प्रिययेष्टया ।
रेमे स्वाराममधीराणामृषभः सीतया किल ॥३५॥

tasmin sa bhagavān rāmaḥ
snigdhayā priyayeṣṭayā
reme svārāma-dhīrāṇām
ṛṣabhaḥ sītayā kila

tasmin—in that celestial palace; *saḥ*—He; *bhagavān*—the Supreme Personality of Godhead; *rāmaḥ*—Lord Rāmacandra; *snigdhayā*—always pleased by her behavior; *priyayā iṣṭayā*—with His dearmost wife; *reme*—enjoyed; *sva-ārāma*—personal pleasure; *dhīrāṇām*—of the greatest learned persons; *ṛṣabhaḥ*—the chief; *sītayā*—with mother Sītā; *kila*—indeed.

TRANSLATION

Lord Rāmacandra, the Supreme Personality of Godhead, chief of the best learned scholars, resided in that palace with His pleasure potency, mother Sītā, and enjoyed complete peace.

TEXT 36

बुभुजे च यथाकालं कामान् धर्ममपीडयन् ।
वर्षपूगान् बहून् नृणामभिध्याताङ्घ्रिपल्लवः ॥३६॥

bubhuje ca yathā-kālaṁ
kāmān dharmam apīḍayan
varṣa-pūgān bahūn nṝṇām
abhidhyātāṅghri-pallavaḥ

bubhuje—He enjoyed; *ca*—also; *yathā-kālam*—as long as required; *kāmān*—all enjoyment; *dharmam*—religious principles; *apīḍayan*—without transgressing; *varṣa-pūgān*—duration of years; *bahūn*—many; *nṝṇām*—of the people in general; *abhidhyāta*—being meditated upon; *aṅghri-pallavaḥ*—His lotus feet.

TRANSLATION

Without transgressing the religious principles, Lord Rāmacandra, whose lotus feet are worshiped by devotees in meditation,

enjoyed with all the paraphernalia of transcendental pleasure for as long as needed.

Thus end the Bhaktivedanta purports of the Ninth Canto, Eleventh Chapter, of the Śrīmad-Bhāgavatam, *entitled "Lord Rāmacandra Rules the World."*

CHAPTER TWELVE

The Dynasty of Kuśa, the Son of Lord Rāmacandra

This chapter describes the dynasty of Kuśa, the son of Lord Rāmacandra. The members of this dynasty are descendants of Śaśāda, the son of Mahārāja Ikṣvāku.

Following in the genealogical table of Lord Rāmacandra's dynasty, Kuśa, the Lord's son, was followed consecutively by Atithi, Niṣadha, Nabha, Puṇḍarīka, Kṣemadhanvā, Devānīka, Anīha, Pāriyātra, Balasthala, Vajranābha, Sagaṇa and Vidhṛti. These personalities ruled the world. From Vidhṛti came Hiraṇyanābha, who later became the disciple of Jaimini and propounded the system of mystic *yoga* in which Yājñavalkya was initiated. Following in this dynasty were Puṣpa, Dhruvasandhi, Sudarśana, Agnivarṇa, Śīghra and Maru. Maru attained full perfection in the practice of *yoga*, and he still lives in the village of Kalāpa. At the end of this age of Kali, he will revive the dynasty of the sun-god. Next in the dynasty were Prasuśruta, Sandhi, Amarṣaṇa, Mahasvān, Viśvabāhu, Prasenajit, Takṣaka and Bṛhadbala, who was later killed by Abhimanyu. Śukadeva Gosvāmī said that these were all kings who had passed away. The future descendants of Bṛhadbala will be Bṛhadraṇa, Ūrukriya, Vatsavṛddha, Prativyoma, Bhānu, Divāka, Sahadeva, Bṛhadaśva, Bhānumān, Pratīkāśva, Supratīka, Marudeva, Sunakṣatra, Puṣkara, Antarikṣa, Sutapā, Amitrajit, Bṛhadrāja, Barhi, Kṛtañjaya, Raṇañjaya, Sañjaya, Śākya, Śuddhoda, Lāṅgala, Prasenajit, Kṣudraka, Raṇaka, Suratha and Sumitra. All of them will become kings one after another. Sumitra, coming in this age of Kali, will be the last king in the Ikṣvāku dynasty; after him, the dynasty will be extinguished.

TEXT 1

श्रीशुक उवाच

कुशस्य चातिथिस्तस्मान्निषधस्तत्सुतो नभः ।
पुण्डरीकोऽथ तत्पुत्रः क्षेमधन्वाभवत्ततः ॥ १ ॥

śrī-śuka uvāca
kuśasya cātithis tasmān
niṣadhas tat-suto nabhaḥ
puṇḍarīko 'tha tat-putraḥ
kṣemadhanvābhavat tataḥ

śrī-śukaḥ uvāca—Śrī Śukadeva Gosvāmī said; *kuśasya*—of Kuśa, the son of Lord Rāmacandra; *ca*—also; *atithiḥ*—Atithi; *tasmāt*—from him; *niṣadhaḥ*—Niṣadha; *tat-sutaḥ*—his son; *nabhaḥ*—Nabha; *puṇḍarīkaḥ*—Puṇḍarīka; *atha*—thereafter; *tat-putraḥ*—his son; *kṣemadhanvā*—Kṣemadhanvā; *abhavat*—became; *tataḥ*—thereafter.

TRANSLATION

Śukadeva Gosvāmī said: The son of Rāmacandra was Kuśa, the son of Kuśa was Atithi, the son of Atithi was Niṣadha, and the son of Niṣadha was Nabha. The son of Nabha was Puṇḍarīka, and from Puṇḍarīka came a son named Kṣemadhanvā.

TEXT 2

देवानीकस्ततोऽनीहः पारियात्रोऽथ तत्सुतः ।
ततो बलस्थलस्तस्माद् वज्रनाभोऽर्कसंभवः ॥ २ ॥

devānīkas tato 'nīhaḥ
pāriyātro 'tha tat-sutaḥ
tato balasthalas tasmād
vajranābho 'rka-sambhavaḥ

devānīkaḥ—Devānīka; *tataḥ*—from Kṣemadhanvā; *anīhaḥ*—from Devānīka came the son named Anīha; *pāriyātraḥ*—Pāriyātra; *atha*—thereafter; *tat-sutaḥ*—the son of Anīha; *tataḥ*—from Pāriyātra; *balasthalaḥ*—Balasthala; *tasmāt*—from Balasthala; *vajranābhaḥ*—Vajranābha; *arka-sambhavaḥ*—derived from the sun-god.

TRANSLATION

The son of Kṣemadhanvā was Devānīka, Devānīka's son was Anīha, Anīha's son was Pāriyātra, and Pāriyātra's son was

Balasthala. The son of Balasthala was Vajranābha, who was said to have been born from the effulgence of the sun-god.

TEXTS 3–4

सगणस्तत्सुतस्तस्माद् विधृतिश्चाभवत् सुतः ।
ततो हिरण्यनाभोऽभूद् योगाचार्यस्तु जैमिनेः ॥ ३ ॥
शिष्यः कौशल्य आध्यात्मं याज्ञवल्क्योऽध्यगाद् यतः ।
योगं महोदयमृषिर्हृदयग्रन्थिभेदकम् ॥ ४ ॥

saganas tat-sutas tasmād
vidhṛtiś cābhavat sutaḥ
tato hiraṇyanābho 'bhūd
yogācāryas tu jaimineḥ

śiṣyaḥ kauśalya ādhyātmaṁ
yājñavalkyo 'dhyagād yataḥ
yogaṁ mahodayam ṛṣir
hṛdaya-granthi-bhedakam

saganaḥ—Sagaṇa; *tat*—this (Vajranābha's); *sutaḥ*—son; *tasmāt*—from him; *vidhṛtiḥ*—Vidhṛti; *ca*—also; *abhavat*—was born; *sutaḥ*—his son; *tataḥ*—from him; *hiraṇyanābhaḥ*—Hiraṇyanābha; *abhūt*—became; *yoga-ācāryaḥ*—the propounder of the philosophy of *yoga; tu*—but; *jaimineḥ*—because of accepting Jaimini as his spiritual master; *śiṣyaḥ*—disciple; *kauśalyaḥ*—Kauśalya; *ādhyātmam*—spiritual; *yājña-valkyaḥ*—Yājñavalkya; *adhyagāt*—studied; *yataḥ*—from him (Hiraṇyanābha); *yogam*—the mystic performances; *mahā-udayam*—highly elevated; *ṛṣiḥ*—Yājñavalkya Ṛṣi; *hṛdaya-granthi-bhedakam*—mystic *yoga*, which can loosen the knots of material attachment in the heart.

TRANSLATION

The son of Vajranābha was Sagaṇa, and his son was Vidhṛti. The son of Vidhṛti was Hiraṇyanābha, who became a disciple of Jaimini and became a great ācārya of mystic yoga. It is from Hiraṇyanābha that the great saint Yājñavalkya learned the highly elevated system

of mystic yoga known as ādhyātma-yoga, which can loosen the knots of material attachment in the heart.

TEXT 5

पुष्पो हिरण्यनाभस्य ध्रुवसन्धिस्ततोऽभवत् ।
सुदर्शनोऽथाग्निवर्णः शीघ्रस्तस्य मरुः सुतः ॥ ५ ॥

puṣpo hiraṇyanābhasya
dhruvasandhis tato 'bhavat
sudarśano 'thāgnivarṇaḥ
śīghras tasya maruḥ sutaḥ

puṣpaḥ—Puṣpa; *hiraṇyanābhasya*—the son of Hiraṇyanābha; *dhruvasandhiḥ*—Dhruvasandhi; *tataḥ*—from him; *abhavat*—was born; *sudarśanaḥ*—from Dhruvasandhi, Sudarśana was born; *atha*—thereafter; *agnivarṇaḥ*—Agnivarṇa, the son of Sudarśana; *śīghraḥ*—Śīghra; *tasya*—his (Agnivarṇa's); *maruḥ*—Maru; *sutaḥ*—son.

TRANSLATION

The son of Hiraṇyanābha was Puṣpa, and the son of Puṣpa was Dhruvasandhi. The son of Dhruvasandhi was Sudarśana, whose son was Agnivarṇa. The son of Agnivarṇa was named Śīghra, and his son was Maru.

TEXT 6

सोऽसावास्ते योगसिद्धः कलापग्राममास्थितः ।
कलेरन्ते सूर्यवंशं नष्टं भावयिता पुनः ॥ ६ ॥

so 'sāv āste yoga-siddhaḥ
kalāpa-grāmam āsthitaḥ
kaler ante sūrya-vaṁśaṁ
naṣṭaṁ bhāvayitā punaḥ

saḥ—he; *asau*—the personality known as Maru; *āste*—still existing; *yoga-siddhaḥ*—perfection in the power of mystic *yoga; kalāpa-grāmam*—the place named Kalāpa-grāma; *āsthitaḥ*—he is still living there; *kaleḥ*—of this Kali-yuga; *ante*—at the end; *sūrya-vaṁśam*—the descendants of the sun-god; *naṣṭam*—after being lost; *bhāvayitā*—Maru will begin by begetting a son; *punaḥ*—again.

TRANSLATION

Having achieved perfection in the power of mystic yoga, Maru still lives in a place known as Kalāpa-grāma. At the end of Kali-yuga, he will revive the lost Sūrya dynasty by begetting a son.

PURPORT

At least five thousand years ago, Śrīla Śukadeva Gosvāmī ascertained the existence of Maru in Kalāpa-grāma and said that Maru, having achieved a *yoga-siddha* body, would continue to exist until the end of Kali-yuga, which is calculated to continue for 432,000 years. Such is the perfection of mystic power. By controlling the breath, the perfect *yogī* can continue his life for as long as he likes. Sometimes we hear from the Vedic literature that some personalities from the Vedic age, such as Vyāsadeva and Aśvatthāmā, are still living. Here we understand that Maru is also still living. We are sometimes surprised that a mortal body can live for such a long time. The explanation of this longevity is given here by the word *yoga-siddha.* If one becomes perfect in the practice of *yoga,* he can live as long as he likes. The demonstration of some trifling *yoga-siddha* does not constitute perfection. Here is a factual example of perfection: a *yoga-siddha* can live as long as he likes.

TEXT 7

तस्मात् प्रसुश्रुतस्तस्य सन्धिस्तस्याप्यमर्षणः ।
महस्वांस्तत्सुतस्तस्माद् विश्वबाहुरजायत ॥ ७ ॥

tasmāt prasuśrutas tasya
sandhis tasyāpy amarṣaṇaḥ
mahasvāṁs tat-sutas tasmād
viśvabāhur ajāyata

tasmāt—from Maru; *prasuśrutaḥ*—Prasuśruta, his son; *tasya*—of Prasuśruta; *sandhiḥ*—a son named Sandhi; *tasya*—his (Sandhi's);

api—also; *amarṣaṇaḥ*—a son named Amarṣaṇa; *mahasvān*—the son of Amarṣaṇa; *tat*—his; *sutaḥ*—son; *tasmāt*—from him (Mahasvān); *viśvabāhuḥ*—Viśvabāhu; *ajāyata*—took birth.

TRANSLATION

From Maru was born a son named Prasuśruta, from Prasuśruta came Sandhi, from Sandhi came Amarṣaṇa, and from Amarṣaṇa a son named Mahasvān. From Mahasvān, Viśvabāhu took his birth.

TEXT 8

ततः प्रसेनजित् तस्मात् तक्षको भविता पुनः ।
ततो बृहद्बलो यस्तु पित्रा ते समरे हतः ॥ ८ ॥

tataḥ prasenajit tasmāt
takṣako bhavitā punaḥ
tato bṛhadbalo yas tu
pitrā te samare hataḥ

tataḥ—from Viśvabāhu; *prasenajit*—a son named Prasenajit was born; *tasmāt*—from him; *takṣakaḥ*—Takṣaka; *bhavitā*—would take birth; *punaḥ*—again; *tataḥ*—from him; *bṛhadbalaḥ*—a son named Bṛhadbala; *yaḥ*—he who; *tu*—but; *pitrā*—by father; *te*—your; *samare*—in the fight; *hataḥ*—killed.

TRANSLATION

From Viśvabāhu came a son named Prasenajit, from Prasenajit came Takṣaka, and from Takṣaka came Bṛhadbala, who was killed in a fight by your father.

TEXT 9

एते हीक्ष्वाकुभूपाला अतीताः शृण्वनागतान् ।
बृहद्बलस्य भविता पुत्रो नाम्ना बृहद्रणः ॥ ९ ॥

ete hīkṣvāku-bhūpālā
atītāḥ śṛṇv anāgatān

bṛhadbalasya bhavitā
putro nāmnā bṛhadraṇaḥ

ete—all of them; *hi*—indeed; *ikṣvāku-bhūpālāḥ*—kings in the dynasty of Ikṣvāku; *atītāḥ*—all of them are dead and gone; *śṛṇu*—just hear; *anāgatān*—those who will come in the future; *bṛhadbalasya*—of Bṛhadbala; *bhavitā*—there will be; *putraḥ*—a son; *nāmnā*—by the name; *bṛhadraṇaḥ*—Bṛhadraṇa.

TRANSLATION

All these kings in the dynasty of Ikṣvāku have passed away. Now please listen as I describe the kings who will be born in the future. From Bṛhadbala will come Bṛhadraṇa.

TEXT 10

ऊरुक्रियः सुतस्तस्य वत्सवृद्धो भविष्यति ।
प्रतिव्योमस्ततो भानुर्दिवाको वाहिनीपतिः ॥१०॥

ūrukriyaḥ sutas tasya
vatsavṛddho bhaviṣyati
prativyomas tato bhānur
divāko vāhinī-patiḥ

ūrukriyaḥ—Ūrukriya; *sutaḥ*—son; *tasya*—of Ūrukriya; *vatsa-vṛddhaḥ*—Vatsavṛddha; *bhaviṣyati*—will take birth; *prativyomaḥ*—Prativyoma; *tataḥ*—from Vatsavṛddha; *bhānuḥ*—(from Prativyoma) a son named Bhānu; *divākaḥ*—from Bhānu a son named Divāka; *vāhinī-patiḥ*—a great commander of soldiers.

TRANSLATION

The son of Bṛhadraṇa will be Ūrukriya, who will have a son named Vatsavṛddha. Vatsavṛddha will have a son named Prativyoma, and Prativyoma will have a son named Bhānu, from whom Divāka, a great commander of soldiers, will take birth.

TEXT 11

सहदेवस्ततो वीरो बृहदश्वोऽथ भानुमान् ।
प्रतीकाश्वो भानुमतः सुप्रतीकोऽथ तत्सुतः ॥११॥

sahadevas tato vīro
bṛhadaśvo 'tha bhānumān
pratīkāśvo bhānumataḥ
supratīko 'tha tat-sutaḥ

sahadevaḥ—Sahadeva; *tataḥ*—from Divāka; *vīraḥ*—a great hero; *bṛhadaśvaḥ*—Bṛhadaśva; *atha*—from him; *bhānumān*—Bhānumān; *pratīkāśvaḥ*—Pratīkāśva; *bhānumataḥ*—from Bhānumān; *supratīkaḥ*—Supratīka; *atha*—thereafter; *tat-sutaḥ*—the son of Pratīkāśva.

TRANSLATION

Thereafter, from Divāka will come a son named Sahadeva, and from Sahadeva a great hero named Bṛhadaśva. From Bṛhadaśva will come Bhānumān, and from Bhānumān will come Pratīkāśva. The son of Pratīkāśva will be Supratīka.

TEXT 12

भविता मरुदेवोऽथ सुनक्षत्रोऽथ पुष्करः ।
तस्यान्तरिक्षस्तत्पुत्रः सुतपास्तदमित्रजित् ॥१२॥

bhavitā marudevo 'tha
sunakṣatro 'tha puṣkaraḥ
tasyāntarikṣas tat-putraḥ
sutapās tad amitrajit

bhavitā—will be born; *marudevaḥ*—Marudeva; *atha*—thereafter; *sunakṣatraḥ*—Sunakṣatra; *atha*—thereafter; *puṣkaraḥ*—Puṣkara, a son of Sunakṣatra; *tasya*—of Puṣkara; *antarikṣaḥ*—Antarikṣa; *tat-putraḥ*—his son; *sutapāḥ*—Sutapā; *tat*—from him; *amitrajit*—a son named Amitrajit.

TRANSLATION

Thereafter, from Supratīka will come Marudeva; from Marudeva, Sunakṣatra; from Sunakṣatra, Puṣkara; and from Puṣkara, Antarikṣa. The son of Antarikṣa will be Sutapā, and his son will be Amitrajit.

TEXT 13

बृहद्राजस्तु तस्यापि बर्हिस्तस्मात् कृतञ्जयः ।
रणञ्जयस्तस्य सुतः सञ्जयो भविता ततः ॥१३॥

bṛhadrājas tu tasyāpi
barhis tasmāt kṛtañjayaḥ
raṇañjayas tasya sutaḥ
sañjayo bhavitā tataḥ

bṛhadrājaḥ—Bṛhadrāja; *tu*—but; *tasya api*—of Amitrajit; *barhiḥ*—Barhi; *tasmāt*—from Barhi; *kṛtañjayaḥ*—Kṛtañjaya; *raṇañjayaḥ*—Raṇañjaya; *tasya*—of Kṛtañjaya; *sutaḥ*—son; *sañjayaḥ*—Sañjaya; *bhavitā*—will take birth; *tataḥ*—from Raṇañjaya.

TRANSLATION

From Amitrajit will come a son named Bṛhadrāja, from Bṛhadrāja will come Barhi, and from Barhi will come Kṛtañjaya. The son of Kṛtañjaya will be known as Raṇañjaya, and from him will come a son named Sañjaya.

TEXT 14

तस्माच्छाक्योऽथ शुद्धोदो लाङ्गलस्तत्सुतः स्मृतः ।
ततः प्रसेनजित् तस्मात् क्षुद्रको भविता ततः ॥१४॥

tasmāc chākyo 'tha śuddhodo
lāṅgalas tat-sutaḥ smṛtaḥ
tataḥ prasenajit tasmāt
kṣudrako bhavitā tataḥ

tasmāt—from Sañjaya; *śākyaḥ*—Śākya; *atha*—thereafter; *śuddhodaḥ*—Śuddhoda; *lāṅgalaḥ*—Lāṅgala; *tat-sutaḥ*—the son of Śuddhoda; *smṛtaḥ*—is well known; *tataḥ*—from him; *prasenajit*—Prasenajit; *tasmāt*—from Prasenajit; *kṣudrakaḥ*—Kṣudraka; *bhavitā*—will take birth; *tataḥ*—thereafter.

TRANSLATION

From Sañjaya will come Śākya, from Śākya will come Śuddhoda, and from Śuddhoda will come Lāṅgala. From Lāṅgala will come Prasenajit, and from Prasenajit, Kṣudraka.

TEXT 15

रणको भविता तस्मात् सुरथस्तनयस्ततः ।
सुमित्रो नाम निष्ठान्त एते बार्हद्बलान्वयाः ॥१५॥

raṇako bhavitā tasmāt
surathas tanayas tataḥ
sumitro nāma niṣṭhānta
ete bārhadbalānvayāḥ

raṇakaḥ—Raṇaka; *bhavitā*—will take birth; *tasmāt*—from Kṣudraka; *surathaḥ*—Suratha; *tanayaḥ*—the son; *tataḥ*—thereafter; *sumitraḥ*—Sumitra, the son of Suratha; *nāma*—by the name; *niṣṭhā-antaḥ*—the end of the dynasty; *ete*—all the above-mentioned kings; *bārhadbala-anvayāḥ*—in the dynasty of King Bṛhadbala.

TRANSLATION

From Kṣudraka will come Raṇaka, from Raṇaka will come Suratha, and from Suratha will come Sumitra, ending the dynasty. This is a description of the dynasty of Bṛhadbala.

TEXT 16

इक्ष्वाकूणामयं वंशः सुमित्रान्तो भविष्यति ।
यतस्तं प्राप्य राजानं संस्थां प्राप्स्यति वै कलौ ॥१६॥

ikṣvākūṇām ayaṁ vaṁśaḥ
sumitrānto bhaviṣyati
yatas taṁ prāpya rājānaṁ
saṁsthāṁ prāpsyati vai kalau

ikṣvākūṇām—of the dynasty of King Ikṣvāku; *ayam*—this (what has been described); *vaṁśaḥ*—descendants; *sumitra-antaḥ*—Sumitra being the last king of this dynasty; *bhaviṣyati*—will appear in the future, while the Kali-yuga still continues; *yataḥ*—because; *tam*—him, Mahārāja Sumitra; *prāpya*—getting; *rājānam*—as a king in that dynasty; *saṁsthām*—culmination; *prāpsyati*—gets; *vai*—indeed; *kalau*—at the end of Kali-yuga.

TRANSLATION

The last king in the dynasty of Ikṣvāku will be Sumitra; after Sumitra there will be no more sons in the dynasty of the sun-god, and thus the dynasty will end.

Thus end the Bhaktivedanta purports of the Ninth Canto, Twelfth Chapter, of the Śrīmad-Bhāgavatam, *entitled "The Dynasty of Kuśa, the Son of Lord Rāmacandra."*

CHAPTER THIRTEEN

The Dynasty of Mahārāja Nimi

This chapter describes the dynasty in which the great and learned scholar Janaka was born. This is the dynasty of Mahārāja Nimi, who is said to have been the son of Ikṣvāku.

When Mahārāja Nimi began performing great sacrifices, he appointed Vasiṣṭha to be chief priest, but Vasiṣṭha refused, for he had already agreed to be priest in performing a *yajña* for Lord Indra. Vasiṣṭha therefore requested Mahārāja Nimi to wait until Lord Indra's sacrifice was finished, but Mahārāja Nimi did not wait. He thought, "Life is very short, so there is no need to wait." He therefore appointed another priest to perform the *yajña*. Vasiṣṭha was very angry at King Nimi and cursed him, saying, "May your body fall down." Cursed in that way, Mahārāja Nimi also became very angry, and he retaliated by saying, "May your body also fall down." As a result of this cursing and countercursing, both of them died. After this incident, Vasiṣṭha took birth again, begotten by Mitra and Varuṇa, who were agitated by Urvaśī.

The priests who were engaged in the sacrifice for King Nimi preserved Nimi's body in fragrant chemicals. When the sacrifice was over, the priests prayed for Nimi's life to all the demigods who had come to the arena of *yajña*, but Mahārāja Nimi refused to take birth again in a material body because he considered the material body obnoxious. The great sages then churned Nimi's body, and as a result of this churning, Janaka was born.

The son of Janaka was Udāvasu, and the son of Udāvasu was Nandivardhana. The son of Nandivardhana was Suketu, and his descendants continued as follows: Devarāta, Bṛhadratha, Mahāvīrya, Sudhṛti, Dhṛṣṭaketu, Haryaśva, Maru, Pratīpaka, Kṛtaratha, Devamīḍha, Viśruta, Mahādhṛti, Kṛtirāta, Mahāromā, Svarṇaromā, Hrasvaromā and Śīradhvaja. All these sons appeared in the dynasty one after another. From Śīradhvaja, mother Sītādevī was born. Śīradhvaja's son was Kuśadhvaja, and the son of Kuśadhvaja was Dharmadhvaja. The sons of Dharmadhvaja were Kṛtadhvaja and Mitadhvaja. The son of Kṛtadhvaja was Keśidhvaja, and the son of Mitadhvaja was Khāṇḍikya. Keśidhvaja was a self-realized soul, and his son was Bhānumān, whose descendants were as follows: Śatadyumna, Śuci, Sanadvāja, Ūrjaketu, Aja, Purujit, Ariṣṭanemi, Śrutāyu, Supārśvaka, Citraratha, Kṣemādhi, Samaratha, Satyaratha, Upaguru, Upagupta, Vasvananta, Yuyudha, Subhāṣaṇa, Śruta, Jaya, Vijaya, Ṛta, Śunaka, Vītahavya, Dhṛti, Bahulāśva, Kṛti and Mahāvaśī. All of these sons were great self-controlled personalities. This completes the list of the entire dynasty.

TEXT 1

श्रीशुक उवाच
निमिरिक्ष्वाकुतनयो वसिष्ठमवृतर्त्विजम् ।
आरभ्य सत्रं सोऽप्याह शक्रेण प्राग्वृतोऽस्मि भोः ॥१॥

śrī-śuka uvāca
nimir ikṣvāku-tanayo
vasiṣṭham avṛtartvijam
ārabhya satraṁ so 'py āha
śakreṇa prāg vṛto 'smi bhoḥ

śrī-śukaḥ uvāca—Śrī Śukadeva Gosvāmī said; *nimiḥ*—King Nimi; *ikṣvāku-tanayaḥ*—the son of Mahārāja Ikṣvāku; *vasiṣṭham*—the great sage Vasiṣṭha; *avṛta*—appointed; *ṛtvijam*—the chief priest of the sacrifice; *ārabhya*—beginning; *satram*—the sacrifice; *saḥ*—he, Vasiṣṭha; *api*—also; *āha*—said; *śakreṇa*—by Lord Indra; *prāk*—before; *vṛtaḥ asmi*—I was appointed; *bhoḥ*—O Mahārāja Nimi.

TRANSLATION

Śrīla Śukadeva Gosvāmī said: After beginning sacrifices, Mahārāja Nimi, the son of Ikṣvāku, requested the great sage Vasiṣṭha to take the post of chief priest. At that time, Vasiṣṭha replied, "My dear Mahārāja Nimi, I have already accepted the same post in a sacrifice begun by Lord Indra.

TEXT 2

तं निर्वर्त्यागमिष्यामि तावन्मां प्रतिपालय ।
तूष्णीमासीद् गृहपतिः सोऽपीन्द्रस्याकरोन्मखम् ॥२॥

taṁ nirvartyāgamiṣyāmi
tāvan māṁ pratipālaya
tūṣṇīm āsīd gṛha-patiḥ
so 'pīndrasyākaron makham

tam—that sacrifice; *nirvartya*—after finishing; *āgamiṣyāmi*—I shall come back; *tāvat*—until that time; *mām*—me (Vasiṣṭha); *pratipālaya*—wait for; *tūṣṇīm*—silent; *āsīt*—remained; *gṛha-patiḥ*—Mahārāja Nimi; *saḥ*—he, Vasiṣṭha; *api*—also; *indrasya*—of Lord Indra; *akarot*—executed; *makham*—the sacrifice.

TRANSLATION

"I shall return here after finishing the yajña for Indra. Kindly wait for me until then." Mahārāja Nimi remained silent, and Vasiṣṭha began to perform the sacrifice for Lord Indra.

TEXT 3

निमिश्चलमिदं विद्वान् सत्रमारभतात्मवान् ।
ऋत्विग्भिरपरैस्तावन्नागमद् यावता गुरुः ॥३॥

nimiś calam idaṁ vidvān
satram ārabhatātmavān
ṛtvigbhir aparais tāvan
nāgamad yāvatā guruḥ

nimiḥ—Mahārāja Nimi; *calam*—flickering, subject to end at any moment; *idam*—this (life); *vidvān*—being completely aware of this fact; *satram*—the sacrifice; *ārabhata*—inaugurated; *ātmavān*—self-realized person; *ṛtvigbhiḥ*—by priests; *aparaiḥ*—other than Vasiṣṭha; *tāvat*—for the time being; *na*—not; *āgamat*—returned; *yāvatā*—so long; *guruḥ*—his spiritual master (Vasiṣṭha).

TRANSLATION

Mahārāja Nimi, being a self-realized soul, considered that this life is flickering. Therefore, instead of waiting long for Vasiṣṭha, he began performing the sacrifice with other priests.

PURPORT

Cāṇakya Paṇḍita says, *śarīraṁ kṣaṇa-vidhvāṁsi kalpānta-sthāyino guṇāḥ:* "The duration of one's life in the material world may end at any moment, but if within this life one does something worthy, that qualification is depicted in history eternally." Here is a great personality, Mahārāja Nimi, who knew this fact. In the human form of life one should perform activities in such a way that at the end he goes back home, back to Godhead. This is self-realization.

TEXT 4

शिष्यव्यतिक्रमं वीक्ष्य तं निर्वर्त्यागतो गुरुः।
अशपत् पतताद् देहो निमेः पण्डितमानिनः ॥ ४ ॥

śiṣya-vyatikramaṁ vīkṣya
taṁ nirvartyāgato guruḥ
aśapat patatād deho
nimeḥ paṇḍita-māninaḥ

śiṣya-vyatikramam—the disciple's deviation from the order of the *guru; vīkṣya*—observing; *tam*—the performance of *yajña* by Indra; *nirvartya*—after finishing; *āgataḥ*—when he returned; *guruḥ*—Vasiṣṭha Muni; *aśapat*—he cursed Nimi Mahārāja; *patatāt*—may it fall down; *dehaḥ*—the material body; *nimeḥ*—of Mahārāja Nimi; *paṇḍita-māninaḥ*—who considers himself so learned (as to disobey the order of his spiritual master).

TRANSLATION

After completing the sacrificial performance for King Indra, the spiritual master Vasiṣṭha returned and found that his disciple Mahārāja Nimi had disobeyed his instructions. Thus Vasiṣṭha

cursed him, saying, "May the material body of Nimi, who considers himself learned, immediately fall."

TEXT 5

निमिः प्रतिददौ शापं गुरवेऽधर्मवर्तिने ।
तवापि पतताद् देहो लोभाद् धर्ममजानतः ॥ ५ ॥

nimiḥ pratidadau śāpaṁ
gurave 'dharma-vartine
tavāpi patatād deho
lobhād dharmam ajānataḥ

nimiḥ—Mahārāja Nimi; *pratidadau śāpam*—countercursed; *gurave*—unto his spiritual master, Vasiṣṭha; *adharma-vartine*—who was induced to irreligious principles (because he cursed his offenseless disciple); *tava*—of you; *api*—also; *patatāt*—let it fall; *dehaḥ*—the body; *lobhāt*—because of greed; *dharmam*—religious principles; *ajānataḥ*—not knowing.

TRANSLATION

For unnecessarily cursing him when he had committed no offense, Mahārāja Nimi countercursed his spiritual master. "For the sake of getting contributions from the King of heaven," he said, "you have lost your religious intelligence. Therefore I pronounce this curse: your body also will fall."

PURPORT

The religious principle for a *brāhmaṇa* is that he should not be greedy at all. In this case, however, for the sake of more lucrative remunerations from the King of heaven, Vasiṣṭha neglected Mahārāja Nimi's request on this planet, and when Nimi performed the sacrifices with other priests, Vasiṣṭha unnecessarily cursed him. When one is infected by contaminated activities, his power, material or spiritual, reduces. Although Vasiṣṭha was the spiritual master of Mahārāja Nimi, because of his greed he became fallen.

TEXT 6

इत्युत्ससर्ज स्वं देहं निमिरध्यात्मकोविदः ।
मित्रावरुणयोर्जज्ञे उर्वश्यां प्रपितामहः ॥ ६ ॥

ity utsasarja svaṁ dehaṁ
nimir adhyātma-kovidaḥ
mitrā-varuṇayor jajñe
urvaśyāṁ prapitāmahaḥ

iti—thus; *utsasarja*—gave up; *svam*—his own; *deham*—body; *nimiḥ*—Mahārāja Nimi; *adhyātma-kovidaḥ*—fully conversant with spiritual knowledge; *mitrā-varuṇayoḥ*—from the semen of Mitra and Varuṇa (discharged from seeing the beauty of Urvaśī); *jajñe*—was born; *urvaśyām*—through Urvaśī, a prostitute of the heavenly kingdom; *prapitāmahaḥ*—Vasiṣṭha, who was known as the great-grandfather.

TRANSLATION

After saying this, Mahārāja Nimi, who was expert in the science of spiritual knowledge, gave up his body. Vasiṣṭha, the great-grandfather, gave up his body also, but through the semen discharged by Mitra and Varuṇa when they saw Urvaśī, he was born again.

PURPORT

Mitra and Varuṇa chanced to meet Urvaśī, the most beautiful prostitute of the heavenly kingdom, and they became lusty. Because they were great saints, they tried to control their lust, but they could not do so, and thus they discharged semen. This semen was kept carefully in a waterpot, and Vasiṣṭha was born from it.

TEXT 7

गन्धवस्तुषु तद्देहं निधाय मुनिसत्तमाः ।
समाप्ते सत्रयागे च देवानूचुः समागतान् ॥ ७ ॥

gandha-vastuṣu tad-dehaṁ
nidhāya muni-sattamāḥ

samāpte satra-yāge ca
devān ūcuḥ samāgatān

gandha-vastuṣu—in things very fragrant; *tat-deham*—the body of Mahārāja Nimi; *nidhāya*—having preserved; *muni-sattamāḥ*—all the great sages gathered there; *samāpte satra-yāge*—at the end of the sacrifice known by the name Satra; *ca*—also; *devān*—to all the demigods; *ūcuḥ*—requested or spoke; *samāgatān*—who were assembled there.

TRANSLATION

During the performance of the yajña, the body relinquished by Mahārāja Nimi was preserved in fragrant substances, and at the end of the Satra-yāga the great saints and brāhmaṇas made the following request to all the demigods assembled there.

TEXT 8

राज्ञो जीवतु देहोऽयं प्रसन्नाः प्रभवो यदि ।
तथेत्युक्ते निमिः प्राह मा भून्मे देहबन्धनम् ॥ ८ ॥

rājño jīvatu deho 'yaṁ
prasannāḥ prabhavo yadi
tathety ukte nimiḥ prāha
mā bhūn me deha-bandhanam

rājñaḥ—of the King; *jīvatu*—may again be enlivened; *dehaḥ ayam*—this body (now preserved); *prasannāḥ*—very much pleased; *prabhavaḥ*—all able to do it; *yadi*—if; *tathā*—let it be so; *iti*—thus; *ukte*—when it was replied (by the demigods); *nimiḥ*—Mahārāja Nimi; *prāha*—said; *mā bhūt*—do not do it; *me*—my; *deha-bandhanam*—imprisonment again in a material body.

TRANSLATION

"If you are satisfied with this sacrifice and if you are actually able to do so, kindly bring Mahārāja Nimi back to life in this body." The demigods said yes to this request by the sages, but Mahārāja Nimi said, "Please do not imprison me again in a material body."

PURPORT

The demigods are in a position many times higher than that of human beings. Therefore, although the great saints and sages were also powerful *brāhmaṇas*, they requested the demigods to revive Mahārāja Nimi's body, which had been preserved in various perfumed balms. One should not think that the demigods are powerful only in enjoying the senses; they are also powerful in such deeds as bringing life back to a dead body. There are many similar instances in the Vedic literature. For example, according to the history of Sāvitrī and Satyavān, Satyavān died and was being taken away by Yamarāja, but on the request of his wife, Sāvitrī, Satyavān was revived in the same body. This is an important fact about the power of the demigods.

TEXT 9

यस्य योगं न वाञ्छन्ति वियोगभयकातराः ।
भजन्ति चरणाम्भोजं मुनयो हरिमेधसः ॥ ९ ॥

yasya yogaṁ na vāñchanti
viyoga-bhaya-kātarāḥ
bhajanti caraṇāmbhojaṁ
munayo hari-medhasaḥ

yasya—with the body; *yogam*—contact; *na*—do not; *vāñchanti*—*jñānīs* desire; *viyoga-bhaya-kātarāḥ*—being afraid of giving up the body again; *bhajanti*—offer transcendental loving service; *caraṇa-ambhojam*—to the lotus feet of the Lord; *munayaḥ*—great saintly persons; *hari-medhasaḥ*—whose intelligence is always absorbed in thoughts of Hari, the Supreme Personality of Godhead.

TRANSLATION

Mahārāja Nimi continued: Māyāvādīs generally want freedom from accepting a material body because they fear having to give it up again. But devotees whose intelligence is always filled with the service of the Lord are unafraid. Indeed, they take advantage of the body to render transcendental loving service.

PURPORT

Mahārāja Nimi did not want to accept a material body, which would be a cause of bondage; because he was a devotee, he wanted a body by which he could render devotional service to the Lord. Śrīla Bhaktivinoda Ṭhākura sings:

janmāobi more icchā yadi tora
bhakta-gṛhe jani janma ha-u mora
kīṭa-janma ha-u yathā tuyā dāsa

"My Lord, if You want me to take birth and accept a material body again, kindly do me this favor: allow me to take birth in the home of Your servant, Your devotee. I do not mind being born there even as an insignificant creature like an insect." Śrī Caitanya Mahāprabhu also said:

na dhanaṁ na janaṁ na sundarīṁ
kavitāṁ vā jagadīśa kāmaye
mama janmani janmanīśvare
bhavatād bhaktir ahaitukī tvayi

"O Lord of the universe, I do not desire material wealth, materialistic followers, a beautiful wife or fruitive activities described in flowery language. All I want, life after life, is unmotivated devotional service to You." (*Śikṣāṣṭaka* 4) By saying "life after life" (*janmani janmani*), the Lord referred not to an ordinary birth but a birth in which to remember the lotus feet of the Lord. Such a body is desirable. A devotee does not think like *yogīs* and *jñānīs*, who want to refuse a material body and become one with the impersonal Brahman effulgence. A devotee does not like this idea. On the contrary, he will accept any body, material or spiritual, for he wants to serve the Lord. This is real liberation.

If one has a strong desire to serve the Lord, even if he accepts a material body, there is no cause of anxiety, since a devotee, even in a material body, is a liberated soul. This is confirmed by Śrīla Rūpa Gosvāmī:

īhā yasya harer dāsye
karmaṇā manasā girā
nikhilāsv apy avasthāsu
jīvan-muktaḥ sa ucyate

"A person acting in Kṛṣṇa consciousness (or, in other words, in the service of Kṛṣṇa) with his body, mind, intelligence and words is a liberated person even within the material world, although he may be engaged in many so-called material activities." The desire to serve the Lord establishes one as liberated in any condition of life, whether in a spiritual body or a material body. In a spiritual body the devotee becomes a direct associate of the Lord, but even though a devotee may superficially appear to be in a material body, he is always liberated and is engaged in the same duties of service to the Lord as a devotee in Vaikuṇṭhaloka. There is no distinction. It is said, *sādhur jīvo vā maro vā.* Whether a devotee is alive or dead, his only concern is to serve the Lord. *Tyaktvā dehaṁ punar janma naiti mām eti.* When he gives up his body, he goes directly to become an associate of the Lord and serve Him, although he does the same thing even in a material body in the material world.

For a devotee there is no pain, pleasure or material perfection. One may argue that at the time of death a devotee also suffers because of giving up his material body. But in this connection the example may be given that a cat carries a mouse in its mouth and also carries a kitten in its mouth. Both the mouse and the kitten are carried in the same mouth, but the perception of the mouse is different from that of the kitten. When a devotee gives up his body (*tyaktvā deham*), he is ready to go back home, back to Godhead. Thus his perception is certainly different from that of a person being taken away by Yamarāja for punishment. A person whose intelligence is always concentrated upon the service of the Lord is unafraid of accepting a material body, whereas a nondevotee, having no engagement in the service of the Lord, is very much afraid of accepting a material body or giving up his present one. Therefore, we should follow the instruction of Caitanya Mahāprabhu: *mama janmani janmanīśvare bhavatād bhaktir ahaitukī tvayi.* It doesn't matter whether we accept a material body or a spiritual body; our only ambition should be to serve the Supreme Personality of Godhead.

TEXT 10

देहं नावरुरुत्सेऽहं दुःखशोकभयावहम् ।
सर्वत्रास्य यतो मृत्युर्मत्स्यानामुदके यथा ॥१०॥

deharà nāvarurutse 'haṁ
duḥkha-śoka-bhayāvaham
sarvatrāsya yato mṛtyur
matsyānām udake yathā

deham—a material body; *na*—not; *avarurutse*—desire to accept; *aham*—I; *duḥkha-śoka-bhaya-āvaham*—which is the cause of all kinds of distress, lamentation and fear; *sarvatra*—always and everywhere within this universe; *asya*—of the living entities who have accepted material bodies; *yataḥ*—because; *mṛtyuḥ*—death; *matsyānām*—of the fish; *udake*—living within the water; *yathā*—like.

TRANSLATION

I do not wish to accept a material body, for such a body is the source of all distress, lamentation and fear, everywhere in the universe, just as it is for a fish in the water, which lives always in anxiety because of fear of death.

PURPORT

The material body, whether in the higher or lower planetary system, is destined to die. In the lower planetary system or lower species of life one may die soon, and in the higher planets or higher species one may live for a long, long time, but death is inevitable. This fact should be understood. In the human form of life one should take the opportunity to put an end to birth, death, old age and disease by performing *tapasya.* This is the aim of human civilization: to stop the repetition of birth and death, which is called *mṛtyu-saṁsāra-vartmani.* This can be done only when one is Kṛṣṇa conscious, or has achieved the service of the lotus feet of the Lord. Otherwise one must rot in this material world and accept a material body subject to birth, death, old age and disease.

The example given here is that water is a very nice place for a fish, but the fish is never free from anxiety about death, since big fish are always eager to eat the small fish. *Phalgūni tatra mahatām:* all living entities are eaten by bigger living entities. This is the way of material nature.

ahastāni sahastānām
apadāni catuṣ-padām
phalgūni tatra mahatāṁ
jīvo jīvasya jīvanam

"Those who are devoid of hands are prey for those who have hands; those devoid of legs are prey for the four-legged. The weak are the subsistence of the strong, and the general rule holds that one living being is food for another." (*Bhāg.* 1.13.47) The Supreme Personality of Godhead has created the material world in such a way that one living entity is food for another. Thus there is a struggle for existence, but although we speak of survival of the fittest, no one can escape death without becoming a devotee of the Lord. *Hariṁ vinā naiva sṛtiṁ taranti:* one cannot escape the cycle of birth and death without becoming a devotee. This is also confirmed in *Bhagavad-gītā* (9.3). *Aprāpya māṁ nivartante mṛtyu-saṁsāra-vartmani.* One who does not attain shelter at the lotus feet of Kṛṣṇa must certainly wander up and down within the cycle of birth and death.

TEXT 11

देवा ऊचुः
विदेह उष्यतां कामं लोचनेषु शरीरिणाम् ।
उन्मेषणनिमेषाभ्यां लक्षितोऽध्यात्मसंस्थितः ॥११॥

devā ūcuḥ
videha uṣyatāṁ kāmaṁ
locaneṣu śarīriṇām
unmeṣaṇa-nimeṣābhyāṁ
lakṣito 'dhyātma-saṁsthitaḥ

devāḥ ūcuḥ—the demigods said; *videhaḥ*—without any material body; *uṣyatām*—you live; *kāmam*—as you like; *locaneṣu*—in the vision; *śarīriṇām*—of those who have material bodies; *unmeṣaṇa-nimeṣābhyām*—become manifest and unmanifest as you desire; *lakṣitaḥ*—being seen; *adhyātma-saṁsthitaḥ*—situated in a spiritual body.

TRANSLATION

The demigods said: Let Mahārāja Nimi live without a material body. Let him live in a spiritual body as a personal associate of the Supreme Personality of Godhead, and, according to his desire, let him be manifest or unmanifest to common materially embodied people.

PURPORT

The demigods wanted Mahārāja Nimi to come to life, but Mahārāja Nimi did not want to accept another material body. Under the circumstances, the demigods, having been requested by the saintly persons, gave him the benediction that he would be able to stay in his spiritual body. There are two kinds of spiritual bodies, as generally understood by common men. The term "spiritual body" is sometimes taken to refer to a ghostly body. An impious man who dies after sinful activities is sometimes condemned so that he cannot possess a gross material body of five material elements, but must live in a subtle body of mind, intelligence and ego. However, as explained in *Bhagavad-gītā*, devotees can give up the material body and attain a spiritual body free from all material tinges, gross and subtle (*tyaktvā dehaṁ punar janma naiti mām eti so 'rjuna*). Thus the demigods gave King Nimi the benediction that he would be able to stay in a purely spiritual body, free from all gross and subtle material contamination.

The Supreme Personality of Godhead can be seen or unseen according to His own transcendental desire; similarly, a devotee, being *jīvan-mukta*, can be seen or not, as he chooses. As stated in *Bhagavad-gītā*, *nāhaṁ prakāśaḥ sarvasya yogamāyā-samāvṛtaḥ:* the Supreme Personality of Godhead, Kṛṣṇa, is not manifest to everyone and anyone. To the common man He is unseen. *Ataḥ śrī-kṛṣṇa-nāmādi na bhaved grāhyam indriyaiḥ:* Kṛṣṇa and His name, fame, qualities and paraphernalia cannot be materially understood. Unless one is advanced in spiritual life (*sevonmukhe hi jihvādau*), one cannot see Kṛṣṇa. Therefore the ability to see Kṛṣṇa depends on Kṛṣṇa's mercy. The same privilege of being seen or unseen according to one's own desire was given to Mahārāja Nimi. Thus he lived in his original, spiritual body as an associate of the Supreme Personality of Godhead.

TEXT 12

अराजकभयं नृणां मन्यमाना महर्षयः ।
देहं ममन्थुः स्म निमेः कुमारः समजायत ॥१२॥

arājaka-bhayaṁ nṛṇāṁ
manyamānā maharṣayaḥ
dehaṁ mamanthuḥ sma nimeḥ
kumāraḥ samajāyata

arājaka-bhayam—due to fear of the danger of an unregulated government; *nṛṇām*—for the people in general; *manyamānāḥ*—considering this situation; *mahā-ṛṣayaḥ*—the great sages; *deham*—the body; *mamanthuḥ*—churned; *sma*—in the past; *nimeḥ*—of Mahārāja Nimi; *kumāraḥ*—one son; *samajāyata*—was thus born.

TRANSLATION

Thereafter, to save the people from the danger of an unregulated government, the sages churned Mahārāja Nimi's material body, from which, as a result, a son was born.

PURPORT

Arājaka-bhayam. If the government is unsteady and unregulated, there is danger of fear for the people. At the present moment this danger always exists because of government by the people. Here we can see that the great sages got a son from Nimi's material body to guide the citizens properly, for such guidance is the duty of a *kṣatriya* king. A *kṣatriya* is one who saves the citizens from being injured. In the so-called people's government there is no trained *kṣatriya* king; as soon as someone strong accumulates votes, he becomes the minister or president, without training from the learned *brāhmaṇas* expert in the *śāstras.* Indeed, we see that in some countries the government changes from party to party, and therefore the men in charge of the government are more eager to protect their position than to see that the citizens are happy. The Vedic civilization prefers monarchy. People liked the government of Lord Rāmacandra, the government of Mahārāja Yudhiṣṭhira and the governments of Mahārāja Parīkṣit, Mahārāja Ambarīṣa and Mahārāja Prahlāda.

There are many instances of excellent government under a monarch. Gradually the democratic government is becoming unfit for the needs of the people, and therefore some parties are trying to elect a dictator. A dictatorship is the same as a monarchy, but without a trained leader. Actually people will be happy when a trained leader, whether a monarch or a dictator, takes control of the government and rules the people according to the standard regulations of the authorized scriptures.

TEXT 13

जन्मना जनकः सोऽभूद् वैदेहस्तु विदेहजः ।
मिथिलो मथनाज्जातो मिथिला येन निर्मिता ॥१३॥

janmanā janakaḥ so 'bhūd
vaidehas tu videhajaḥ
mithilo mathanāj jāto
mithilā yena nirmitā

janmanā—by birth; *janakaḥ*—born uncommonly, not by the usual process; *saḥ*—he; *abhūt*—became; *vaidehaḥ*—also known as Vaideha; *tu*—but; *videha-jaḥ*—because of being born from the body of Mahārāja Nimi, who had left his material body; *mithilaḥ*—he also became known as Mithila; *mathanāt*—because of being born from the churning of his father's body; *jātaḥ*—thus born; *mithilā*—the kingdom called Mithilā; *yena*—by whom (Janaka); *nirmitā*—was constructed.

TRANSLATION

Because he was born in an unusual way, the son was called Janaka, and because he was born from the dead body of his father, he was known as Vaideha. Because he was born from the churning of his father's material body, he was known as Mithila, and because he constructed a city as King Mithila, the city was called Mithilā.

TEXT 14

तस्मादुदावसुस्तस्य पुत्रोऽभून्नन्दिवर्धनः ।
ततः सुकेतुस्तस्यापि देवरातो महीपते ॥१४॥

tasmād udāvasus tasya
putro 'bhūn nandivardhanaḥ
tataḥ suketus tasyāpi
devarāto mahīpate

tasmāt—from Mithila; *udāvasuḥ*—a son named Udāvasu; *tasya*—of him (Udāvasu); *putraḥ*—son; *abhūt*—was born; *nandivardhanaḥ*—Nandivardhana; *tataḥ*—from him (Nandivardhana); *suketuḥ*—a son named Suketu; *tasya*—of him (Suketu); *api*—also; *devarātaḥ*—a son named Devarāta; *mahīpate*—O King Parīkṣit.

TRANSLATION

O King Parīkṣit, from Mithila came a son named Udāvasu; from Udāvasu, Nandivardhana; from Nandivardhana, Suketu; and from Suketu, Devarāta.

TEXT 15

तस्माद् बृहद्रथस्तस्य महावीर्यः सुधृत्पिता ।
सुधृतेर्धृष्टकेतुर्वै हर्यश्वोऽथ मरुस्ततः ॥१५॥

tasmād bṛhadrathas tasya
mahāvīryaḥ sudhṛt-pitā
sudhṛter dhṛṣṭaketur vai
haryaśvo 'tha marus tataḥ

tasmāt—from Devarāta; *bṛhadrathaḥ*—a son named Bṛhadratha; *tasya*—of him (Bṛhadratha); *mahāvīryaḥ*—a son named Mahāvīrya; *sudhṛt-pitā*—he became the father of King Sudhṛti; *sudhṛteḥ*—from Sudhṛti; *dhṛṣṭaketuḥ*—a son named Dhṛṣṭaketu; *vai*—indeed; *haryaśvaḥ*—his son was Haryaśva; *atha*—thereafter; *maruḥ*—Maru; *tataḥ*—thereafter.

TRANSLATION

From Devarāta came a son named Bṛhadratha and from Bṛhadratha a son named Mahāvīrya, who became the father of Sudhṛti. The son of Sudhṛti was known as Dhṛṣṭaketu, and from

Dhṛṣṭaketu came Haryaśva. From Haryaśva came a son named Maru.

TEXT 16

मरोः प्रतीपकस्तस्माज्जातः कृतरथो यतः ।
देवमीढस्तस्य पुत्रो विश्रुतोऽथ महाधृतिः ॥१६॥

maroḥ pratīpakas tasmāj
jātaḥ kṛtaratho yataḥ
devamīḍhas tasya putro
viśruto 'tha mahādhṛtiḥ

maroḥ—of Maru; *pratīpakaḥ*—a son named Pratīpaka; *tasmāt*—from Pratīpaka; *jātaḥ*—was born; *kṛtarathaḥ*—a son named Kṛtaratha; *yataḥ*—and from Kṛtaratha; *devamīḍhaḥ*—Devamīḍha; *tasya*—of Devamīḍha; *putraḥ*—a son; *viśrutaḥ*—Viśruta; *atha*—from him; *mahādhṛtiḥ*—a son named Mahādhṛti.

TRANSLATION

The son of Maru was Pratīpaka, and the son of Pratīpaka was Kṛtaratha. From Kṛtaratha came Devamīḍha; from Devamīḍha, Viśruta; and from Viśruta, Mahādhṛti.

TEXT 17

कृतिरातस्ततस्तस्मान्महारोमा च तत्सुतः ।
स्वर्णरोमा सुतस्तस्य ह्रस्वरोमा व्यजायत ॥१७॥

kṛtirātas tatas tasmān
mahāromā ca tat-sutaḥ
svarṇaromā sutas tasya
hrasvaromā vyajāyata

kṛtirātaḥ—Kṛtirāta; *tataḥ*—from Mahādhṛti; *tasmāt*—from Kṛtirāta; *mahāromā*—a son named Mahāromā; *ca*—also; *tat-sutaḥ*—his son; *svarṇaromā*—Svarṇaromā; *sutaḥ tasya*—his son; *hrasvaromā*—Hrasvaromā; *vyajāyata*—were all born.

TRANSLATION

From Mahādhṛti was born a son named Kṛtirāta, from Kṛtirāta was born Mahāromā, from Mahāromā came a son named Svarṇaromā, and from Svarṇaromā came Hrasvaromā.

TEXT 18

ततः शीरध्वजो जज्ञे यज्ञार्थं कर्षतो महीम् ।
सीता शीराग्रतो जाता तस्मात् शीरध्वजः स्मृतः ॥१८॥

tataḥ śīradhvajo jajñe
yajñārthaṁ karṣato mahīm
sītā śīrāgrato jātā
tasmāt śīradhvajaḥ smṛtaḥ

tataḥ—from Hrasvaromā; *śīradhvajaḥ*—a son named Śīradhvaja; *jajñe*—was born; *yajña-artham*—for performing sacrifices; *karṣataḥ*—while plowing the field; *mahīm*—the earth; *sītā*—mother Sītā, the wife of Lord Rāmacandra; *śīra-agrataḥ*—from the front portion of the plow; *jātā*—was born; *tasmāt*—therefore; *śīradhvajaḥ*—was known as Śīradhvaja; *smṛtaḥ*—celebrated.

TRANSLATION

From Hrasvaromā came a son named Śīradhvaja [also called Janaka]. When Śīradhvaja was plowing a field, from the front of his plow [śīra] appeared a daughter named Sītādevī, who later became the wife of Lord Rāmacandra. Thus he was known as Śīradhvaja.

TEXT 19

कुशध्वजस्तस्य पुत्रस्ततो धर्मध्वजो नृपः ।
धर्मध्वजस्य द्वौ पुत्रौ कृतध्वजमितध्वजौ ॥१९॥

kuśadhvajas tasya putras
tato dharmadhvajo nṛpaḥ
dharmadhvajasya dvau putrau
kṛtadhvaja-mitadhvajau

kuśadhvajaḥ—Kuśadhvaja; *tasya*—of Śīradhvaja; *putraḥ*—son; *tataḥ*—from him; *dharmadhvajaḥ*—Dharmadhvaja; *nṛpaḥ*—the king; *dharmadhvajasya*—from this Dharmadhvaja; *dvau*—two; *putrau*—sons; *kṛtadhvaja-mitadhvajau*—Kṛtadhvaja and Mitadhvaja.

TRANSLATION

The son of Śīradhvaja was Kuśadhvaja, and the son of Kuśadhvaja was King Dharmadhvaja, who had two sons, namely Kṛtadhvaja and Mitadhvaja.

TEXTS 20–21

कृतध्वजात् केशिध्वजः खाण्डिक्यस्तु मितध्वजात् ।
कृतध्वजसुतो राजन्नात्मविद्याविशारदः ॥२०॥
खाण्डिक्यः कर्मतत्त्वज्ञो भीतः केशिध्वजाद् द्रुतः ।
भानुमांस्तस्य पुत्रोऽभूच्छतद्युम्नस्तु तत्सुतः ॥२१॥

kṛtadhvajāt keśidhvajaḥ
khāṇḍikyas tu mitadhvajāt
kṛtadhvaja-suto rājann
ātma-vidyā-viśāradaḥ

khāṇḍikyaḥ karma-tattva-jño
bhītaḥ keśidhvajād drutaḥ
bhānumāṁs tasya putro 'bhūc
chatadyumnas tu tat-sutaḥ

kṛtadhvajāt—from Kṛtadhvaja; *keśidhvajaḥ*—a son named Keśidhvaja; *khāṇḍikyaḥ tu*—also a son named Khāṇḍikya; *mitadhvajāt*—from Mitadhvaja; *kṛtadhvaja-sutaḥ*—the son of Kṛtadhvaja; *rājan*—O King; *ātma-vidyā-viśāradaḥ*—expert in transcendental science; *khāṇḍikyaḥ*—King Khāṇḍikya; *karma-tattva-jñaḥ*—expert in Vedic ritualistic ceremonies; *bhītaḥ*—fearing; *keśidhvajāt*—because of Keśidhvaja; *drutaḥ*—he fled; *bhānumān*—Bhānumān; *tasya*—of Keśidhvaja; *putraḥ*—son; *abhūt*—there was; *śatadyumnaḥ*—Śatadyumna; *tu*—but; *tat-sutaḥ*—the son of Bhānumān.

TRANSLATION

O Mahārāja Parīkṣit, the son of Kṛtadhvaja was Keśidhvaja, and the son of Mitadhvaja was Khāṇḍikya. The son of Kṛtadhvaja was expert in spiritual knowledge, and the son of Mitadhvaja was expert in Vedic ritualistic ceremonies. Khāṇḍikya fled in fear of Keśidhvaja. The son of Keśidhvaja was Bhānumān, and the son of Bhānumān was Śatadyumna.

TEXT 22

शुचिस्तुतनयस्तस्मात् सनद्वाजः सुतोऽभवत् ।
ऊर्जकेतुः सनद्वाजादजोऽथ पुरुजित्सुतः ॥२२॥

śucis tu tanayas tasmāt
sanadvājaḥ suto 'bhavat
ūrjaketuḥ sanadvājād
ajo 'tha purujit sutaḥ

śuciḥ—Śuci; *tu*—but; *tanayaḥ*—a son; *tasmāt*—from him; *sanadvājaḥ*—Sanadvāja; *sutaḥ*—a son; *abhavat*—was born; *ūrjaketuḥ*—Ūrjaketu; *sanadvājāt*—from Sanadvāja; *ajaḥ*—Aja; *atha*—thereafter; *purujit*—Purujit; *sutaḥ*—a son.

TRANSLATION

The son of Śatadyumna was named Śuci. From Śuci, Sanadvāja was born, and from Sanadvāja came a son named Ūrjaketu. The son of Ūrjaketu was Aja, and the son of Aja was Purujit.

TEXT 23

अरिष्टनेमिस्तस्यापि श्रुतायुस्तत्सुपार्श्वकः ।
ततश्चित्ररथो यस्य क्षेमाधिर्मिथिलाधिपः ॥२३॥

ariṣṭanemis tasyāpi
śrutāyus tat supārśvakaḥ
tataś citraratho yasya
kṣemādhir mithilādhipaḥ

ariṣṭanemiḥ—Ariṣṭanemi; *tasya api*—of Purujit also; *śrutāyuḥ*—a son named Śrutāyu; *tat*—and from him; *supārśvakaḥ*—Supārśvaka; *tataḥ*—from Supārśvaka; *citrarathaḥ*—Citraratha; *yasya*—of whom (Citraratha); *kṣemādhiḥ*—Kṣemādhi; *mithilā-adhipaḥ*—became the king of Mithilā.

TRANSLATION

The son of Purujit was Ariṣṭanemi, and his son was Śrutāyu. Śrutāyu begot a son named Supārśvaka, and Supārśvaka begot Citraratha. The son of Citraratha was Kṣemādhi, who became the king of Mithilā.

TEXT 24

तस्मात् समरथस्तस्य सुतः सत्यरथस्ततः ।
आसीदुपगुरुस्तस्मादुपगुप्तोऽग्निसम्भवः ॥२४॥

tasmāt samarathas tasya
sutaḥ satyarathas tataḥ
āsīd upagurus tasmād
upagupto 'agni-sambhavaḥ

tasmāt—from Kṣemādhi; *samarathaḥ*—a son named Samaratha; *tasya*—from Samaratha; *sutaḥ*—son; *satyarathaḥ*—Satyaratha; *tataḥ*—from him (Satyaratha); *āsīt*—was born; *upaguruḥ*—Upaguru; *tasmāt*—from him; *upaguptaḥ*—Upagupta; *agni-sambhavaḥ*—a partial expansion of the demigod Agni.

TRANSLATION

The son of Kṣemādhi was Samaratha, and his son was Satyaratha. The son of Satyaratha was Upaguru, and the son of Upaguru was Upagupta, a partial expansion of the fire-god.

TEXT 25

वस्वनन्तोऽथ तत्पुत्रो युयुधो यत् सुभाषणः ।
श्रुतस्ततो जयस्तस्माद् विजयोऽस्माद्दतः सुतः ॥२५॥

vasvananto 'tha tat-putro
yuyudho yat subhāṣaṇaḥ
śrutas tato jayas tasmād
vijayo 'smād ṛtaḥ sutaḥ

vasvanantaḥ—Vasvananta; *atha*—thereafter (the son of Upagupta); *tat-putraḥ*—his son; *yuyudhaḥ*—by the name Yuyudha; *yat*—from Yuyudha; *subhāṣaṇaḥ*—a son named Subhāṣaṇa; *śrutaḥ tataḥ*—and the son of Subhāṣaṇa was Śruta; *jayaḥ tasmāt*—the son of Śruta was Jaya; *vijayaḥ*—a son named Vijaya; *asmāt*—from Jaya; *ṛtaḥ*—Ṛta; *sutaḥ*—a son.

TRANSLATION

The son of Upagupta was Vasvananta, the son of Vasvananta was Yuyudha, the son of Yuyudha was Subhāṣaṇa, and the son of Subhāṣaṇa was Śruta. The son of Śruta was Jaya, from whom there came Vijaya. The son of Vijaya was Ṛta.

TEXT 26

शुनकस्तत्सुतो जज्ञे वीतहव्यो धृतिस्ततः ।
बहुलाश्वो धृतेस्तस्य कृतिरस्य महावशी ॥२६॥

śunakas tat-suto jajñe
vītahavyo dhṛtis tataḥ
bahulāśvo dhṛtes tasya
kṛtir asya mahāvaśī

śunakaḥ—Śunaka; *tat-sutaḥ*—the son of Ṛta; *jajñe*—was born; *vītahavyaḥ*—Vītahavya; *dhṛtiḥ*—Dhṛti; *tataḥ*—the son of Vītahavya; *bahulāśvaḥ*—Bahulāśva; *dhṛteḥ*—from Dhṛti; *tasya*—his son; *kṛtiḥ*—Kṛti; *asya*—of Kṛti; *mahāvaśī*—there was a son named Mahāvaśī.

TRANSLATION

The son of Ṛta was Śunaka, the son of Śunaka was Vītahavya, the son of Vītahavya was Dhṛti, and the son of Dhṛti was Bahulāśva. The son of Bahulāśva was Kṛti, and his son was Mahāvaśī.

TEXT 27

एते वै मैथिला राजन्नात्मविद्याविशारदाः ।
योगेश्वरप्रसादेन द्वन्द्वैर्मुक्ता गृहेष्वपि ॥२७॥

ete vai maithilā rājann
ātma-vidyā-viśāradāḥ
yogeśvara-prasādena
dvandvair muktā gṛheṣv api

ete—all of them; *vai*—indeed; *maithilāḥ*—the descendants of Mithila; *rājan*—O King; *ātma-vidyā-viśāradāḥ*—expert in spiritual knowledge; *yogeśvara-prasādena*—by the grace of Yogeśvara, the Supreme Personality of Godhead, Kṛṣṇa; *dvandvaiḥ muktāḥ*—they were all freed from the duality of the material world; *gṛheṣu api*—even though staying at home.

TRANSLATION

Śukadeva Gosvāmī said: My dear King Parīkṣit, all the kings of the dynasty of Mithila were completely in knowledge of their spiritual identity. Therefore, even though staying at home, they were liberated from the duality of material existence.

PURPORT

This material world is called *dvaita,* or duality. The *Caitanya-caritāmṛta* (*Antya* 4.176) says:

'dvaite' bhadrābhadra-jñāna, saba——'manodharma'
'ei bhāla, ei manda,'——ei saba 'bhrama'

In the world of duality—that is to say, in the material world—so-called goodness and badness are both the same. Therefore, in this world, to distinguish between good and bad, happiness and distress, is meaningless because they are both mental concoctions (*manodharma*). Because everything here is miserable and troublesome, to create an artificial situation and pretend it to be full of happiness is simply illusion. The liberated person, being above the influence of the three modes of material nature, is unaffected by such dualities in all circumstances. He remains Kṛṣṇa conscious by tolerating so-called happiness and distress. This is also confirmed in *Bhagavad-gītā* (2.14):

mātrā-sparśās tu kaunteya
śītoṣṇa-sukha-duḥkhadāḥ
āgamāpāyino 'nityās
tāṁs titikṣasva bhārata

"O son of Kuntī, the nonpermanent appearance of happiness and distress, and their disappearance in due course, are like the appearance and disappearance of winter and summer seasons. They arise from sense perception, O scion of Bharata, and one must learn to tolerate them without being disturbed." Those who are liberated, being on the transcendental platform of rendering service to the Lord, do not care about so-called happiness and distress. They know that these are like changing seasons, which are perceivable by contact with the material body. Happiness and distress come and go. Therefore a *paṇḍita*, a learned man, is not concerned with them. As it is said, *gatāsūn agatāsūṁś ca nānuśocanti paṇḍitāḥ*. The body is dead from the very beginning because it is a lump of matter. It has no feelings of happiness and distress. Because the soul within the body is in the bodily concept of life, he suffers happiness and distress, but these come and go. It is understood herewith that the kings born in the dynasty of Mithila were all liberated persons, unaffected by the so-called happiness and distress of this world.

Thus end the Bhaktivedanta purports of the Ninth Canto, Thirteenth Chapter, of the Śrīmad-Bhāgavatam, *entitled "The Dynasty of Mahārāja Nimi."*

CHAPTER FOURTEEN

King Purūravā Enchanted by Urvaśī

The summary of this Fourteenth Chapter is given as follows. This chapter describes Soma and how he kidnapped the wife of Bṛhaspati and begot in her womb a son named Budha. Budha begot Purūravā, who begot six sons, headed by Āyu, in the womb of Urvaśī.

Lord Brahmā was born from the lotus that sprouted from the navel of Garbhodakaśāyī Viṣṇu. Brahmā had a son named Atri, and Atri's son was Soma, the king of all drugs and stars. Soma became the conqueror of the entire universe, and, being inflated with pride, he kidnapped Tārā, who was the wife of Bṛhaspati, the spiritual master of the demigods. A great fight ensued between the demigods and the *asuras*, but Brahmā rescued Bṛhaspati's wife from the clutches of Soma and returned her to her husband, thus stopping the fighting. In the womb of Tārā, Soma begot a son named Budha, who later begot in the womb of Ilā a son named Aila, or Purūravā. Urvaśī was captivated by Purūravā's beauty, and therefore she lived with him for some time, but when she left his company he became almost like a madman. While traveling all over the world, he met Urvaśī again at Kurukṣetra, but she agreed to join with him for only one night in a year.

One year later, Purūravā saw Urvaśī at Kurukṣetra and was glad to be with her for one night, but when he thought of her leaving him again, he was overwhelmed by grief. Urvaśī then advised Purūravā to worship the Gandharvas. Being satisfied with Purūravā, the Gandharvas gave him a woman known as Agnisthālī. Purūravā mistook Agnisthālī for Urvaśī, but while he was wandering in the forest his misunderstanding was cleared, and he immediately gave up her company. After returning home and meditating upon Urvaśī all night, he wanted to perform a Vedic ritualistic ceremony to satisfy his desire. Thereafter he went to the same place where he had left Agnisthālī, and there he saw that from the womb of a *śamī* tree had come an *aśvattha* tree. Purūravā made two sticks from this tree and thus produced a fire. By such a fire one can satisfy all lusty desires. The fire was considered the son of Purūravā. In Satya-yuga there was only one social division, called *haṁsa;* there were no divisions of *varṇa* like *brāhmaṇa*, *kṣatriya*, *vaiśya* and *śūdra*. The *Veda* was the *oṁkāra*. The various demigods were not worshiped, for only the Supreme Personality of Godhead was the worshipable Deity.

TEXT 1

श्रीशुक उवाच
अथातः श्रूयतां राजन् वंशः सोमस्य पावनः ।
यस्मिन्नैलादयो भूपाः कीर्त्यन्ते पुण्यकीर्तयः ॥ १ ॥

śrī-śuka uvāca
athātaḥ śrūyatāṁ rājan
vaṁśaḥ somasya pāvanaḥ
yasminn ailādayo bhūpāḥ
kīrtyante puṇya-kīrtayaḥ

śrī-śukaḥ uvāca—Śrī Śukadeva Gosvāmī said; *atha*—now (after hearing the history of the dynasty of the sun); *ataḥ*—therefore; *śrūyatām*—just hear from me; *rājan*—O King (Mahārāja Parīkṣit); *vaṁśaḥ*—the dynasty; *somasya*—of the moon-god; *pāvanaḥ*—which is purifying to hear about; *yasmin*—in which (dynasty); *aila-ādayaḥ*—headed by Aila (Purūravā); *bhūpāḥ*—kings; *kīrtyante*—are described; *puṇya-kīrtayaḥ*—persons of whom it is glorious to hear.

TRANSLATION

Śrīla Śukadeva Gosvāmī said to Mahārāja Parīkṣit: O King, thus far you have heard the description of the dynasty of the sun-god. Now hear the most glorious and purifying description of the dynasty of the moon-god. This description mentions kings like Aila [Purūravā] of whom it is glorious to hear.

TEXT 2

सहस्रशिरसः पुंसो नाभिह्रदसरोरुहात् ।
जातस्यासीत् सुतो धातुरत्रिः पितृसमो गुणैः ॥ २ ॥

sahasra-śirasaḥ puṁso
nābhi-hrada-saroruhāt

jātasyāsīt suto dhātur
atriḥ pitṛ-samo guṇaiḥ

sahasra-śirasaḥ—who has thousands of heads; *puṁsaḥ*—of Lord Viṣṇu (Garbhodakaśāyī Viṣṇu); *nābhi-hrada-saroruhāt*—from the lotus produced from the lake of the navel; *jātasya*—who appeared; *āsīt*—there was; *sutaḥ*—a son; *dhātuḥ*—of Lord Brahmā; *atriḥ*—by the name Atri; *pitṛ-samaḥ*—like his father; *guṇaiḥ*—qualified.

TRANSLATION

Lord Viṣṇu [Garbhodakaśāyī Viṣṇu] is also known as Sahasraśīrṣā Puruṣa. From the lake of His navel sprang a lotus, on which Lord Brahmā was generated. Atri, the son of Lord Brahmā, was as qualified as his father.

TEXT 3

तस्य दृग्भ्योऽभवत् पुत्रः सोमोऽमृतमयः किल ।
विप्रौषध्युडुगणानां ब्रह्मणा कल्पितः पतिः ॥ ३ ॥

tasya dṛgbhyo 'bhavat putraḥ
somo 'mṛtamayaḥ kila
viprauṣadhy-uḍu-gaṇānāṁ
brahmaṇā kalpitaḥ patiḥ

tasya—of him, Atri, the son of Brahmā; *dṛgbhyaḥ*—from the tears of jubilation from the eyes; *abhavat*—was born; *putraḥ*—a son; *somaḥ*—the moon-god; *amṛta-mayaḥ*—full of soothing rays; *kila*—indeed; *vipra*—of the *brāhmaṇas; oṣadhi*—of the drugs; *uḍu-gaṇānām*—and of the luminaries; *brahmaṇā*—by Lord Brahmā; *kalpitaḥ*—was appointed or designated; *patiḥ*—the supreme director.

TRANSLATION

From Atri's tears of jubilation was born a son named Soma, the moon, who was full of soothing rays. Lord Brahmā appointed him the director of the brāhmaṇas, drugs and luminaries.

PURPORT

According to the Vedic description, Soma, the moon-god, was born from the mind of the Supreme Personality of Godhead (*candramā manaso jātaḥ*). But here we find that Soma was born from the tears in the eyes of Atri. This appears contradictory to the Vedic information, but actually it is not, for this birth of the moon is understood to have taken place in another millennium. When tears appear in the eyes because of jubilation, the tears are soothing. Śrīla Viśvanātha Cakravartī Ṭhākura says, *dṛgbhya ānandāśrubhya ata evāmṛtamayaḥ:* "Here the word *dṛgbhyaḥ* means 'from tears of jubilation.' Therefore the moon-god is called *amṛtamayaḥ*, 'full of soothing rays.' " In the Fourth Canto of *Śrīmad-Bhāgavatam* (4.1.15) we find this verse:

atreḥ patny anasūyā trīñ
jajñe suyaśasaḥ sutān
dattaṁ durvāsasaṁ somam
ātmeśa-brahma-sambhavān

This verse describes that Anasūyā, the wife of Atri Ṛṣi, bore three sons—Soma, Durvāsā and Dattātreya. It is said that at the time of conception Anasūyā was impregnated by the tears of Atri.

TEXT 4

सोऽयजद् राजसूयेन विजित्य भुवनत्रयम् ।
पत्नीं बृहस्पतेर्दर्पात् तारां नामाहरद् बलात् ॥ ४ ॥

so 'yajad rājasūyena
vijitya bhuvana-trayam
patnīṁ bṛhaspater darpāt
tārāṁ nāmāharad balāt

saḥ—he, Soma; *ayajat*—performed; *rājasūyena*—the sacrifice known as Rājasūya; *vijitya*—after conquering; *bhuvana-trayam*—the three worlds (Svarga, Martya and Pātāla); *patnīm*—the wife; *bṛhaspateḥ*—of Bṛhaspati, the spiritual master of the demigods; *darpāt*—out of pride; *tārām*—Tārā; *nāma*—by name; *aharat*—took away; *balāt*—by force.

TRANSLATION

After conquering the three worlds [the upper, middle and lower planetary systems], Soma, the moon-god, performed a great sacrifice known as the Rājasūya-yajña. Because he was very much puffed up, he forcibly kidnapped Bṛhaspati's wife, whose name was Tārā.

TEXT 5

यदा स देवगुरुणा याचितोऽभीक्ष्णशो मदात् ।
नात्यजत् तत्कृते जज्ञे सुरदानवविग्रहः ॥ ५ ॥

yadā sa deva-guruṇā
yācito 'bhīkṣṇaśo madāt
nātyajat tat-kṛte jajñe
sura-dānava-vigrahaḥ

yadā—when; *saḥ*—he (Soma, the moon-god); *deva-guruṇā*—by the spiritual master of the demigods, Bṛhaspati; *yācitaḥ*—was begged; *abhīkṣṇaśaḥ*—again and again; *madāt*—because of false pride; *na*—not; *atyajat*—did deliver; *tat-kṛte*—because of this; *jajñe*—there was; *sura-dānava*—between the demigods and the demons; *vigrahaḥ*—a fight.

TRANSLATION

Although requested again and again by Bṛhaspati, the spiritual master of the demigods, Soma did not return Tārā. This was due to his false pride. Consequently, a fight ensued between the demigods and the demons.

TEXT 6

शुक्रो बृहस्पतेर्द्वेषादग्रहीत् सासुरोडुपम् ।
हरो गुरुसुतं स्नेहात् सर्वभूतगणावृतः ॥ ६ ॥

śukro bṛhaspater dveṣād
agrahīt sāsuroḍupam
haro guru-sutaṁ snehāt
sarva-bhūta-gaṇāvṛtaḥ

śukraḥ—the demigod named Śukra; *bṛhaspateḥ*—unto Bṛhaspati; *dveṣāt*—because of enmity; *agrahīt*—took; *sa-asura*—with the demons; *uḍupam*—the side of the moon-god; *haraḥ*—Lord Śiva; *guru-sutam*—the side of his spiritual master's son; *snehāt*—because of affection; *sarva-bhūta-gaṇa-āvṛtaḥ*—accompanied by all kinds of ghosts and hobgoblins.

TRANSLATION

Because of enmity between Bṛhaspati and Śukra, Śukra took the side of the moon-god and was joined by the demons. But Lord Śiva, because of affection for the son of his spiritual master, joined the side of Bṛhaspati and was accompanied by all the ghosts and hobgoblins.

PURPORT

The moon-god is one of the demigods, but to fight against the other demigods he took the assistance of the demons. Śukra, being an enemy of Bṛhaspati, also joined the moon-god to retaliate in wrath against Bṛhaspati. To counteract this situation, Lord Śiva, who was affectionate toward Bṛhaspati, joined Bṛhaspati. The father of Bṛhaspati was Aṅgirā, from whom Lord Śiva had received knowledge. Therefore Lord Śiva had some affection for Bṛhaspati and joined his side in this fight. Śrīdhara Svāmī remarks, *aṅgirasaḥ sakāśāt prāpta-vidyo hara iti prasiddhaḥ:* "Lord Śiva is well known to have received knowledge from Aṅgirā."

TEXT 7

सर्वदेवगणोपेतो महेन्द्रो गुरुमन्वयात् ।
सुरासुरविनाशोऽभूत् समरस्तारकामयः ॥ ७ ॥

sarva-deva-gaṇopeto
mahendro gurum anvayāt
surāsura-vināśo 'bhūt
samaras tārakāmayaḥ

sarva-deva-gaṇa—by all the different demigods; *upetaḥ*—joined; *mahendraḥ*—Mahendra, the King of heaven, Indra; *gurum*—his spiritual master; *anvayāt*—followed; *sura*—of the demigods; *asura*—and of the demons; *vināśaḥ*—causing destruction; *abhūt*—there was;

samaraḥ—a fight; *tārakā-mayaḥ*—simply because of Tārā, a woman, the wife of Bṛhaspati.

TRANSLATION

King Indra, accompanied by all kinds of demigods, joined the side of Bṛhaspati. Thus there was a great fight, destroying both demons and demigods, only for the sake of Tārā, Bṛhaspati's wife.

TEXT 8

निवेदितोऽथाङ्गिरसा सोमं निर्भर्त्स्य विश्वकृत् ।
तारां स्वभर्त्रे प्रायच्छदन्तर्वत्नीमवैत् पतिः ॥ ८ ॥

nivedito 'thāṅgirasā
somaṁ nirbhartsya viśva-kṛt
tārāṁ sva-bhartre prāyacchad
antarvatnīm avait patiḥ

niveditaḥ—being fully informed; *atha*—thus; *aṅgirasā*—by Aṅgirā Muni; *somam*—the moon-god; *nirbhartsya*—chastising severely; *viśva-kṛt*—Lord Brahmā; *tārām*—Tārā, the wife of Bṛhaspati; *sva-bhartre*—unto her husband; *prāyacchat*—delivered; *antarvatnīm*—pregnant; *avait*—could understand; *patiḥ*—the husband (Bṛhaspati).

TRANSLATION

When Lord Brahmā was fully informed by Aṅgirā about the entire incident, he severely chastised the moon-god, Soma. Thus Lord Brahmā delivered Tārā to her husband, who could then understand that she was pregnant.

TEXT 9

त्यज त्यजाशु दुष्प्रज्ञे मत्क्षेत्रादाहितं परैः ।
नाहं त्वां भस्मसात् कुर्यां स्त्रियं सान्तानिकेऽसति ॥ ९ ॥

tyaja tyajāśu duṣprajñe
mat-kṣetrād āhitaṁ paraiḥ

nāhaṁ tvāṁ bhasmasāt kuryāṁ
striyaṁ sāntānike 'sati

tyaja—deliver; *tyaja*—deliver; *āśu*—immediately; *duṣprajñe*—you foolish woman; *mat-kṣetrāt*—from the womb meant for me to impregnate; *āhitam*—begotten; *paraiḥ*—by others; *na*—not; *aham*—I; *tvām*—you; *bhasmasāt*—burnt to ashes; *kuryām*—shall make; *striyam*—because you are a woman; *sāntānike*—wanting a child; *asati*—although you are unchaste.

TRANSLATION

Bṛhaspati said: You foolish woman, your womb, which was meant for me to impregnate, has been impregnated by someone other than me. Immediately deliver your child! Immediately deliver it! Be assured that after the child is delivered, I shall not burn you to ashes. I know that although you are unchaste, you wanted a son. Therefore I shall not punish you.

PURPORT

Tārā was married to Bṛhaspati, and therefore as a chaste woman she should have been impregnated by him. But instead she preferred to be impregnated by Soma, the moon-god, and therefore she was unchaste. Although Bṛhaspati accepted Tārā from Brahmā, when he saw that she was pregnant he wanted her to deliver a son immediately. Tārā certainly very much feared her husband, and she thought she might be punished after giving birth. Thus Bṛhaspati assured her that he would not punish her, for although she was unchaste and had become pregnant illicitly, she wanted a son.

TEXT 10

तत्याज व्रीडिता तारा कुमारं कनकप्रभम् ।
स्पृहामाङ्गिरसश्चक्रे कुमारे सोम एव च ॥१०॥

tatyāja vrīḍitā tārā
kumāraṁ kanaka-prabham

spṛhām āṅgirasaś cakre
kumāre soma eva ca

tatyāja—gave delivery; *vrīḍitā*—being very much ashamed; *tārā*—Tārā, the wife of Bṛhaspati; *kumāram*—to a child; *kanaka-prabham*—having a bodily effulgence like gold; *spṛhām*—aspiration; *āṅgirasaḥ*—Bṛhaspati; *cakre*—made; *kumāre*—unto the child; *somaḥ*—the moon-god; *eva*—indeed; *ca*—also.

TRANSLATION

Śukadeva Gosvāmī continued: By Bṛhaspati's order, Tārā, who was very much ashamed, immediately gave birth to the child, who was very beautiful, with a golden bodily hue. Both Bṛhaspati and the moon-god, Soma, desired the beautiful child.

TEXT 11

ममायं न तवेत्युच्चैस्तस्मिन् विवदमानयोः ।
पप्रच्छुर्ऋषयो देवा नैवोचे व्रीडिता तु सा ॥११॥

mamāyaṁ na tavety uccais
tasmin vivadamānayoḥ
papracchur ṛṣayo devā
naivoce vrīḍitā tu sā

mama—mine; *ayam*—this (child); *na*—not; *tava*—yours; *iti*—thus; *uccaiḥ*—very loudly; *tasmin*—for the child; *vivadamānayoḥ*—when the two parties were fighting; *papracchuḥ*—inquired (from Tārā); *ṛṣayaḥ*—all the saintly persons; *devāḥ*—all the demigods; *na*—not; *eva*—indeed; *uce*—said anything; *vrīḍitā*—being ashamed; *tu*—indeed; *sā*—Tārā.

TRANSLATION

Fighting again broke out between Bṛhaspati and the moon-god, both of whom claimed, "This is my child, not yours!" All the saints and demigods present asked Tārā whose child the newborn baby actually was, but because she was ashamed she could not immediately answer.

TEXT 12

कुमारो मातरं प्राह कुपितोऽलीकलज्जया ।
किं न वचस्यसद्वृत्ते आत्मावद्यं वदाशु मे ॥१२॥

kumāro mātaraṁ prāha
kupito 'līka-lajjayā
kiṁ na vacasy asad-vṛtte
ātmāvadyaṁ vadāśu me

kumāraḥ—the child; *mātaram*—unto his mother; *prāha*—said; *kupitaḥ*—being very angry; *alīka*—unnecessary; *lajjayā*—with shame; *kim*—why; *na*—not; *vacasi*—you say; *asat-vṛtte*—O unchaste woman; *ātma-avadyam*—the fault you have committed; *vada*—say; *āśu*—immediately; *me*—unto me.

TRANSLATION

The child then became very angry and demanded that his mother immediately tell the truth. "You unchaste woman," he said, "what is the use of your unnecessary shame? Why do you not admit your fault? Immediately tell me about your faulty behavior."

TEXT 13

ब्रह्मा तां रह आहूय समप्राक्षीच्च सान्त्वयन् ।
सोमस्येत्याह शनकैः सोमस्तं तावदग्रहीत् ॥१३॥

brahmā tāṁ raha āhūya
samaprākṣīc ca sāntvayan
somasyety āha śanakaiḥ
somas taṁ tāvad agrahīt

brahmā—Lord Brahmā; *tām*—unto her, Tārā; *rahaḥ*—in a secluded place; *āhūya*—putting her; *samaprākṣīt*—inquired in detail; *ca*—and; *sāntvayan*—pacifying; *somasya*—this son belongs to Soma, the moon-god; *iti*—thus; *āha*—she replied; *śanakaiḥ*—very slowly; *somaḥ*—Soma; *tam*—the child; *tāvat*—immediately; *agrahīt*—took charge of.

TRANSLATION

Lord Brahmā then brought Tārā to a secluded place, and after pacifying her he asked to whom the child actually belonged. She replied very slowly, "This is the son of Soma, the moon-god." Then the moon-god immediately took charge of the child.

TEXT 14

तस्यात्मयोनिरकृत बुध इत्यभिधां नृप ।
बुद्‍ध्या गम्भीरया येन पुत्रेणापोडुराण् मुदम् ॥१४॥

tasyātma-yonir akṛta
budha ity abhidhāṁ nṛpa
buddhyā gambhīrayā yena
putreṇāpoḍurāṇ mudam

tasya—of the child; *ātma-yoniḥ*—Lord Brahmā; *akṛta*—made; *budhaḥ*—Budha; *iti*—thus; *abhidhām*—the name; *nṛpa*—O King Parīkṣit; *buddhyā*—by intelligence; *gambhīrayā*—very deeply situated; *yena*—by whom; *putreṇa*—by such a son; *āpa*—he got; *uḍurāṭ*—the moon-god; *mudam*—jubilation.

TRANSLATION

O Mahārāja Parīkṣit, when Lord Brahmā saw that the child was deeply intelligent, he gave the child the name Budha. The moon-god, the ruler of the stars, enjoyed great jubilation because of this son.

TEXTS 15–16

ततः पुरूरवा जज्ञे इलायां य उदाहृतः ।
तस्य रूपगुणौदार्यशीलद्रविणविक्रमान् ॥१५॥
श्रुत्वोर्वशीन्द्रभवने गीयमानान् सुरर्षिणा ।
तदन्तिकमुपेयाय देवी स्मरशरार्दिता ॥१६॥

tataḥ purūravā jajñe
ilāyāṁ ya udāhṛtaḥ

tasya rūpa-guṇaudārya-
śīla-draviṇa-vikramān

śrutvorvaśīndra-bhavane
gīyamānān surarṣiṇā
tad-antikam upeyāya
devī smara-śarārditā

tataḥ—from him (Budha); *purūravāḥ*—the son named Purūravā; *jajñe*—was born; *ilāyām*—in the womb of Ilā; *yaḥ*—one who; *udāhṛtaḥ*—has already been described (in the beginning of the Ninth Canto); *tasya*—his (Purūravā's); *rūpa*—beauty; *guṇa*—qualities; *audārya*—magnanimity; *śīla*—behavior; *draviṇa*—wealth; *vikramān*—power; *śrutvā*—by hearing; *urvaśī*—the celestial woman named Urvaśī; *indra-bhavane*—in the court of King Indra; *gīyamānān*—when they were being described; *sura-ṛṣiṇā*—by Nārada; *tat-antikam*—near him; *upeyāya*—approached; *devī*—Urvaśī; *smara-śara*—by the arrows of Cupid; *arditā*—being stricken.

TRANSLATION

Thereafter, from Budha, through the womb of Ilā, a son was born named Purūravā, who was described in the beginning of the Ninth Canto. When his beauty, personal qualities, magnanimity, behavior, wealth and power were described by Nārada in the court of Lord Indra, the celestial woman Urvaśī was attracted to him. Pierced by the arrow of Cupid, she thus approached him.

TEXTS 17–18

मित्रावरुणयोः शापादापन्ना नरलोकताम् ।
निशम्य पुरुषश्रेष्ठं कन्दर्पमिव रूपिणम् ॥१७॥
धृतिं विष्टभ्य ललना उपतस्थे तदन्तिके ।
स तां विलोक्य नृपतिर्हर्षेणोत्फुल्ललोचनः ।
उवाच श्लक्ष्णया वाचा देवीं हृष्टतनूरुहः ॥१८॥

mitrā-varuṇayoḥ śāpād
āpannā nara-lokatām
niśamya puruṣa-śreṣṭhaṁ
kandarpam iva rūpiṇam

dhṛtiṁ viṣṭabhya lalanā
upatasthe tad-antike
sa tāṁ vilokya nṛpatir
harṣeṇotphulla-locanaḥ
uvāca ślakṣṇayā vācā
devīṁ hṛṣṭa-tanūruhaḥ

mitrā-varuṇayoḥ—of Mitra and Varuṇa; *śāpāt*—by the curse; *āpannā*—having obtained; *nara-lokatām*—the habits of a human being; *niśamya*—thus seeing; *puruṣa-śreṣṭham*—the best of males; *kandarpam iva*—like Cupid; *rūpiṇam*—having beauty; *dhṛtim*—patience, forbearance; *viṣṭabhya*—accepting; *lalanā*—that woman; *upatasthe*—approached; *tat-antike*—near to him; *saḥ*—he, Purūravā; *tām*—her; *vilokya*—by seeing; *nṛpatiḥ*—the King; *harṣeṇa*—with great jubilation; *utphulla-locanaḥ*—whose eyes became very bright; *uvāca*—said; *ślakṣṇayā*—very mild; *vācā*—by words; *devīm*—unto the demigoddess; *hṛṣṭa-tanūruhaḥ*—the hairs on whose body were standing in jubilation.

TRANSLATION

Having been cursed by Mitra and Varuṇa, the celestial woman Urvaśī had acquired the habits of a human being. Therefore, upon seeing Purūravā, the best of males, whose beauty resembled that of Cupid, she controlled herself and then approached him. When King Purūravā saw Urvaśī, his eyes became jubilant in the ecstasy of joy, and the hairs on his body stood on end. With mild, pleasing words, he spoke to her as follows.

TEXT 19

श्रीराजोवाच
स्वागतं ते वरारोहे आस्यतां करवाम किम् ।
संरमस्व मया साकं रतिर्नौ शाश्वतीः समाः ॥१९॥

śrī-rājovāca
svāgataṁ te varārohe
āsyatāṁ karavāma kim
saṁramasva mayā sākaṁ
ratir nau śāśvatīḥ samāḥ

śrī-rājā uvāca—the King (Purūravā) said; *svāgatam*—welcome; *te*—unto you; *varārohe*—O best of beautiful women; *āsyatām*—kindly take your seat; *karavāma kim*—what can I do for you; *saṁramasva*—just become my companion; *mayā sākam*—with me; *ratiḥ*—a sexual relationship; *nau*—between us; *śāśvatīḥ samāḥ*—for many years.

TRANSLATION

King Purūravā said: O most beautiful woman, you are welcome. Please sit here and tell me what I can do for you. You may enjoy with me as long as you desire. Let us pass our life happily in a sexual relationship.

TEXT 20

उर्वश्युवाच
कस्यास्त्वयि न सज्जेत मनो दृष्टिश्च सुन्दर ।
यदङ्गान्तरमासाद्य च्यवते ह रिरंसया ॥२०॥

urvaśy uvāca
kasyās tvayi na sajjeta
mano dṛṣṭiś ca sundara
yad-aṅgāntaram āsādya
cyavate ha riraṁsayā

urvaśī uvāca—Urvaśī replied; *kasyāḥ*—of which woman; *tvayi*—unto you; *na*—not; *sajjeta*—would become attracted; *manaḥ*—the mind; *dṛṣṭiḥ ca*—and sight; *sundara*—O most beautiful man; *yat-aṅgāntaram*—whose chest; *āsādya*—enjoying; *cyavate*—gives up; *ha*—indeed; *riraṁsayā*—for sexual enjoyment.

TRANSLATION

Urvaśī replied: O most handsome man, who is the woman whose mind and sight would not be attracted by you? If a woman takes shelter of your chest, she cannot refuse to enjoy with you in a sexual relationship.

PURPORT

When a beautiful man and a beautiful woman unite together and embrace one another, how within these three worlds can they check their sexual relationship? Therefore *Śrīmad-Bhāgavatam* (7.9.45) says, *yan maithunādi-gṛhamedhi-sukhaṁ hi tuccham.*

TEXT 21

एतावुरणकौ राजन् न्यासौ रक्षस्व मानद ।
संरंस्ये भवता साकं श्लाघ्यः स्त्रीणां वरः स्मृतः ॥२१॥

etāv uraṇakau rājan
nyāsau rakṣasva mānada
saṁraṁsye bhavatā sākaṁ
ślāghyaḥ strīṇāṁ varaḥ smṛtaḥ

etau—to these two; *uraṇakau*—lambs; *rājan*—O King Purūravā; *nyāsau*—who have fallen down; *rakṣasva*—please give protection; *māna-da*—O one who gives all honor to a guest or visitor; *saṁraṁsye*—I shall enjoy sexual union; *bhavatā sākam*—in your company; *ślāghyaḥ*—superior; *strīṇām*—of a woman; *varaḥ*—husband; *smṛtaḥ*—it is said.

TRANSLATION

My dear King Purūravā, please give protection to these two lambs, who have fallen down with me. Although I belong to the heavenly planets and you belong to earth, I shall certainly enjoy sexual union with you. I have no objection to accepting you as my husband, for you are superior in every respect.

PURPORT

As stated in the *Brahma-saṁhitā* (5.40), *yasya prabhā prabhavato jagad-aṇḍa-koṭi-koṭiṣv aśeṣa-vasudhādi-vibhūti-bhinnam.* There are various planets and various atmospheres within this universe. The atmosphere of the heavenly planet from which Urvaśī descended after being cursed by Mitra and Varuṇa was different from the atmosphere of this earth. Indeed, the inhabitants of the heavenly planets are certainly far superior to the inhabitants of earth. Nonetheless, Urvaśī agreed to remain the consort of Purūravā, although she belonged to a superior community. A woman who finds a man with superior qualities may accept such a man as her husband. Similarly, if a man finds a woman who is from an inferior family but who has good qualities, he can accept such a brilliant wife, as advised by Śrī Cāṇakya Paṇḍita (*strī-ratnaṁ duṣkulād api*). The combination of male and female is worthwhile if the qualities of both are on an equal level.

TEXT 22

घृतं मे वीर भक्ष्यं स्यान्नेक्षे त्वान्यत्र मैथुनात् ।
विवाससं तत् तथेति प्रतिपेदे महामनाः ॥२२॥

ghṛtaṁ me vīra bhakṣyaṁ syān
nekṣe tvānyatra maithunāt
vivāsasaṁ tat tatheti
pratipede mahāmanāḥ

ghṛtam—clarified butter or nectar; *me*—my; *vīra*—O hero; *bhakṣyam*—eatable; *syāt*—shall be; *na*—not; *īkṣe*—I shall see; *tvā*—you; *anyatra*—any other time; *maithunāt*—except at the time of sexual intercourse; *vivāsasam*—without any dress (naked); *tat*—that; *tathā iti*—shall be like that; *pratipede*—promised; *mahāmanāḥ*—King Purūravā.

TRANSLATION

Urvaśī said: "My dear hero, only preparations made in ghee [clarified butter] will be my eatables, and I shall not want to see you naked at any time, except at the time of sexual intercourse." The great-minded King Purūravā accepted these proposals.

TEXT 23

अहो रूपमहो भावो नरलोकविमोहनम् ।
को न सेवेत मनुजो देवीं त्वां स्वयमागताम् ॥२३॥

aho rūpam aho bhāvo
nara-loka-vimohanam
ko na seveta manujo
devīṁ tvāṁ svayam āgatām

aho—wonderful; *rūpam*—beauty; *aho*—wonderful; *bhāvaḥ*—postures; *nara-loka*—in human society or on the planet earth; *vimohanam*—so attractive; *kaḥ*—who; *na*—not; *seveta*—can accept; *manujaḥ*—among human beings; *devīm*—a demigoddess; *tvām*—like you; *svayam āgatām*—who has personally arrived.

TRANSLATION

Purūravā replied: O beautiful one, your beauty is wonderful and your gestures are also wonderful. Indeed, you are attractive to all human society. Therefore, since you have come of your own accord from the heavenly planets, who on earth would not agree to serve a demigoddess such as you.

PURPORT

It appears from the words of Urvaśī that the standard of living, eating, behavior and speech are all different on the heavenly planets from the standards on this planet earth. The inhabitants of the heavenly planets do not eat such abominable things as meat and eggs; everything they eat is prepared in clarified butter. Nor do they like to see either men or women naked, except at the time of sexual intercourse. To live naked or almost naked is uncivilized, but on this planet earth it has now become fashionable to dress half naked, and sometimes those like hippies live completely naked. Indeed, there are many clubs and societies for this purpose. Such conduct is not allowed, however, on the heavenly planets. The inhabitants of the heavenly planets, aside from being very beautiful, both in complexion and bodily features, are well behaved and long-living, and they eat first-class food in goodness. These are some of the distinctions between the inhabitants of the heavenly planets and the inhabitants of earth.

TEXT 24

तया स पुरुषश्रेष्ठो रमयन्त्या यथार्हतः ।
रेमे सुरविहारेषु कामं चैत्ररथादिषु ॥२४॥

tayā sa puruṣa-śreṣṭho
ramayantyā yathārhataḥ
reme sura-vihāreṣu
kāmaṁ caitrarathādiṣu

tayā—with her; *saḥ*—he; *puruṣa-śreṣṭhaḥ*—the best of human beings (Purūravā); *ramayantyā*—enjoying; *yathā-arhataḥ*—as far as possible; *reme*—enjoyed; *sura-vihāreṣu*—in places resembling the heavenly parks; *kāmam*—according to his desire; *caitraratha-ādiṣu*—in the best gardens, like Caitraratha.

TRANSLATION

Śukadeva Gosvāmī continued: The best of human beings, Purūravā, began freely enjoying the company of Urvaśī, who engaged in sexual activities with him in many celestial places, such as Caitraratha and Nandana-kānana, where the demigods enjoy.

TEXT 25

रममाणस्तया देव्या पद्मकिञ्जल्कगन्धया ।
तन्मुखामोदमुषितो मुमुदेऽहर्गणान् बहून् ॥२५॥

ramamāṇas tayā devyā
padma-kiñjalka-gandhayā
tan-mukhāmoda-muṣito
mumude 'har-gaṇān bahūn

ramamāṇaḥ—enjoying sex; *tayā*—with her; *devyā*—the heavenly goddess; *padma*—of a lotus; *kiñjalka*—like the saffron; *gandhayā*—the fragrance of whom; *tat-mukha*—her beautiful face; *āmoda*—by the fragrance; *muṣitaḥ*—being enlivened more and more; *mumude*—enjoyed life; *ahaḥ-gaṇān*—days after days; *bahūn*—many.

TRANSLATION

Urvaśī's body was as fragrant as the saffron of a lotus. Being enlivened by the fragrance of her face and body, Purūravā enjoyed her company for many days with great jubilation.

TEXT 26

अपश्यन्नुर्वशीमिन्द्रो गन्धर्वान् समचोदयत् ।
उर्वशीरहितं मह्यमास्थानं नातिशोभते ॥२६॥

apaśyann urvaśīm indro
gandharvān samacodayat
urvaśī-rahitaṁ mahyam
āsthānaṁ nātiśobhate

apaśyan—without seeing; *urvaśīm*—Urvaśī; *indraḥ*—the King of the heavenly planet; *gandharvān*—unto the Gandharvas; *samacodayat*—instructed; *urvaśī-rahitam*—without Urvaśī; *mahyam*—my; *āsthānam*—place; *na*—not; *atiśobhate*—appears beautiful.

TRANSLATION

Not seeing Urvaśī in his assembly, the King of heaven, Lord Indra, said, "Without Urvaśī my assembly is no longer beautiful." Considering this, he requested the Gandharvas to bring her back to his heavenly planet.

TEXT 27

ते उपेत्य महारात्रे तमसि प्रत्युपस्थिते ।
उर्वश्या उरणौ जह्रुर्न्यस्तौ राजनि जायया ॥२७॥

te upetya mahā-rātre
tamasi pratyupasthite

urvaśyā uraṇau jahrur
nyastau rājani jāyayā

te—they, the Gandharvas; *upetya*—coming there; *mahā-rātre*—in the dead of night; *tamasi*—when the darkness; *pratyupasthite*—appeared; *urvaśyā*—by Urvaśī; *uraṇau*—two lambs; *jahruḥ*—stole; *nyastau*—given in charge; *rājani*—unto the King; *jāyayā*—by his wife, Urvaśī.

TRANSLATION

Thus the Gandharvas came to earth, and at midnight, when everything was dark, they appeared in the house of Purūravā and stole the two lambs entrusted to the King by his wife, Urvaśī.

PURPORT

"The dead of night" refers to midnight. The *mahā-niśā* is described in this *smṛti-mantra: mahā-niśā dve ghaṭike rātrer madhyama-yāmayoḥ*, "Twelve o'clock midnight is called the dead of night."

TEXT 28

निशम्याक्रन्दितं देवी पुत्रयोर्नीयमानयोः ।
हतास्म्यहं कुनाथेन नपुंसा वीरमानिना ॥२८॥

niśamyākranditaṁ devī
putrayor nīyamānayoḥ
hatāsmy ahaṁ kunāthena
napuṁsā vīra-māninā

niśamya—by hearing; *ākranditam*—crying (because of being stolen); *devī*—Urvaśī; *putrayoḥ*—of those two lambs, which she treated as sons; *nīyamānayoḥ*—as they were being taken away; *hatā*—killed; *asmi*—am; *aham*—I; *ku-nāthena*—under the protection of a bad husband; *na-puṁsā*—by the eunuch; *vīra-māninā*—although considering himself a hero.

TRANSLATION

Urvaśī treated the two lambs like her own sons. Therefore, when they were being taken by the Gandharvas and began crying, Urvaśī heard them and rebuked her husband. "Now I am being killed," she said, "under the protection of an unworthy husband, who is a coward and a eunuch although he thinks himself a great hero.

TEXT 29

यद्विश्रम्भादहं नष्टा हृतापत्या च दस्युभिः ।
यः शेते निशि संत्रस्तो यथा नारी दिवा पुमान् ॥२९॥

yad-viśrambhād ahaṁ naṣṭā
hṛtāpatyā ca dasyubhiḥ
yaḥ śete niśi santrasto
yathā nārī divā pumān

yat-viśrambhāt—because of depending upon whom; *aham*—I (am); *naṣṭā*—lost; *hṛta-apatyā*—bereft of my two sons, the lambs; *ca*—also; *dasyubhiḥ*—by the plunderers; *yaḥ*—he who (my so-called husband); *śete*—lies down; *niśi*—at night; *santrastaḥ*—being afraid; *yathā*—as; *nārī*—a woman; *divā*—during the daytime; *pumān*—male.

TRANSLATION

"Because I depended on him, the plunderers have deprived me of my two sons the lambs, and therefore I am now lost. My husband lies down at night in fear, exactly like a woman, although he appears to be a man during the day."

TEXT 30

इति वाक्सायकैर्बिद्धः प्रतोत्त्रैरिव कुञ्जरः ।
निशि निस्त्रिंशमादाय विवस्त्रोऽभ्यद्रवद् रुषा ॥३०॥

iti vāk-sāyakair biddhaḥ
pratottrair iva kuñjaraḥ

niśi nistriṁśam ādāya
vivastro 'bhyadravad ruṣā

iti—thus; *vāk-sāyakaiḥ*—by the arrows of strong words; *biddhaḥ*—being pierced; *pratottraiḥ*—by the goads; *iva*—like; *kuñjaraḥ*—an elephant; *niśi*—in the night; *nistriṁśam*—a sword; *ādāya*—taking in hand; *vivastraḥ*—naked; *abhyadravat*—went out; *ruṣā*—in anger.

TRANSLATION

Purūravā, stricken by the sharp words of Urvaśī like an elephant struck by its driver's pointed rod, became very angry. Not even dressing himself properly, he took a sword in hand and went out naked into the night to follow the Gandharvas who had stolen the lambs.

TEXT 31

ते विसृज्योरणौ तत्र व्यद्योतन्त स्म विद्युतः ।
आदाय मेषावायान्तं नग्नमैक्षत सा पतिम् ॥३१॥

te visṛjyoraṇau tatra
vyadyotanta sma vidyutaḥ
ādāya meṣāv āyāntaṁ
nagnam aikṣata sā patim

te—they, the Gandharvas; *visṛjya*—after giving up; *uraṇau*—the two lambs; *tatra*—on the spot; *vyadyotanta sma*—illuminated; *vidyutaḥ*—shining like lightning; *ādāya*—taking in hand; *meṣau*—the two lambs; *āyāntam*—returning; *nagnam*—naked; *aikṣata*—saw; *sā*—Urvaśī; *patim*—her husband.

TRANSLATION

After giving up the two lambs, the Gandharvas shone brightly like lightning, thus illuminating the house of Purūravā. Urvaśī then saw her husband returning with the lambs in hand, but he was naked, and therefore she left.

TEXT 32

ऐलोऽपि शयने जायामपश्यन् विमना इव ।
तच्चित्तो विह्वलः शोचन् बभ्रामोन्मत्तवन्महीम् ॥३२॥

ailo 'pi śayane jāyām
apaśyan vimanā iva
tac-citto vihvalaḥ śocan
babhrāmonmattavan mahīm

ailaḥ—Purūravā; *api*—also; *śayane*—on the bedstead; *jāyām*—his wife; *apaśyan*—not seeing; *vimanāḥ*—morose; *iva*—like that; *tat-cittaḥ*—being too much attached to her; *vihvalaḥ*—disturbed in mind; *śocan*—lamenting; *babhrāma*—traveled; *unmatta-vat*—like a madman; *mahīm*—on the earth.

TRANSLATION

No longer seeing Urvaśī on his bed, Purūravā was most aggrieved. Because of his great attraction for her, he was very much disturbed. Thus, lamenting, he began traveling about the earth like a madman.

TEXT 33

स तां वीक्ष्य कुरुक्षेत्रे सरस्वत्यां च तत्सखीः ।
पञ्च प्रहृष्टवदनः प्राह सूक्तं पुरूरवाः ॥३३॥

sa tāṁ vīkṣya kurukṣetre
sarasvatyāṁ ca tat-sakhīḥ
pañca prahṛṣṭa-vadanaḥ
prāha sūktaṁ purūravāḥ

saḥ—he, Purūravā; *tām*—Urvaśī; *vīkṣya*—observing; *kurukṣetre*—at the place known as Kurukṣetra; *sarasvatyām*—on the bank of the Sarasvatī; *ca*—also; *tat-sakhīḥ*—her companions; *pañca*—five; *prahṛṣṭa-vadanaḥ*—being very happy and smiling; *prāha*—said; *sūktam*—sweet words; *purūravāḥ*—King Purūravā.

TRANSLATION

Once during his travels all over the world, Purūravā saw Urvaśī, accompanied by five companions, on the bank of the Sarasvatī at Kurukṣetra. With jubilation in his face, he then spoke to her in sweet words as follows.

TEXT 34

अहो जाये तिष्ठ तिष्ठ घोरे न त्यक्तुमर्हसि ।
मां त्वमद्याप्यनिर्वृत्य वचांसि कृणवावहै ॥३४॥

aho jāye tiṣṭha tiṣṭha
ghore na tyaktum arhasi
māṁ tvam adyāpy anirvṛtya
vacāṁsi kṛṇavāvahai

aho—hello; *jāye*—O my dear wife; *tiṣṭha tiṣṭha*—kindly stay, stay; *ghore*—O most cruel one; *na*—not; *tyaktum*—to give up; *arhasi*—you ought; *mām*—me; *tvam*—you; *adya api*—until now; *anirvṛtya*—having not gotten any happiness from me; *vacāṁsi*—some words; *kṛṇavāvahai*—let us talk for some time.

TRANSLATION

O my dear wife, O most cruel one, kindly stay, kindly stay. I know that I have never made you happy until now, but you should not give me up for that reason. This is not proper for you. Even if you have decided to give up my company, let us nonetheless talk for some time.

TEXT 35

सुदेहोऽयं पतत्यत्र देवि दूरं हृतस्त्वया ।
खादन्त्येनं वृका गृध्रास्त्वत्प्रसादस्य नास्पदम् ॥३५॥

sudeho 'yaṁ pataty atra
devi dūraṁ hṛtas tvayā
khādanty enaṁ vṛkā gṛdhrās
tvat-prasādasya nāspadam

su-dehaḥ—very beautiful body; *ayam*—this; *patati*—will now fall down; *atra*—on the spot; *devi*—O Urvaśī; *dūram*—far, far away from home; *hṛtaḥ*—taken away; *tvayā*—by you; *khādanti*—they will eat; *enam*—this (body); *vṛkāḥ*—foxes; *gṛdhrāḥ*—vultures; *tvat*—your; *prasādasya*—in mercy; *na*—not; *āspadam*—suitable.

TRANSLATION

O goddess, now that you have refused me, my beautiful body will fall down here, and because it is unsuitable for your pleasure, it will be eaten by foxes and vultures.

TEXT 36

उर्वश्युवाच
मा मृथाः पुरुषोऽसि त्वं मा स्म त्वाद्युर्वृका इमे ।
क्वापि सख्यं न वै स्त्रीणां वृकाणां हृदयं यथा ॥३६॥

urvaśy uvāca
mā mṛthāḥ puruṣo 'si tvaṁ
mā sma tvādyur vṛkā ime
kvāpi sakhyaṁ na vai strīṇāṁ
vṛkāṇāṁ hṛdayaṁ yathā

urvaśī uvāca—Urvaśī said; *mā*—do not; *mṛthāḥ*—give up your life; *puruṣaḥ*—male; *asi*—are; *tvam*—you; *mā sma*—do not allow it; *tvā*—unto you; *adyuḥ*—may eat; *vṛkāḥ*—the foxes; *ime*—these senses (do not be under the control of your senses); *kva api*—anywhere; *sakhyam*—friendship; *na*—not; *vai*—indeed; *strīṇām*—of women; *vṛkāṇām*—of the foxes; *hṛdayam*—the heart; *yathā*—as.

TRANSLATION

Urvaśī said: My dear King, you are a man, a hero. Don't be impatient and give up your life. Be sober and don't allow the senses to overcome you like foxes. Don't let the foxes eat you. In other words, you should not be controlled by your senses. Rather, you should know that the heart of a woman is like that of a fox. There is no use making friendship with women.

PURPORT

Cāṇakya Paṇḍita has advised, *viśvāso naiva kartavyaḥ strīṣu rāja-kuleṣu ca:* "Never place your faith in a woman or a politician." Unless elevated to spiritual consciousness, everyone is conditioned and fallen, what to speak of women, who are less intelligent than men. Women have been compared to *śūdras* and *vaiśyas* (*striyo vaiśyās tathā śūdrāḥ*). On the spiritual platform, however, when one is elevated to the platform of Kṛṣṇa consciousness, whether one is a man, woman, *śūdra* or whatever, everyone is equal. Otherwise, Urvaśī, who was a woman herself and who knew the nature of women, said that a woman's heart is like that of a sly fox. If a man cannot control his senses, he becomes a victim of such sly foxes. But if one can control the senses, there is no chance of his being victimized by sly, foxlike women. Cāṇakya Paṇḍita has also advised that if one has a wife like a sly fox, he must immediately give up his life at home and go to the forest.

mātā yasya gṛhe nāsti
bhāryā cāpriya-vādinī
araṇyaṁ tena gantavyaṁ
yathāraṇyaṁ tathā gṛham

(*Cāṇakya-śloka* 57)

Kṛṣṇa conscious *gṛhasthas* must be very careful of the sly fox woman. If the wife at home is obedient and follows her husband in Kṛṣṇa consciousness, the home is welcome. Otherwise one should give up one's home and go to the forest.

hitvātma-pātaṁ gṛham andha-kūpaṁ
vanaṁ gato yad dharim āśrayeta

(*Bhāg.* 7.5.5)

One should go to the forest and take shelter of the lotus feet of Hari, the Supreme Personality of Godhead.

TEXT 37

स्त्रियो ह्यकरुणाः क्रूरा दुर्मर्षाः प्रियसाहसाः ।
घ्नन्त्यल्पार्थेऽपि विश्रब्धं पतिं भ्रातरमप्युत ॥३७॥

striyo hy akaruṇāḥ krūrā
durmarṣāḥ priya-sāhasāḥ
ghnanty alpārthe 'pi viśrabdhaṁ
patiṁ bhrātaram apy uta

striyaḥ—women; *hi*—indeed; *akaruṇāḥ*—merciless; *krūrāḥ*—cunning; *durmarṣāḥ*—intolerant; *priya-sāhasāḥ*—for their own pleasure they can do anything; *ghnanti*—they kill; *alpa-arthe*—for a slight reason; *api*—indeed; *viśrabdham*—faithful; *patim*—husband; *bhrātaram*—brother; *api*—also; *uta*—it is said.

TRANSLATION

Women as a class are merciless and cunning. They cannot tolerate even a slight offense. For their own pleasure they can do anything irreligious, and therefore they do not fear killing even a faithful husband or brother.

PURPORT

King Purūravā was greatly attached to Urvaśī. Yet despite his faithfulness to her, she had left him. Now, considering that the King was wasting his rarely achieved human form of life, Urvaśī frankly explained the nature of a woman. Because of her nature, a woman can respond to even a slight offense from her husband by not only leaving him but even killing him if required. To say nothing of her husband, she can even kill her brother. That is a woman's nature. Therefore, in the material world, unless women are trained to be chaste and faithful to their husbands, there cannot be peace or prosperity in society.

TEXT 38

विधायालीकविश्रम्भमज्ञेषु त्यक्तसौहृदाः ।
नवं नवमभीप्सन्त्यः पुंश्चल्यः स्वैरवृत्तयः ॥३८॥

vidhāyālīka-viśrambham
ajñeṣu tyakta-sauhṛdāḥ
navaṁ navam abhīpsantyaḥ
puṁścalyaḥ svaira-vṛttayaḥ

vidhāya—by establishing; *alīka*—false; *viśrambham*—faithfulness; *ajñeṣu*—unto the foolish men; *tyakta-sauhṛdāḥ*—who have given up the company of well-wishers; *navam*—new; *navam*—new; *abhīpsantyaḥ*—desiring; *puṁścalyaḥ*—women very easily allured by other men; *svaira*—independently; *vṛttayaḥ*—professional.

TRANSLATION

Women are very easily seduced by men. Therefore, polluted women give up the friendship of a man who is their well-wisher and establish false friendship among fools. Indeed, they seek newer and newer friends, one after another.

PURPORT

Because women are easily seduced, the *Manu-saṁhitā* enjoins that they should not be given freedom. A woman must always be protected, either by her father, by her husband, or by her elderly son. If women are given freedom to mingle with men like equals, which they now claim to be, they cannot keep their propriety. The nature of a woman, as personally described by Urvaśī, is to establish false friendship with someone and then seek new male companions, one after another, even if this means giving up the company of a sincere well-wisher.

TEXT 39

संवत्सरान्ते हि भवानेकरात्रं मयेश्वरः।
रंस्यत्यपत्यानि च ते भविष्यन्त्यपराणि भोः ॥३९॥

saṁvatsarānte hi bhavān
eka-rātraṁ mayeśvaraḥ
raṁsyaty apatyāni ca te
bhaviṣyanty aparāṇi bhoḥ

saṁvatsara-ante—at the end of every year; *hi*—indeed; *bhavān*—your good self; *eka-rātram*—one night only; *mayā*—with me; *īśvaraḥ*—my husband; *raṁsyati*—will enjoy sex life; *apatyāni*—children; *ca*—also; *te*—your; *bhaviṣyanti*—will generate; *aparāṇi*—others, one after another; *bhoḥ*—O my dear King.

TRANSLATION

O my dear King, you will be able to enjoy with me as my husband at the end of every year, for one night only. In this way you will have other children, one after another.

PURPORT

Although Urvaśī had adversely explained the nature of woman, Mahārāja Purūravā was very much attached to her, and therefore she wanted to give the King some concession by agreeing to be his wife for one night at the end of each year.

TEXT 40

अन्तर्वत्नीमुपालक्ष्य देवीं स प्रययौ पुरीम् ।
पुनस्तत्र गतोऽब्दान्ते उर्वशीं वीरमातरम् ॥४०॥

antarvatnīm upālakṣya
devīṁ sa prayayau purīm
punas tatra gato 'bdānte
urvaśīṁ vīra-mātaram

antarvatnīm—pregnant; *upālakṣya*—by observing; *devīm*—Urvaśī; *saḥ*—he, King Purūravā; *prayayau*—returned; *purīm*—to his palace; *punaḥ*—again; *tatra*—at that very spot; *gataḥ*—went; *abda-ante*—at the end of the year; *urvaśīm*—Urvaśī; *vīra-mātaram*—the mother of one *kṣatriya* son.

TRANSLATION

Understanding that Urvaśī was pregnant, Purūravā returned to his palace. At the end of the year, there at Kurukṣetra, he again obtained the association of Urvaśī, who was then the mother of a heroic son.

TEXT 41

उपलभ्य मुदा युक्तः समुवास तया निशाम् ।
अथैनमुर्वशी प्राह कृपणं विरहातुरम् ॥४१॥

upalabhya mudā yuktaḥ
samuvāsa tayā niśām
athainam urvaśī prāha
kṛpaṇaṁ virahāturam

upalabhya—getting the association; *mudā*—in great jubilation; *yuktaḥ*—being united; *samuvāsa*—enjoyed her company in sex; *tayā*—with her; *niśām*—that night; *atha*—thereafter; *enam*—unto King Purūravā; *urvaśī*—the woman named Urvaśī; *prāha*—said; *kṛpaṇam*—to he who was poor-hearted; *viraha-āturam*—afflicted by the thought of separation.

TRANSLATION

Having regained Urvaśī at the end of the year, King Purūravā was most jubilant, and he enjoyed her company in sex for one night. But then he was very sorry at the thought of separation from her, so Urvaśī spoke to him as follows.

TEXT 42

गन्धर्वानुपधावेमांस्तुभ्यं दास्यन्ति मामिति ।
तस्य संस्तुवतस्तुष्टा अग्निस्थालीं ददुर्नृप ।
उर्वशीं मन्यमानस्तां सोऽबुध्यत चरन् वने ॥४२॥

gandharvān upadhāvemāṁs
tubhyaṁ dāsyanti mām iti
tasya saṁstuvatas tuṣṭā
agni-sthālīṁ dadur nṛpa
urvaśīṁ manyamānas tāṁ
so 'budhyata caran vane

gandharvān—unto the Gandharvas; *upadhāva*—go take shelter; *imān*—these; *tubhyam*—unto you; *dāsyanti*—will deliver; *mām iti*—exactly like me, or me factually; *tasya*—by him; *saṁstuvataḥ*—offering prayers; *tuṣṭāḥ*—being satisfied; *agni-sthālīm*—a girl produced from fire; *daduḥ*—delivered; *nṛpa*—O King; *urvaśīm*—Urvaśī; *manya-*

mānaḥ—thinking; *tām*—her; *saḥ*—he (Purūravā); *abudhyata*—understood factually; *caran*—while walking; *vane*—in the forest.

TRANSLATION

Urvaśī said: "My dear King, seek shelter of the Gandharvas, for they will be able to deliver me to you again." In accordance with these words, the King satisfied the Gandharvas by prayers, and the Gandharvas, being pleased with him, gave him an Agnisthālī girl who looked exactly like Urvaśī. Thinking that the girl was Urvaśī, the King began walking with her in the forest, but later he could understand that she was not Urvaśī but Agnisthālī.

PURPORT

Śrīla Viśvanātha Cakravartī Ṭhākura remarks that Purūravā was very lusty. Immediately after getting the Agnisthālī girl, he wanted to have sex with her, but during sexual intercourse he could understand that the girl was Agnisthālī, not Urvaśī. This indicates that every man attached to a particular woman knows the particular characteristics of that woman during sex life. Thus Purūravā understood during sexual intercourse that the Agnisthālī girl was not Urvaśī.

TEXT 43

स्थालीं न्यस्य वने गत्वा गृहानाध्यायतो निशि ।
त्रेतायां संप्रवृत्तायां मनसि त्रय्यवर्तत ॥४३॥

sthālīṁ nyasya vane gatvā
gṛhān ādhyāyato niśi
tretāyāṁ sampravṛttāyāṁ
manasi trayy avartata

sthālīm—the woman Agnisthālī; *nyasya*—immediately giving up; *vane*—in the forest; *gatvā*—on returning; *gṛhān*—at home; *ādhyāyataḥ*—began to meditate; *niśi*—the whole night; *tretāyām*—when the Tretā millennium; *sampravṛttāyām*—was just on the point of beginning; *manasi*—in his mind; *trayī*—the principles of the three *Vedas; avartata*—became revealed.

TRANSLATION

King Purūravā then left Agnisthālī in the forest and returned home, where he meditated all night upon Urvaśī. In the course of his meditation, the Tretā millennium began, and therefore the principles of the three Vedas, including the process of performing yajña to fulfill fruitive activities, appeared within his heart.

PURPORT

It is said, *tretāyāṁ yajato makhaiḥ:* in Tretā-yuga, if one performed *yajñas,* he would get the results of those *yajñas.* By performing *viṣṇu-yajña* specifically, one could even achieve the lotus feet of the Supreme Personality of Godhead. Of course, *yajña* is intended to please the Supreme Personality of Godhead. While Purūravā was meditating upon Urvaśī, the Tretā-yuga began, and therefore the Vedic *yajñas* were revealed in his heart. But Purūravā was a materialistic man, especially interested in enjoying the senses. *Yajñas* for enjoyment of the senses are called *karma-kāṇḍīya-yajñas.* Therefore, he decided to perform *karma-kāṇḍīya-yajñas* to fulfill his lusty desires. In other words, *karma-kāṇḍīya-yajñas* are meant for sensuous persons, whereas *yajña* should actually be performed to please the Supreme Personality of Godhead. To please the Supreme Personality of Godhead in Kali-yuga, the *saṅkīrtana-yajña* is recommended. *Yajñaiḥ saṅkīrtana-prāyair yajanti hi sumedhasaḥ.* Only those who are very intelligent take to *saṅkīrtana-yajña* to fulfill all their desires, material and spiritual, whereas those who are lusty for sense enjoyment perform *karma-kāṇḍīya-yajñas.*

TEXTS 44–45

स्थालीस्थानं गतोऽश्वत्थं शमीगर्भं विलक्ष्य सः ।
तेन द्वे अरणी कृत्वा उर्वशीलोककाम्यया ॥४४॥
उर्वशीं मन्त्रतो ध्यायन्नधरारणिमुत्तराम् ।
आत्मानमुभयोर्मध्ये यत् तत् प्रजननं प्रभुः ॥४५॥

sthālī-sthānaṁ gato 'śvatthaṁ
śamī-garbhaṁ vilakṣya saḥ

tena dve araṇī kṛtvā
urvaśī-loka-kāmyayā

urvaśīṁ mantrato dhyāyann
adharāraṇim uttarām
ātmānam ubhayor madhye
yat tat prajananaṁ prabhuḥ

sthālī-sthānam—the place where Agnisthālī was left; *gataḥ*—going there; *aśvattham*—an *aśvattha* tree; *śamī-garbham*—produced from the womb of the *śamī* tree; *vilakṣya*—seeing; *saḥ*—he, Purūravā; *tena*—from that; *dve*—two; *araṇī*—pieces of wood required for igniting a fire for sacrifice; *kṛtvā*—making; *urvaśī-loka-kāmyayā*—desiring to go to the planet where Urvaśī was present; *urvaśīm*—Urvaśī; *mantrataḥ*—by chanting the required *mantra; dhyāyan*—meditating upon; *adhara*—lower; *araṇim*—*araṇi* wood; *uttarām*—and the upper one; *ātmānam*—himself; *ubhayoḥ madhye*—in between the two; *yat tat*—that which (he meditated upon); *prajananam*—as a son; *prabhuḥ*—the King.

TRANSLATION

When the process of fruitive yajña became manifest within his heart, King Purūravā went to the same spot where he had left Agnisthālī. There he saw that from the womb of a śamī tree, an aśvattha tree had grown. He then took a piece of wood from that tree and made it into two araṇis. Desiring to go to the planet where Urvaśī resided, he chanted mantras, meditating upon the lower araṇi as Urvaśī, the upper one as himself, and the piece of wood between them as his son. In this way he began to ignite a fire.

PURPORT

The Vedic fire for performing *yajña* was not ignited with ordinary matches or similar devices. Rather, the Vedic sacrificial fire was ignited by the *araṇis*, or two sacred pieces of wood, which produced fire by friction with a third. Such a fire is necessary for the performance of *yajña*. If successful, a *yajña* will fulfill the desire of its performer. Thus Purūravā took advantage of the process of *yajña* to fulfill his lusty desires. He thought of the lower *araṇi* as Urvaśī, the upper one as himself, and the middle one as his son. A relevant Vedic *mantra* quoted herein by Viśvanātha Cakravartī Ṭhākura is *śamī-garbhād agniṁ mantha.* A similar *mantra* is *urvaśyām urasi purūravāḥ.* Purūravā wanted to have children continuously by the womb of Urvaśī. His only ambition was to have sex life with Urvaśī and thereby get a son. In other words, he had so much lust in his heart that even while performing *yajña* he thought of Urvaśī, instead of thinking of the master of *yajña*, Yajñeśvara, Lord Viṣṇu.

TEXT 46

तस्य निर्मन्थनाज्जातो जातवेदा विभावसुः ।
त्रय्या स विद्यया राज्ञा पुत्रत्वे कल्पितस्त्रिवृत् ॥४६॥

tasya nirmanthanāj jāto
jāta-vedā vibhāvasuḥ
trayyā sa vidyayā rājñā
putratve kalpitas tri-vṛt

tasya—of Purūravā; *nirmanthanāt*—because of interaction; *jātaḥ*—was born; *jāta-vedāḥ*—meant for material enjoyment according to the Vedic principles; *vibhāvasuḥ*—a fire; *trayyā*—following the Vedic principles; *saḥ*—the fire; *vidyayā*—by such a process; *rājñā*—by the King; *putratve*—a son's being born; *kalpitaḥ*—it so became; *tri-vṛt*—the three letters *a-u-m* combined together as *oṁ.*

TRANSLATION

From Purūravā's rubbing of the araṇis came a fire. By such a fire one can achieve all success in material enjoyment and be purified in seminal birth, initiation and in the performance of sacrifice, which are invoked with the combined letters a-u-m. Thus the fire was considered the son of King Purūravā.

PURPORT

According to the Vedic process, one can get a son through semen (*śukra*), one can get a bona fide disciple through initiation (*sāvitra*), or one can get a son or disciple through the fire of sacrifice (*yajña*). Thus when Mahārāja Purūravā generated the fire by rubbing the *araṇis*, the fire became his son. Either by semen, by initiation or by *yajña* one may get a son. The Vedic *mantra oṁkāra*, or *praṇava*, consisting of the letters *a-u-m*, can call each of these three methods into existence. Therefore the words *nirmanthanāj jātaḥ* indicate that by the rubbing of the *araṇis* a son was born.

TEXT 47

तेनायजत यज्ञेशं भगवन्तमधोक्षजम् ।
उर्वशीलोकमन्विच्छन् सर्वदेवमयं हरिम् ॥४७॥

tenāyajata yajñeśaṁ
bhagavantam adhokṣajam
urvaśī-lokam anvicchan
sarva-devamayaṁ harim

tena—by generating such a fire; *ayajata*—he worshiped; *yajña-īśam*—the master or enjoyer of the *yajña; bhagavantam*—the Supreme Personality of Godhead; *adhokṣajam*—beyond the perception of the senses; *urvaśī-lokam*—to the planet where Urvaśī was staying; *anvicchan*—although desiring to go; *sarva-deva-mayam*—the reservoir of all demigods; *harim*—the Supreme Personality of Godhead.

TRANSLATION

By means of that fire, Purūravā, who desired to go to the planet where Urvaśī resided, performed a sacrifice, by which he satisfied the Supreme Personality of Godhead, Hari, the enjoyer of the results of sacrifice. Thus he worshiped the Lord, who is beyond the perception of the senses and is the reservoir of all the demigods.

PURPORT

As stated in *Bhagavad-gītā, bhoktāraṁ yajña-tapasāṁ sarva-loka-maheśvaram:* any *loka*, or planet, to which one wants to go is the property of the Supreme Personality of Godhead, the enjoyer of the performance of sacrifice. The purpose of *yajña* is to satisfy the Supreme

Personality of Godhead. In this age, as we have explained many times, the *yajña* of chanting the Hare Kṛṣṇa *mahā-mantra* is the only sacrifice that can satisfy the Supreme Lord. When the Lord is satisfied, one can fulfill any desire, material or spiritual. *Bhagavad-gītā* (3.14) also says, *yajnād bhavati parjanyaḥ:* by offering sacrifices to Lord Viṣṇu, one can have sufficient rainfall. When there is sufficient rainfall, the earth becomes fit to produce everything (*sarva-kāma-dughā mahī*). If one can utilize the land properly, one can get all the necessities of life from the land, including food grains, fruits, flowers and vegetables. Everything one gets for material wealth is produced from the earth, and therefore it is said, *sarva-kāma-dughā mahī* (*Bhāg.* 1.10.4). Everything is possible by performing *yajña.* Therefore although Purūravā desired something material, he factually performed *yajña* to please the Supreme Personality of Godhead. The Lord is *adhokṣaja,* beyond the perception of Purūravā and everyone else. Consequently, some kind of *yajña* must be performed to fulfill the desires of the living entity. *Yajñas* can be performed in human society only when society is divided by *varṇāśrama-dharma* into four *varṇas* and four *āśramas.* Without such a regulative process, no one can perform *yajñas,* and without the performance of *yajñas,* no material plans can make human society happy at any time. Everyone should therefore be induced to perform *yajñas.* In this age of Kali, the *yajña* recommended is *saṅkīrtana,* the individual or collective chanting of the Hare Kṛṣṇa *mahā-mantra.* This will bring the fulfillment of all necessities for human society.

TEXT 48

एक एव पुरा वेदः प्रणवः सर्ववाङ्मयः ।
देवो नारायणो नान्य एकोऽग्निर्वर्ण एव च ॥४८॥

eka eva purā vedaḥ
praṇavaḥ sarva-vāṅmayaḥ
devo nārāyaṇo nānya
eko 'gnir varṇa eva ca

ekaḥ—only one; *eva*—indeed; *purā*—formerly; *vedaḥ*—book of transcendental knowledge; *praṇavaḥ*—*oṁkāra; sarva-vāk-mayaḥ*—

consisting of all Vedic *mantras; devaḥ*—the Lord, God; *nārāyaṇaḥ*—only Nārāyaṇa (was worshipable in the Satya-yuga); *na anyaḥ*—no other; *ekaḥ agniḥ*—one division only for *agni; varṇaḥ*—order of life; *eva ca*—and certainly.

TRANSLATION

In the Satya-yuga, the first millennium, all the Vedic mantras were included in one mantra—praṇava, the root of all Vedic mantras. In other words, the Atharva Veda alone was the source of all Vedic knowledge. The Supreme Personality of Godhead Nārāyaṇa was the only worshipable Deity; there was no recommendation for worship of the demigods. Fire was one only, and the only order of life in human society was known as haṁsa.

PURPORT

In Satya-yuga there was only one *Veda*, not four. Later, before the beginning of Kali-yuga, this one *Veda*, the *Atharva Veda* (or, some say, the *Yajur Veda*), was divided into four—*Sāma, Yajur, Ṛg* and *Atharva*—for the facility of human society. In Satya-yuga the only *mantra* was *oṁkāra* (*oṁ tat sat*). The same name *oṁkāra* is manifest in the *mantra* Hare Kṛṣṇa, Hare Kṛṣṇa, Kṛṣṇa Kṛṣṇa, Hare Hare/ Hare Rāma, Hare Rāma, Rāma Rāma, Hare Hare. Unless one is a *brāhmaṇa*, one cannot utter *oṁkāra* and get the desired result. But in Kali-yuga almost everyone is a *śūdra*, unfit for pronouncing the *praṇava, oṁkāra*. Therefore the *śāstras* have recommended the chanting of the Hare Kṛṣṇa *mahā-mantra. Oṁkāra* is a *mantra*, or *mahā-mantra*, and Hare Kṛṣṇa is also a *mahā-mantra*. The purpose of pronouncing *oṁkāra* is to address the Supreme Personality of Godhead, Vāsudeva (*oṁ namo bhagavate vāsudevāya*). And the purpose of chanting the Hare Kṛṣṇa *mantra* is the same. *Hare:* "O energy of the Lord!" *Kṛṣṇa:* "O Lord Kṛṣṇa!" *Hare:* "O energy of the Lord!" *Rāma:* "O Supreme Lord, O supreme enjoyer!" The only worshipable Lord is Hari, who is the goal of the *Vedas* (*vedaiś ca sarvair aham eva vedyaḥ*). By worshiping the demigods, one worships the different parts of the Lord, just as one might water the branches and twigs of a tree. But worshiping Nārāyaṇa, the all-inclusive Supreme Personality of Godhead, is like pouring water on the root of the tree, thus supplying water to the trunk, branches, twigs, leaves and so on. In Satya-yuga people knew how to fulfill the necessities of life simply by worshiping Nārāyaṇa, the Supreme Personality of Godhead. The same purpose can be served in this age of Kali by the chanting of the Hare Kṛṣṇa *mantra*, as recommended in the *Bhāgavatam. Kīrtanād eva kṛṣṇasya mukta-saṅgaḥ paraṁ vrajet.* Simply by chanting the Hare Kṛṣṇa *mantra*, one becomes free from the bondage of material existence and thus becomes eligible to return home, back to Godhead.

TEXT 49

पुरूरवस एवासीत् त्रयी त्रेतामुखे नृप ।
अग्निना प्रजया राजा लोकं गान्धर्वमेयिवान् ॥४९॥

purūravasa evāsīt
trayī tretā-mukhe nṛpa
agninā prajayā rājā
lokaṁ gāndharvam eyivān

purūravasaḥ—from King Purūravā; *eva*—thus; *āsīt*—there was; *trayī*—the Vedic principles of *karma, jñāna* and *upāsanā; tretā-mukhe*—in the beginning of the Tretā-yuga; *nṛpa*—O King Parīkṣit; *agninā*—simply by generating the fire of sacrifice; *prajayā*—by his son; *rājā*—King Purūravā; *lokam*—to the planet; *gāndharvam*—of the Gandharvas; *eyivān*—achieved.

TRANSLATION

O Mahārāja Parīkṣit, at the beginning of Tretā-yuga, King Purūravā inaugurated a karma-kāṇḍa sacrifice. Thus Purūravā, who considered the yajñic fire his son, was able to go to Gandharvaloka as he desired.

PURPORT

In Satya-yuga, Lord Nārāyaṇa was worshiped by meditation (*kṛte yad dhyāyato viṣṇum*). Indeed, everyone always meditated upon Lord Viṣṇu, Nārāyaṇa, and achieved every success by this process of meditation. In the next *yuga*, Tretā-yuga, the performance of *yajña* began (*tretāyāṁ yajato mukhaiḥ*). Therefore this verse says, *trayī tretā-mukhe.* Ritualistic ceremonies are generally called fruitive activities. Śrīla Viśvanātha Cakravartī Ṭhākura says that in Tretā-yuga, beginning in the Svāyambhuva-manvantara, ritualistic fruitive activities were similarly manifested from Priyavrata, etc.

Thus end the Bhaktivedanta purports of the Ninth Canto, Fourteenth Chapter, of the Śrīmad-Bhāgavatam, *entitled "King Purūravā Enchanted by Urvaśī."*

CHAPTER FIFTEEN

Paraśurāma, the Lord's Warrior Incarnation

This chapter describes the history of Gādhi in the dynasty of Aila.

From the womb of Urvaśī came six sons, named Āyu, Śrutāyu, Satyāyu, Raya, Jaya and Vijaya. The son of Śrutāyu was Vasumān, the son of Satyāyu was Śrutañjaya, the son of Raya was Eka, the son of Jaya was Amita, and the son of Vijaya was Bhīma. Bhīma's son was named Kāñcana, the son of Kāñcana was Hotraka, and the son of Hotraka was Jahnu, who was celebrated for having drunk all the water of the Ganges in one sip. The descendants of Jahnu, one after another, were Puru, Balāka, Ajaka and Kuśa. The sons of Kuśa were Kuśāmbu, Tanaya, Vasu and Kuśanābha. From Kuśāmbu came Gādhi, who had a daughter named Satyavatī. Satyavatī married Ṛcīka Muni after the *muni* contributed a substantial dowry, and from the womb of Satyavatī by Ṛcīka Muni, Jamadagni was born. The son of Jamadagni was Rāma, or Paraśurāma. When a king named Kārtavīryārjuna stole Jamadagni's desire cow, Paraśurāma, who is ascertained by learned experts to be a *saktyāveśa* incarnation of the Supreme Personality of Godhead, killed Kārtavīryārjuna. Later, he annihilated the *kṣatriya* dynasty twenty-one times. After Paraśurāma killed Kārtavīryārjuna, Jamadagni told him that killing a king is sinful and that as a *brāhmaṇa* he should have tolerated the offense. Therefore Jamadagni advised Paraśurāma to atone for his sin by traveling to various holy places.

TEXT 1

श्रीबादरायणिरुवाच
ऐलस्य चोर्वशीगर्भात् षडासन्नात्मजा नृप ।
आयुः श्रुतायुः सत्यायू रयोऽथ विजयो जयः ॥ १ ॥

śrī-bādarāyaṇir uvāca
ailasya corvaśī-garbhāt
ṣaḍ āsann ātmajā nṛpa

āyuḥ śrutāyuḥ satyāyū
rayo 'tha vijayo jayaḥ

śrī-bādarāyaṇiḥ uvāca—Śrī Śukadeva Gosvāmī said; *ailasya*—of Purūravā; *ca*—also; *urvaśī-garbhāt*—from the womb of Urvaśī; *ṣaṭ*—six; *āsan*—there were; *ātmajāḥ*—sons; *nṛpa*—O King Parīkṣit; *āyuḥ*—Āyu; *śrutāyuḥ*—Śrutāyu; *satyāyuḥ*—Satyāyu; *rayaḥ*—Raya; *atha*—as well as; *vijayaḥ*—Vijaya; *jayaḥ*—Jaya.

TRANSLATION

Śukadeva Gosvāmī continued: O King Parīkṣit, from the womb of Urvaśī, six sons were generated by Purūravā. Their names were Āyu, Śrutāyu, Satyāyu, Raya, Vijaya and Jaya.

TEXTS 2–3

श्रुतायोर्वसुमान् पुत्रः सत्यायोश्च श्रुतञ्जयः ।
रयस्य सुत एकश्च जयस्य तनयोऽमितः ॥ २ ॥
भीमस्तु विजयस्याथ काञ्चनो होत्रकस्ततः ।
तस्य जह्नुः सुतो गङ्गां गण्डूषीकृत्य योऽपिबत् ॥ ३ ॥

śrutāyor vasumān putraḥ
satyāyoś ca śrutañjayaḥ
rayasya suta ekaś ca
jayasya tanayo 'mitaḥ

bhīmas tu vijayasyātha
kāñcano hotrakas tataḥ
tasya jahnuḥ suto gaṅgāṁ
gaṇḍūṣī-kṛtya yo 'pibat

śrutāyoḥ—of Śrutāyu; *vasumān*—Vasumān; *putraḥ*—a son; *satyāyoḥ*—of Satyāyu; *ca*—also; *śrutañjayaḥ*—a son named Śrutañjaya; *rayasya*—of Raya; *sutaḥ*—a son; *ekaḥ*—by the name Eka; *ca*—and; *jayasya*—of Jaya; *tanayaḥ*—the son; *amitaḥ*—by the name Amita; *bhīmaḥ*—by the name Bhīma; *tu*—indeed; *vijayasya*—of Vijaya; *atha*—thereafter; *kāñcanaḥ*—Kāñcana, the son of Bhīma; *hotrakaḥ*—

Hotraka, the son of Kāñcana; *tataḥ*—then; *tasya*—of Hotraka; *jahnuḥ*—by the name Jahnu; *sutaḥ*—a son; *gaṅgām*—all the water of the Ganges; *gaṇḍūṣī-kṛtya*—by one sip; *yaḥ*—he who (Jahnu); *apibat*—drank.

TRANSLATION

The son of Śrutāyu was Vasumān; the son of Satyāyu, Śrutañjaya; the son of Raya, Eka; the son of Jaya, Amita; and the son of Vijaya, Bhīma. The son of Bhīma was Kāñcana; the son of Kāñcana was Hotraka; and the son of Hotraka was Jahnu, who drank all the water of the Ganges in one sip.

TEXT 4

जह्नोस्तु पुरुस्तस्याथ बलाकश्चात्मजोऽजकः ।
ततः कुशः कुशस्यापि कुशाम्बुस्तनयो वसुः ।
कुशनाभश्च चत्वारो गाधिरासीत्कुशाम्बुजः ॥ ४ ॥

jahnos tu purus tasyātha
balākaś cātmajo 'jakaḥ
tataḥ kuśaḥ kuśasyāpi
kuśāmbus tanayo vasuḥ
kuśanābhaś ca catvāro
gādhir āsīt kuśāmbujaḥ

jahnoḥ—of Jahnu; *tu*—indeed; *puruḥ*—a son named Puru; *tasya*—of Puru; *atha*—thereafter; *balākaḥ*—a son named Balāka; *ca*—and; *ātmajaḥ*—Balāka's son; *ajakaḥ*—of the name Ajaka; *tataḥ*—thereafter; *kuśaḥ*—Kuśa; *kuśasya*—of Kuśa; *api*—then; *kuśāmbuḥ*—Kuśāmbu; *tanayaḥ*—Tanaya; *vasuḥ*—Vasu; *kuśanābhaḥ*—Kuśanābha; *ca*—and; *catvāraḥ*—four (sons); *gādhiḥ*—Gādhi; *āsīt*—there was; *kuśāmbujaḥ*—the son of Kuśāmbu.

TRANSLATION

The son of Jahnu was Puru, the son of Puru was Balāka, the son of Balāka was Ajaka, and the son of Ajaka was Kuśa. Kuśa had four sons, named Kuśāmbu, Tanaya, Vasu and Kuśanābha. The son of Kuśāmbu was Gādhi.

TEXTS 5–6

तस्य सत्यवतीं कन्यामृचीकोऽयाचत द्विजः ।
वरं विसदृशं मत्वा गाधिर्भार्गवमब्रवीत् ॥ ५ ॥
एकतः श्यामकर्णानां हयानां चन्द्रवर्चसाम् ।
सहस्रं दीयतां शुल्कं कन्यायाः कुशिका वयम् ॥ ६ ॥

tasya satyavatīṁ kanyām
ṛcīko 'yācata dvijaḥ
varaṁ visadṛśaṁ matvā
gādhir bhārgavam abravīt

ekataḥ śyāma-karṇānāṁ
hayānāṁ candra-varcasām
sahasraṁ dīyatāṁ śulkaṁ
kanyāyāḥ kuśikā vayam

tasya—of Gādhi; *satyavatīm*—Satyavatī; *kanyām*—the daughter; *ṛcīkaḥ*—the great sage Ṛcīka; *ayācata*—requested; *dvijaḥ*—the *brāhmaṇa; varam*—as her husband; *visadṛśam*—not equal or fit; *matvā*—thinking like that; *gādhiḥ*—King Gādhi; *bhārgavam*—unto Ṛcīka; *abravīt*—replied; *ekataḥ*—by one; *śyāma-karṇānām*—whose ear is black; *hayānām*—horses; *candra-varcasām*—as brilliant as the moonshine; *sahasram*—one thousand; *dīyatām*—please deliver; *śulkam*—as a dowry; *kanyāyāḥ*—to my daughter; *kuśikāḥ*—in the family of Kuśa; *vayam*—we (are).

TRANSLATION

King Gādhi had a daughter named Satyavatī, whom a brāhmaṇa sage named Ṛcīka requested from the King to be his wife. King Gādhi, however, regarded Ṛcīka as an unfit husband for his daughter, and therefore he told the brāhmaṇa, "My dear sir, I belong to the dynasty of Kuśa. Because we are aristocratic kṣatriyas, you have to give some dowry for my daughter. Therefore, bring at least one thousand horses, each as brilliant as moonshine and each having one black ear, whether right or left."

PURPORT

The son of King Gādhi was Viśvāmitra, who was said to be a *brāhmaṇa* and *kṣatriya* combined. Viśvāmitra attained the status of a *brahmarṣi*, as explained later. From the marriage of Satyavatī with Ṛcīka Muni would come a son with the spirit of a *kṣatriya*. King Gādhi demanded that an uncommon request be fulfilled before the *brāhmaṇa* Ṛcīka could marry his daughter.

TEXT 7

इत्युक्तस्तन्मतं ज्ञात्वा गतः स वरुणान्तिकम् ।
आनीय दत्त्वा तानश्वानुपयेमे वराननाम् ॥ ७ ॥

ity uktas tan-mataṁ jñātvā
gataḥ sa varuṇāntikam
ānīya dattvā tān aśvān
upayeme varānanām

iti—thus; *uktaḥ*—having been requested; *tat-matam*—his mind; *jñātvā*—(the sage) could understand; *gataḥ*—went; *saḥ*—he; *varuṇa-antikam*—to the place of Varuṇa; *ānīya*—having brought; *dattvā*—and after delivering; *tān*—those; *aśvān*—horses; *upayeme*—married; *vara-ānanām*—the beautiful daughter of King Gādhi.

TRANSLATION

When King Gādhi made this demand, the great sage Ṛcīka could understand the King's mind. Therefore he went to the demigod Varuṇa and brought from him the one thousand horses that Gādhi had demanded. After delivering these horses, the sage married the King's beautiful daughter.

TEXT 8

स ऋषिः प्रार्थितः पत्न्या श्वश्र्वा चापत्यकाम्यया ।
श्रपयित्वोभयैर्मन्त्रैश्चरुं स्नातुं गतो मुनिः ॥ ८ ॥

sa ṛṣiḥ prārthitaḥ patnyā
śvaśrvā cāpatya-kāmyayā

śrapayitvobhayair mantraiś
caruṁ snātuṁ gato muniḥ

saḥ—he (Ṛcīka); *ṛṣiḥ*—the great saint; *prārthitaḥ*—being requested; *patnyā*—by his wife; *śvaśrvā*—by his mother-in-law; *ca*—also; *apatya-kāmyayā*—desiring a son; *śrapayitvā*—after cooking; *ubhayaiḥ*—both; *mantraiḥ*—by chanting particular *mantras; carum*—a preparation for offering in a sacrifice; *snātum*—to bathe; *gataḥ*—went out; *muniḥ*—the great sage.

TRANSLATION

Thereafter, Ṛcīka Muni's wife and mother-in-law, each desiring a son, requested the Muni to prepare an oblation. Thus Ṛcīka Muni prepared one oblation for his wife with a brāhmaṇa mantra and another for his mother-in-law with a kṣatriya mantra. Then he went out to bathe.

TEXT 9

तावत् सत्यवती मात्रा स्वचरुं याचिता सती ।
श्रेष्ठं मत्वा तयायच्छन्मात्रे मातुरदत् स्वयम् ॥ ९ ॥

tāvat satyavatī mātrā
sva-caruṁ yācitā satī
śreṣṭhaṁ matvā tayāyacchan
mātre mātur adat svayam

tāvat—in the meantime; *satyavatī*—Satyavatī, the wife of Ṛcīka; *mātrā*—by her mother; *sva-carum*—the oblation meant for herself (Satyavatī); *yācitā*—asked to give; *satī*—being; *śreṣṭham*—better; *matvā*—thinking; *tayā*—by her; *ayacchat*—delivered; *mātre*—to her mother; *mātuḥ*—of the mother; *adat*—ate; *svayam*—personally.

TRANSLATION

Meanwhile, because Satyavatī's mother thought that the oblation prepared for her daughter, Ṛcīka's wife, must be better, she asked her daughter for that oblation. Satyavatī therefore gave her own oblation to her mother and ate her mother's oblation herself.

PURPORT

A husband naturally has some affection for his wife. Therefore Satyavatī's mother thought that the oblation prepared for Satyavatī by the sage Ṛcīka must have been better than her own oblation. In Ṛcīka's absence, the mother took the better oblation from Satyavatī and ate it.

TEXT 10

तद् विदित्वा मुनिः प्राह पत्नीं कष्टमकारषीः ।
घोरो दण्डधरः पुत्रो भ्राता ते ब्रह्मवित्तमः ॥१०॥

tad viditvā muniḥ prāha
patnīṁ kaṣṭam akārasīḥ
ghoro daṇḍa-dharaḥ putro
bhrātā te brahma-vittamaḥ

tat—this fact; *viditvā*—having learned; *muniḥ*—the great sage; *prāha*—said; *patnīm*—unto his wife; *kaṣṭam*—very regrettable; *akārasīḥ*—you have done; *ghoraḥ*—fierce; *daṇḍa-dharaḥ*—a great personality who can punish others; *putraḥ*—such a son; *bhrātā*—brother; *te*—your; *brahma-vittamaḥ*—a learned scholar in spiritual science.

TRANSLATION

When the great sage Ṛcīka returned home after bathing and understood what had happened in his absence, he said to his wife, Satyavatī, "You have done a great wrong. Your son will be a fierce kṣatriya, able to punish everyone, and your brother will be a learned scholar in spiritual science."

PURPORT

A *brāhmaṇa* is highly qualified when he can control his senses and mind, when he is a learned scholar in spiritual science and when he is tolerant and forgiving. A *kṣatriya*, however, is highly qualified when he is fierce in giving punishment to wrongdoers. These qualities are stated in *Bhagavad-gītā* (18.42–43). Because Satyavatī, instead of eating her own oblation, had eaten that which was meant for her mother, she would give birth to a son imbued with the *kṣatriya* spirit. This was undesirable. The son of a *brāhmaṇa* is generally expected to become a *brāhmaṇa*, but if such a son becomes fierce like a *kṣatriya*, he is designated according to the description of the four *varṇas* in *Bhagavad-gītā* (*cātur-varṇyaṁ mayā sṛṣṭaṁ guṇa-karma-vibhāgaśaḥ*). If the son of a *brāhmaṇa* does not become like a *brāhmaṇa*, he may be called a *kṣatriya*, *vaiśya* or *śūdra*, according to his qualifications. The basic principle for dividing society is not a person's birth but his qualities and actions.

TEXT 11

प्रसादितः सत्यवत्या मैवं भूरिति भार्गवः ।
अथ तर्हि भवेत् पौत्रो जमदग्निस्ततोऽभवत् ॥११॥

prasāditaḥ satyavatyā
maivaṁ bhūr iti bhārgavaḥ
atha tarhi bhavet pautro
jamadagnis tato 'bhavat

prasāditaḥ—pacified; *satyavatyā*—by Satyavatī; *mā*—not; *evam*—thus; *bhūḥ*—let it be; *iti*—thus; *bhārgavaḥ*—the great sage; *atha*—if your son should not become like that; *tarhi*—then; *bhavet*—should become like that; *pautraḥ*—the grandson; *jamadagniḥ*—Jamadagni; *tataḥ*—thereafter; *abhavat*—was born.

TRANSLATION

Satyavatī, however, pacified Ṛcīka Muni with peaceful words and requested that her son not be like a fierce kṣatriya. Ṛcīka Muni replied, "Then your grandson will be of a kṣatriya spirit." Thus Jamadagni was born as the son of Satyavatī.

PURPORT

The great sage Ṛcīka was very angry, but somehow or other Satyavatī pacified him, and at her request he changed his mind. It is indicated here that the son of Jamadagni would be born as Paraśurāma.

TEXTS 12–13

सा चाभूत्सुमहत्पुण्या कौशिकी लोकपावनी ।
रेणोः सुतां रेणुकां वै जमदग्निरुवाह याम् ॥१२॥
तस्यां वै भार्गवऋषेः सुता वसुमदादयः ।
यवीयाञ्जज्ञ एतेषां राम इत्यभिविश्रुतः ॥१३॥

sā cābhūt sumahat-puṇyā
kauśikī loka-pāvanī
reṇoḥ sutāṁ reṇukāṁ vai
jamadagnir uvāha yām

tasyāṁ vai bhārgava-ṛṣeḥ
sutā vasumad-ādayaḥ
yavīyāñ jajña eteṣāṁ
rāma ity abhiviśrutaḥ

sā—she (Satyavatī); *ca*—also; *abhūt*—became; *sumahat-puṇyā*—very great and sacred; *kauśikī*—the river by the name Kauśikī; *loka-pāvanī*—purifying the whole world; *reṇoḥ*—of Reṇu; *sutām*—the daughter; *reṇukām*—by the name Reṇukā; *vai*—indeed; *jamadagniḥ*—Satyavatī's son, Jamadagni; *uvāha*—married; *yām*—whom; *tasyām*—in the womb of Reṇukā; *vai*—indeed; *bhārgava-ṛṣeḥ*—by the semen of Jamadagni; *sutāḥ*—sons; *vasumat-ādayaḥ*—many, headed by Vasumān; *yavīyān*—the youngest; *jajñe*—was born; *eteṣām*—among them; *rāmaḥ*—Paraśurāma; *iti*—thus; *abhiviśrutaḥ*—was known everywhere.

TRANSLATION

Satyavatī later became the sacred river Kauśikī to purify the entire world, and her son, Jamadagni, married Reṇukā, the daughter of Reṇu. By the semen of Jamadagni, many sons, headed by Vasumān, were born from the womb of Reṇukā. The youngest of them was named Rāma, or Paraśurāma.

TEXT 14

यमाहुर्वासुदेवांशं हैहयानां कुलान्तकम् ।
त्रिःसप्तकृत्वो य इमां चक्रे निःक्षत्रियां महीम् ॥१४॥

yam āhur vāsudevāṁśaṁ
haihayānāṁ kulāntakam
triḥ-sapta-kṛtvo ya imāṁ
cakre niḥkṣatriyāṁ mahīm

yam—whom (Paraśurāma); *āhuḥ*—all the learned scholars say; *vāsudeva-aṁśam*—an incarnation of Vāsudeva, the Supreme Personality of Godhead; *haihayānām*—of the Haihayas; *kula-antakam*—the annihilator of the dynasty; *triḥ-sapta-kṛtvaḥ*—twenty-one times; *yaḥ*—who (Paraśurāma); *imām*—this; *cakre*—made; *niḥkṣatriyām*—devoid of *kṣatriyas; mahīm*—the earth.

TRANSLATION

Learned scholars accept this Paraśurāma as the celebrated incarnation of Vāsudeva who annihilated the dynasty of Kārtavīrya. Paraśurāma killed all the kṣatriyas on earth twenty-one times.

TEXT 15

दृप्तं क्षत्रं भुवो भारमब्रह्मण्यमनीनशत् ।
रजस्तमोवृतमहन् फल्गुन्यपि कृतेऽंहसि ॥१५॥

dṛptaṁ kṣatraṁ bhuvo bhāram
abrahmaṇyam anīnaśat
rajas-tamo-vṛtam ahan
phalguny api kṛte 'ṁhasi

dṛptam—very proud; *kṣatram*—the *kṣatriyas,* the ruling class; *bhuvaḥ*—of the earth; *bhāram*—burden; *abrahmaṇyam*—sinful, not caring for the religious principles enunciated by the *brāhmaṇas; anīnaśat*—drove away or annihilated; *rajaḥ-tamaḥ*—by the qualities of passion and ignorance; *vṛtam*—covered; *ahan*—he killed; *phalguni*—not very great; *api*—although; *kṛte*—had been committed; *aṁhasi*—an offense.

TRANSLATION

When the royal dynasty, being excessively proud because of the material modes of passion and ignorance, became irreligious and

ceased to care for the laws enacted by the brāhmaṇas, Paraśurāma killed them. Although their offense was not very severe, he killed them to lessen the burden of the world.

PURPORT

The *kṣatriyas*, or the ruling class, must govern the world in accordance with the rules and regulations enacted by great *brāhmaṇas* and saintly persons. As soon as the ruling class becomes irresponsible in regard to the religious principles, it becomes a burden on the earth. As stated here, *rajas-tamo-vṛtaṁ, bhāram abrahmaṇyam:* when the ruling class is influenced by the lower modes of nature, namely ignorance and passion, it becomes a burden to the world and must then be annihilated by superior power. We actually see from modern history that monarchies have been abolished by various revolutions, but unfortunately the monarchies have been abolished to establish the supremacy of third-class and fourth-class men. Although monarchies overpowered by the modes of passion and ignorance have been abolished in the world, the inhabitants of the world are still unhappy, for although the qualities of the former monarchs were degraded by taints of ignorance, these monarchs have been replaced by men of the mercantile and worker classes whose qualities are even more degraded. When the government is actually guided by *brāhmaṇas*, or God conscious men, then there can be real happiness for the people. Therefore in previous times, when the ruling class was degraded to the modes of passion and ignorance, the *brāhmaṇas*, headed by such a *kṣatriya*-spirited *brāhmaṇa* as Paraśurāma, killed them twenty-one consecutive times.

In Kali-yuga, as stated in *Śrīmad-Bhāgavatam* (12.2.13), *dasyu-prāyeṣu rājasu:* the ruling class (*rājanya*) will be no better than plunderers (*dasyus*) because the third-class and fourth-class men will monopolize the affairs of the government. Ignoring the religious principles and brahminical rules and regulations, they will certainly try to plunder the riches of the citizens without consideration. As stated elsewhere in *Śrīmad-Bhāgavatam* (12.1.40):

asaṁskṛtāḥ kriyā-hīnā
rajasā tamasāvṛtāḥ

prajās te bhakṣayiṣyanti
mlecchā rājanya-rūpiṇaḥ

Being unpurified, neglecting to discharge human duties properly, and being influenced by the modes of passion (*rajas*) and ignorance (*tamas*), unclean people (*mlecchas*), posing as members of the government (*rājanya-rūpiṇaḥ*), will swallow the citizens (*prājas te bhakṣayiṣyanti*). And in still another place, *Śrīmad-Bhāgavatam* (12.2.7–8) says:

evaṁ prajābhir duṣṭābhir
ākīrṇe kṣiti-maṇḍale
brahma-viṭ-kṣatra-śūdrāṇāṁ
yo balī bhavitā nṛpaḥ

prajā hi lubdhai rājanyair
nirghṛṇair dasyu-dharmabhiḥ
ācchinna-dāra-draviṇā
yāsyanti giri-kānanam

Human society is naturally grouped into four divisions, as stated in *Bhagavad-gītā* (*cātur-varṇyaṁ mayā sṛṣṭaṁ guṇa-karma-vibhāgaśaḥ*). But if this system is neglected and the qualities and divisions of society are not considered, the result will be *brahma-viṭ-kṣatra-śūdrāṇāṁ yo balī bhavitā nṛpaḥ:* the so-called caste system of *brāhmaṇa, kṣatriya, vaiśya* and *śūdra* will be meaningless. As a result, whoever somehow or other becomes powerful will be the king or president, and thus the *prajās*, or citizens, will be so harassed that they will give up hearth and home and will go to the forest (*yāsyanti giri-kānanam*) to escape harassment by government officials who have no mercy and are addicted to the ways of plunderers. Therefore the *prajās*, or the people in general, must take to the Kṛṣṇa consciousness movement, the Hare Kṛṣṇa movement, which is the sound incarnation of the Supreme Personality of Godhead. *Kali-kāle nāma-rūpe kṛṣṇa-avatāra:* Kṛṣṇa, the Supreme Personality of Godhead, has now appeared as an incarnation by His holy name. Therefore, when the *prajās* become Kṛṣṇa conscious, they can then expect a good government and good society, a perfect life, and liberation from the bondage of material existence.

TEXT 16

श्रीराजोवाच

किं तदंहो भगवतो राजन्यैरजितात्मभिः ।
कृतं येन कुलं नष्टं क्षत्रियाणामभीक्ष्णशः ॥१६॥

śrī-rājovāca
kiṁ tad aṁho bhagavato
rājanyair ajitātmabhiḥ
kṛtaṁ yena kulaṁ naṣṭaṁ
kṣatriyāṇām abhīkṣṇaśaḥ

śrī-rājā uvāca—Mahārāja Parīkṣit inquired; *kim*—what; *tat aṁhaḥ*—that offense; *bhagavataḥ*—unto the Supreme Personality of Godhead; *rājanyaiḥ*—by the royal family; *ajita-ātmabhiḥ*—who could not control their senses and thus were degraded; *kṛtam*—which had been done; *yena*—by which; *kulam*—the dynasty; *naṣṭam*—was annihilated; *kṣatriyāṇām*—of the royal family; *abhīkṣṇaśaḥ*—again and again.

TRANSLATION

King Parīkṣit inquired from Śukadeva Gosvāmī: What was the offense that the kṣatriyas who could not control their senses committed before Lord Paraśurāma, the incarnation of the Supreme Personality of Godhead, for which the Lord annihilated the kṣatriya dynasty again and again?

TEXTS 17–19

श्रीबादरायणिरुवाच

हैहयानामधिपतिरर्जुनः क्षत्रियर्षभः ।
दत्तं नारायणांशांशमाराध्य परिकर्मभिः ॥१७॥
बाहून् दशशतं लेभे दुर्धर्षत्वमरातिषु ।
अव्याहतेन्द्रियौजःश्रीतेजोवीर्ययशोबलम् ॥१८॥
योगेश्वरत्वमैश्वर्यं गुणा यत्राणिमादयः ।
चचाराव्याहतगतिर्लोकेषु पवनो यथा ॥१९॥

śrī-bādarāyaṇir uvāca
haihayānām adhipatir
arjunaḥ kṣatriyarṣabhaḥ
dattaṁ nārāyaṇāṁśāṁśam
ārādhya parikarmabhiḥ

bāhūn daśa-śataṁ lebhe
durdharṣatvam arātiṣu
avyāhatendriyaujaḥ śrī-
tejo-vīrya-yaśo-balam

yogeśvaratvam aiśvaryaṁ
guṇā yatrāṇimādayaḥ
cacārāvyāhata-gatir
lokeṣu pavano yathā

śrī-bādarāyaṇiḥ uvāca—Śrī Śukadeva Gosvāmī replied; *haihayānām adhipatiḥ*—the King of the Haihayas; *arjunaḥ*—by the name Kārtavīryārjuna; *kṣatriya-ṛṣabhaḥ*—the best of the *kṣatriyas; dattam*—unto Dattātreya; *nārāyaṇa-aṁśa-aṁśam*—the plenary portion of the plenary portion of Nārāyaṇa; *ārādhya*—after worshiping; *parikarmabhiḥ*—by worship according to the regulative principles; *bāhūn*—arms; *daśa-śatam*—one thousand (ten times one hundred); *lebhe*—achieved; *durdharṣatvam*—the quality of being very difficult to conquer; *arātiṣu*—in the midst of enemies; *avyāhata*—undefeatable; *indriya-ojaḥ*—strength of the senses; *śrī*—beauty; *tejaḥ*—influence; *vīrya*—power; *yaśaḥ*—fame; *balam*—bodily strength; *yoga-īśvaratvam*—controlling power gained by the practice of mystic *yoga; aiśvaryam*—opulence; *guṇāḥ*—qualities; *yatra*—wherein; *aṇimā-ādayaḥ*—eight kinds of yogic perfection (*aṇimā, laghimā,* etc.); *cacāra*—he went; *avyāhata-gatiḥ*—whose progress was indefatigable; *lokeṣu*—all over the world or universe; *pavanaḥ*—the wind; *yathā*—like.

TRANSLATION

Śukadeva Gosvāmī said: The best of the kṣatriyas, Kārtavīryārjuna, the King of the Haihayas, received one thousand arms by worshiping Dattātreya, the plenary expansion of the Supreme

Personality of Godhead, Nārāyaṇa. He also became undefeatable by enemies and received unobstructed sensory power, beauty, influence, strength, fame and the mystic power by which to achieve all the perfections of yoga, such as aṇimā and laghimā. Thus having become fully opulent, he roamed all over the universe without opposition, just like the wind.

TEXT 20

स्त्रीरत्नैरावृतः क्रीडन् रेवाम्भसि मदोत्कटः ।
वैजयन्तीं स्रजं बिभ्रद् रुरोध सरितं भुजैः ॥२०॥

strī-ratnair āvṛtaḥ krīḍan
revāmbhasi madotkaṭaḥ
vaijayantīṁ srajaṁ bibhrad
rurodha saritaṁ bhujaiḥ

strī-ratnaiḥ—by beautiful women; *āvṛtaḥ*—surrounded; *krīḍan*—enjoying; *revā-ambhasi*—in the water of the River Revā, or Narmadā; *mada-utkaṭaḥ*—too puffed up because of opulence; *vaijayantīm srajam*—the garland of victory; *bibhrat*—being decorated with; *rurodha*—stopped the flow; *saritam*—of the river; *bhujaiḥ*—with his arms.

TRANSLATION

Once while enjoying in the water of the River Narmadā, the puffed-up Kārtavīryārjuna, surrounded by beautiful women and garlanded with a garland of victory, stopped the flow of the water with his arms.

TEXT 21

विप्लावितं स्वशिबिरं प्रतिस्रोतःसरिज्जलैः ।
नामृष्यत् तस्य तद् वीर्यं वीरमानी दशाननः ॥२१॥

viplāvitaṁ sva-śibiraṁ
pratisrotaḥ-sarij-jalaiḥ
nāmṛṣyat tasya tad vīryaṁ
vīramānī daśānanaḥ

viplāvitam—having been inundated; *sva-śibiram*—his own camp; *pratisrotaḥ*—which was flowing in the opposite direction; *sarit-jalaiḥ*—by the water of the river; *na*—not; *amṛṣyat*—could tolerate; *tasya*—of Kārtavīryārjuna; *tat vīryam*—that influence; *vīramānī*—considering himself very heroic; *daśa-ānanaḥ*—the ten-headed Rāvaṇa.

TRANSLATION

Because Kārtavīryārjuna made the water flow in the opposite direction, the camp of Rāvaṇa, which was set up on the bank of the Narmadā near the city of Māhiṣmatī, was inundated. This was unbearable to the ten-headed Rāvaṇa, who considered himself a great hero and could not tolerate Kārtavīryārjuna's power.

PURPORT

Rāvaṇa was out touring to gain victory over all other countries (*dig-vijaya*), and he had camped on the bank of the Narmadā River near the city of Māhiṣmatī.

TEXT 22

गृहीतो लीलया स्त्रीणां समक्षं कृतकिल्बिषः ।
माहिष्मत्यां संनिरुद्धो मुक्तो येन कपिर्यथा ॥२२॥

gṛhīto līlayā strīṇāṁ
samakṣaṁ kṛta-kilbiṣaḥ
māhiṣmatyāṁ sanniruddho
mukto yena kapir yathā

gṛhītaḥ—was arrested by force; *līlayā*—very easily; *strīṇām*—of the women; *samakṣam*—in the presence; *kṛta-kilbiṣaḥ*—thus becoming an offender; *māhiṣmatyām*—in the city known as Māhiṣmatī; *sanniruddhaḥ*—was arrested; *muktaḥ*—released; *yena*—by whom (Kārtavīryārjuna); *kapiḥ yathā*—exactly as done to a monkey.

TRANSLATION

When Rāvaṇa attempted to insult Kārtavīryārjuna in the presence of the women and thus offended him, Kārtavīryārjuna easily

arrested Rāvaṇa and put him in custody in the city of Māhiṣmatī, just as one captures a monkey, and then released him neglectfully.

TEXT 23

स एकदा तु मृगयां विचरन् विजने वने ।
यदृच्छयाश्रमपदं जमदग्नेरुपाविशत् ॥२३॥

sa ekadā tu mṛgayāṁ
vicaran vijane vane
yadṛcchayāśrama-padaṁ
jamadagner upāviśat

saḥ—he, Kārtavīryārjuna; *ekadā*—once upon a time; *tu*—but; *mṛgayām*—while hunting; *vicaran*—wandering; *vijane*—solitary; *vane*—in a forest; *yadṛcchayā*—without any program; *āśrama-padam*—the residential place; *jamadagneḥ*—of Jamadagni Muni; *upāviśat*—he entered.

TRANSLATION

Once while Kārtavīryārjuna was wandering unengaged in a solitary forest and hunting, he approached the residence of Jamadagni.

PURPORT

Kārtavīryārjuna had no business going to the residence of Jamadagni, but because he was puffed-up by his extraordinary power, he went there and offended Paraśurāma. This was the prelude to his being killed by Paraśurāma for his offensive act.

TEXT 24

तस्मै स नरदेवाय मुनिरर्हणमाहरत् ।
ससैन्यामात्यवाहाय हविष्मत्या तपोधनः ॥२४॥

tasmai sa naradevāya
munir arhaṇam āharat

sasainyāmātya-vāhāya
haviṣmatyā tapo-dhanaḥ

tasmai—unto him; *saḥ*—he (Jamadagni); *naradevāya*—unto King Kārtavīryārjuna; *muniḥ*—the great sage; *arhaṇam*—paraphernalia for worship; *āharat*—offered; *sa-sainya*—with his soldiers; *amātya*—his ministers; *vāhāya*—and the chariots, the elephants, the horses or the men who carried the palanquins; *haviṣmatyā*—because of possessing a *kāmadhenu*, a cow that could supply everything; *tapaḥ-dhanaḥ*—the great sage, whose only power was his austerity, or who was engaged in austerity.

TRANSLATION

The sage Jamadagni, who was engaged in great austerities in the forest, received the King very well, along with the King's soldiers, ministers and carriers. He supplied all the necessities to worship these guests, for he possessed a kāmadhenu cow that was able to supply everything.

PURPORT

The *Brahma-saṁhitā* informs us that the spiritual world, and especially the planet Goloka Vṛndāvana, where Kṛṣṇa lives, is full of *surabhi* cows (*surabhīr abhipālayantam*). The *surabhi* cow is also called *kāmadhenu.* Although Jamadagni possessed only one *kāmadhenu*, he was able to get from it everything desirable. Thus he was able to receive the King, along with the King's great number of followers, ministers, soldiers, animals and palanquin carriers. When we speak of a king, we understand that he is accompanied by many followers. Jamadagni was able to receive all the King's followers properly and feed them sumptuously with food prepared in ghee. The King was astonished at how opulent Jamadagni was because of possessing only one cow, and therefore he became envious of the great sage. This was the beginning of his offense. Paraśurāma, the incarnation of the Supreme Personality of Godhead, killed Kārtavīryārjuna because Kārtavīryārjuna was too proud. One may possess unusual opulence in this material world, but if one becomes puffed up and acts whimsically he will be punished by the Supreme Personality of Godhead. This is the lesson to learn from this history, in which Paraśurāma became angry at Kārtavīryārjuna and killed him and rid the entire world of *kṣatriyas* twenty-one times.

TEXT 25

स वैरत्नं तु तद् दृष्ट्वा आत्मैश्वर्यातिशायनम् ।
तन्नाद्रियताग्निहोत्र्यां साभिलाषः सहैहयः ॥२५॥

sa vai ratnaṁ tu tad dṛṣṭvā
ātmaiśvaryātiśāyanam
tan nādriyatāgnihotryāṁ
sābhilāṣaḥ sahaihayaḥ

saḥ—he (Kārtavīryārjuna); *vai*—indeed; *ratnam*—a great source of wealth; *tu*—indeed; *tat*—the *kāmadhenu* in the possession of Jamadagni; *dṛṣṭvā*—by observing; *ātma-aiśvarya*—his own personal opulence; *ati-śāyanam*—which was exceeding; *tat*—that; *na*—not; *ādriyata*—appreciated very much; *agnihotryām*—in that cow, which was useful for executing the *agnihotra* sacrifice; *sa-abhilāṣaḥ*—became desirous; *sa-haihayaḥ*—with his own men, the Haihayas.

TRANSLATION

Kārtavīryārjuna thought that Jamadagni was more powerful and wealthy than himself because of possessing a jewel in the form of the kāmadhenu. Therefore he and his own men, the Haihayas, were not very much appreciative of Jamadagni's reception. On the contrary, they wanted to possess that kāmadhenu, which was useful for the execution of the agnihotra sacrifice.

PURPORT

Jamadagni was more powerful than Kārtavīryārjuna because of performing the *agnihotra-yajña* with clarified butter received from the *kāmadhenu.* Not everyone can be expected to possess such a cow. Nonetheless, an ordinary man may possess an ordinary cow, give protection to this animal, take sufficient milk from it, and engage the milk to produce butter and clarified ghee, especially for performing the *agnihotra-yajña.* This is possible for everyone. Thus we find that in *Bhagavad-gītā* Lord

Kṛṣṇa advises *go-rakṣya*, the protection of cows. This is essential because if cows are cared for properly they will surely supply sufficient milk. We have practical experience in America that in our various ISKCON farms we are giving proper protection to the cows and receiving more than enough milk. In other farms the cows do not deliver as much milk as in our farms; because our cows know very well that we are not going to kill them, they are happy, and they give ample milk. Therefore this instruction given by Lord Kṛṣṇa—*go-rakṣya*—is extremely meaningful. The whole world must learn from Kṛṣṇa how to live happily without scarcity simply by producing food grains (*annād bhavanti bhūtāni*) and giving protection to the cows (*go-rakṣya*). *Kṛṣi-gorakṣya-vāṇijyaṁ vaiśya-karma svabhāvajam.* Those who belong to the third level of human society, namely the mercantile people, must keep land for producing food grains and giving protection to cows. This is the injunction of *Bhagavad-gītā*. In the matter of protecting the cows, the meat-eaters will protest, but in answer to them we may say that since Kṛṣṇa gives stress to cow protection, those who are inclined to eat meat may eat the flesh of unimportant animals like hogs, dogs, goats and sheep, but they should not touch the life of the cows, for this is destructive to the spiritual advancement of human society.

TEXT 26

हविर्धानीमृषेर्दर्पान्नरान् हर्तुमचोदयत् ।
ते च माहिष्मतीं निन्युः सवत्सां क्रन्दतीं बलात् ॥ २६ ॥

havirdhānīm ṛṣer darpān
narān hartum acodayat
te ca māhiṣmatīṁ ninyuḥ
sa-vatsāṁ krandatīṁ balāt

haviḥ-dhānīm—the *kāmadhenu; ṛṣeḥ*—of the great sage Jamadagni; *darpāt*—because of his being puffed up with material power; *narān*—all his men (soldiers); *hartum*—to steal or take away; *acodayat*—encouraged; *te*—the men of Kārtavīryārjuna; *ca*—also; *māhiṣmatīm*—to the capital of Kārtavīryārjuna; *ninyuḥ*—brought; *sa-vatsām*—with the calf; *krandatīm*—crying; *balāt*—because of being taken away by force.

TRANSLATION

Being puffed up by material power, Kārtavīryārjuna encouraged his men to steal Jamadagni's kāmadhenu. Thus the men forcibly took away the crying kāmadhenu, along with her calf, to Māhiṣmatī, Kārtavīryārjuna's capital.

PURPORT

The word *havirdhānīm* is significant in this verse. *Havirdhānīm* refers to a cow required for supplying *havis*, or ghee, for the performance of ritualistic ceremonies in sacrifices. In human life, one should be trained to perform *yajñas*. As we are informed in *Bhagavad-gītā* (3.9), *yajñārthāt karmaṇo 'nyatra loko 'yaṁ karma-bandhanaḥ:* if we do not perform *yajña*, we shall simply work very hard for sense gratification like dogs and hogs. This is not civilization. A human being should be trained to perform *yajña. Yajñād bhavati parjanyaḥ*. If *yajñas* are regularly performed, there will be proper rain from the sky, and when there is regular rainfall, the land will be fertile and suitable for producing all the necessities of life. *Yajña*, therefore, is essential. For performing *yajña*, clarified butter is essential, and for clarified butter, cow protection is essential. Therefore, if we neglect the Vedic way of civilization, we shall certainly suffer. So-called scholars and philosophers do not know the secret of success in life, and therefore they suffer in the hands of *prakṛti*, nature (*prakṛteḥ kriyamāṇāni guṇaiḥ karmāṇi sarvaśaḥ*). Nonetheless, although they are forced to suffer, they think they are advancing in civilization (*ahaṅkāra-vimūḍhātmā kartāham iti manyate*). The Kṛṣṇa consciousness movement is therefore meant to revive a mode of civilization in which everyone will be happy. This is the motive of our Kṛṣṇa consciousness movement. *Yajñe sukhena bhavantu.*

TEXT 27

अथ राजनि निर्याते राम आश्रम आगतः ।
श्रुत्वा तत् तस्य दौरात्म्यं चुक्रोधाहिरिवाहतः ॥२७॥

atha rājani niryāte
rāma āśrama āgataḥ
śrutvā tat tasya daurātmyaṁ
cukrodhāhir ivāhataḥ

atha—thereafter; *rājani*—when the King; *niryāte*—had gone away; *rāmaḥ*—Paraśurāma, the youngest son of Jamadagni; *āśrame*—in the cottage; *āgataḥ*—returned; *śrutvā*—when he heard; *tat*—that; *tasya*—of Kārtavīryārjuna; *daurātmyam*—nefarious act; *cukrodha*—became extremely angry; *ahiḥ*—a snake; *iva*—like; *āhataḥ*—trampled or injured.

TRANSLATION

Thereafter, Kārtavīryārjuna having left with the kāmadhenu, Paraśurāma returned to the āśrama. When Paraśurāma, the youngest son of Jamadagni, heard about Kārtavīryārjuna's nefarious deed, he became as angry as a trampled snake.

TEXT 28

घोरमादाय परशुं सतूणं वर्म कार्मुकम् ।
अन्वधावत दुर्मर्षो मृगेन्द्र इव यूथपम् ॥२८॥

ghoram ādāya paraśuṁ
satūṇaṁ varma kārmukam
anvadhāvata durmarṣo
mṛgendra iva yūthapam

ghoram—extremely fierce; *ādāya*—taking in hand; *paraśum*—a chopper; *sa-tūṇam*—along with a quiver; *varma*—a shield; *kārmukam*—a bow; *anvadhāvata*—followed; *durmarṣaḥ*—Lord Paraśurāma, being exceedingly angry; *mṛgendraḥ*—a lion; *iva*—like; *yūthapam*—(goes to attack) an elephant.

TRANSLATION

Taking up his fierce chopper, his shield, his bow and a quiver of arrows, Lord Paraśurāma, exceedingly angry, chased Kārtavīryārjuna just as a lion chases an elephant.

TEXT 29

तमापतन्तं भृगुवर्यमोजसा
धनुर्धरं बाणपरश्वधायुधम् ।

ऐणेयचर्माम्बरमर्कधामभि-
र्युतं जटाभिर्ददृशे पुरीं विशन् ॥२९॥

tam āpatantaṁ bhṛgu-varyam ojasā
dhanur-dharaṁ bāṇa-paraśvadhāyudham
aiṇeya-carmāmbaram arka-dhāmabhir
yutaṁ jaṭābhir dadṛśe purīṁ viśan

tam—that Lord Paraśurāma; *āpatantam*—coming after him; *bhṛgu-varyam*—the best of the Bhṛgu dynasty, Lord Paraśurāma; *ojasā*—very fiercely; *dhanuḥ-dharam*—carrying a bow; *bāṇa*—arrows; *paraśvadha*—chopper; *āyudham*—having all these weapons; *aiṇeya-carma*—blackish deerskin; *ambaram*—the covering of his body; *arka-dhāmabhiḥ*—appearing like the sunshine; *yutam jaṭābhiḥ*—with locks of hair; *dadṛśe*—he saw; *purīm*—into the capital; *viśan*—entering.

TRANSLATION

As King Kārtavīryārjuna entered his capital, Māhiṣmatī Purī, he saw Lord Paraśurāma, the best of the Bhṛgu dynasty, coming after him, holding a chopper, shield, bow and arrows. Lord Paraśurāma was covered with a black deerskin, and his matted locks of hair appeared like the sunshine.

TEXT 30

अचोदयद्धस्तिरथाश्वपत्तिभि-
र्गदासिबाणर्ष्टिशतघ्निशक्तिभिः ।
अक्षौहिणीः सप्तदशातिभीषणा-
स्ता राम एको भगवानसूदयत् ॥३०॥

acodayad dhasti-rathāśva-pattibhir
gadāsi-bāṇarṣṭi-śataghni-śaktibhiḥ
akṣauhiṇīḥ sapta-daśātibhīṣaṇās
tā rāma eko bhagavān asūdayat

acodayat—he sent for fighting; *hasti*—with elephants; *ratha*—with chariots; *aśva*—with horses; *pattibhiḥ*—and with infantry; *gadā*—with clubs; *asi*—with swords; *bāṇa*—with arrows; *ṛṣṭi*—with the weapons called *ṛṣṭis; śataghni*—with weapons called *śataghnis; śaktibhiḥ*—with weapons called *śaktis; akṣauhiṇīḥ*—whole groups of *akṣauhiṇīs; sapta-daśa*—seventeen; *ati-bhīṣaṇāḥ*—very fierce; *tāḥ*—all of them; *rāmaḥ*—Lord Paraśurāma; *ekaḥ*—alone; *bhagavān*—the Supreme Personality of Godhead; *asūdayat*—killed.

TRANSLATION

Upon seeing Paraśurāma, Kārtavīryārjuna immediately feared him and sent many elephants, chariots, horses and infantry soldiers equipped with clubs, swords, arrows, ṛṣṭis, śataghnis, śaktis, and many similar weapons to fight against him. Kārtavīryārjuna sent seventeen full akṣauhiṇīs of soldiers to check Paraśurāma. But Lord Paraśurāma alone killed all of them.

PURPORT

The word *akṣauhiṇī* refers to a military phalanx consisting of 21,870 chariots and elephants, 109,350 infantry soldiers and 65,610 horses. An exact description is given in the *Mahābhārata, Ādi Parva,* Second Chapter, as follows:

eko ratho gajaś caikaḥ
narāḥ pañca padātayaḥ
trayaś ca turagās taj-jñaiḥ
pattir ity abhidhīyate

pattiṁ tu triguṇām etāṁ
viduḥ senāmukhaṁ budhāḥ
trīṇi senāmukhāny eko
gulma ity adhidhīyate

trayo gulmā gaṇo nāma
vāhinī tu gaṇās trayaḥ
śrutās tisras tu vāhinyaḥ
pṛtaneti vicakṣaṇaiḥ

camūs tu pṛtanās tisraś
caṁvas tisras tv anīkinī
anīkinīṁ daśa-guṇām
āhur akṣauhiṇīṁ budhāḥ

akṣauhiṇyas tu saṅkhyātā
rathānāṁ dvija-sattamāḥ
saṅkhyā-gaṇita-tattvajñaiḥ
sahasrāṇy eka-viṁśati

śatāny upari cāṣṭau ca
bhūyas tathā ca saptatiḥ
gajānāṁ tu parīmāṇaṁ
tāvad evātra nirdiśet

jñeyaṁ śata-sahasraṁ tu
sahasrāṇi tathā nava
narāṇām adhi pañcāśac
chatāni trīṇi cānaghāḥ

pañca-ṣaṣṭi-sahasrāṇi
tathāśvānāṁ śatāni ca
daśottarāṇi ṣaṭ cāhur
yathāvad abhisaṅkhyayā
etām akṣauhiṇīṁ prāhuḥ
saṅkhyā-tattva-vido janāḥ

"One chariot, one elephant, five infantry soldiers and three horses are called a *patti* by those who are learned in the science. The wise also know that a *senāmukha* is three times what a *patti* is. Three *senāmukhas* are known as one *gulma*, three *gulmas* are called a *gaṇa*, and three *gaṇas* are called a *vāhinī*. Three *vāhinīs* have been referred to by the learned as a *pṛtanā*, three *pṛtanās* equal one *camū*, and three *camūs* equal one *anīkinī*. The wise refer to ten *anīkinīs* as one *akṣauhiṇī*. The chariots of an *akṣauhiṇī* have been calculated at 21,870 by those who know the science of such calculations, O best of the twice-born, and the number of elephants is the same. The number of infantry soldiers is 109,350, and the number of horses is 65,610. This is called an *akṣauhiṇī.*"

TEXT 31

यतो यतोऽसौ प्रहरत्परश्वधो
मनोऽनिलौजाः परचक्रसूदनः ।
ततस्ततश्छिन्नभुजोरुकन्धरा
निपेतुरुर्व्यां हतसूतवाहनाः ॥३१॥

yato yato 'sau praharat-paraśvadho
mano-'nilaujāḥ para-cakra-sūdanaḥ
tatas tataś chinna-bhujoru-kandharā
nipetur urvyāṁ hata-sūta-vāhanāḥ

yataḥ—wherever; *yataḥ*—wherever; *asau*—Lord Paraśurāma; *praharat*—slashing; *paraśvadhaḥ*—being expert in using his weapon, the *paraśu,* or chopper; *manaḥ*—like the mind; *anila*—like the wind; *ojāḥ*—being forceful; *para-cakra*—of the enemies' military strength; *sūdanaḥ*—killer; *tataḥ*—there; *tataḥ*—and there; *chinna*—scattered and cut off; *bhuja*—arms; *ūru*—legs; *kandharāḥ*—shoulders; *nipetuḥ*—fell down; *urvyām*—on the ground; *hata*—killed; *sūta*—chariot drivers; *vāhanāḥ*—carrier horses and elephants.

TRANSLATION

Lord Paraśurāma, being expert in killing the military strength of the enemy, worked with the speed of the mind and the wind, slicing his enemies with his chopper [paraśu]. Wherever he went, the enemies fell, their legs, arms and shoulders being severed, their chariot drivers killed, and their carriers, the elephants and horses all annihilated.

PURPORT

In the beginning, when the army of the enemy was full of fighting soldiers, elephants and horses, Lord Paraśurāma proceeded into their midst at the speed of mind to kill them. When somewhat tired, he slowed down to the speed of wind and continued to kill the enemies vigorously. The speed of mind is greater than the speed of the wind.

TEXT 32

दृष्ट्वा स्वसैन्यं रुधिरौघकर्दमे
रणाजिरे रामकुठारसायकैः ।
विवृक्णवर्मध्वजचापविग्रहं
निपातितं हैहय आपतद् रुषा ॥३२॥

dṛṣṭvā sva-sainyaṁ rudhiraugha-kardame
raṇājire rāma-kuṭhāra-sāyakaiḥ
vivṛkṇa-varma-dhvaja-cāpa-vigrahaṁ
nipātitaṁ haihaya āpatad ruṣā

dṛṣṭvā—by seeing; *sva-sainyam*—his own soldiers; *rudhira-ogha-kardame*—which had become muddy due to the flow of blood; *raṇa-ajire*—on the battlefield; *rāma-kuṭhāra*—by the axe of Lord Paraśurāma; *sāyakaiḥ*—and by the arrows; *vivṛkṇa*—scattered; *varma*—the shields; *dhvaja*—the flags; *cāpa*—bows; *vigraham*—the bodies; *nipātitam*—fallen; *haihayaḥ*—Kārtavīryārjuna; *āpatat*—forcefully came there; *ruṣā*—being very angry.

TRANSLATION

By manipulating his axe and arrows, Lord Paraśurāma cut to pieces the shields, flags, bows and bodies of Kārtavīryārjuna's soldiers, who fell on the battlefield, muddying the ground with their blood. Seeing these reverses, Kārtavīryārjuna, infuriated, rushed to the battlefield.

TEXT 33

अथार्जुनः पञ्चशतेषु बाहुभि-
र्धनुःषु बाणान् युगपत् स सन्दधे ।
रामाय रामोऽस्त्रभृतां समग्रणी-
स्तान्येकधन्वेषुभिराच्छिनत् समम् ॥३३॥

athārjunaḥ pañca-śateṣu bāhubhir
dhanuḥṣu bāṇān yugapat sa sandadhe
rāmāya rāmo 'stra-bhṛtāṁ samagraṇīs
tāny eka-dhanveṣubhir ācchinat samam

atha—thereafter; *arjunaḥ*—Kārtavīryārjuna; *pañca-śateṣu*—five hundred; *bāhubhiḥ*—with his arms; *dhanuḥṣu*—on the bows; *bāṇān*—arrows; *yugapat*—simultaneously; *saḥ*—he; *sandadhe*—fixed; *rāmāya*—just to kill Lord Paraśurāma; *rāmaḥ*—Lord Paraśurāma; *astra-bhṛtām*—of all the soldiers who could use weapons; *samagraṇīḥ*—the very best; *tāni*—all the bows of Kārtavīryārjuna; *eka-dhanvā*—possessing one bow; *iṣubhiḥ*—the arrows; *ācchinat*—cut to pieces; *samam*—with.

TRANSLATION

Then Kārtavīryārjuna, with his one thousand arms, simultaneously fixed arrows on five hundred bows to kill Lord Paraśurāma. But Lord Paraśurāma, the best of fighters, released enough arrows with only one bow to cut to pieces immediately all the arrows and bows in the hands of Kārtavīryārjuna.

TEXT 34

पुनः स्वहस्तैरचलान् मृधेऽङ्घ्रिपा-
नुत्क्षिप्य वेगादभिधावतो युधि ।
भुजान् कुठारेण कठोरनेमिना
चिच्छेद रामः प्रसभं त्वहेरिव ॥३४॥

punaḥ sva-hastair acalān mṛdhe 'ṅghripān
utkṣipya vegād abhidhāvato yudhi
bhujān kuṭhāreṇa kaṭhora-neminā
ciccheda rāmaḥ prasabhaṁ tv aher iva

punaḥ—again; *sva-hastaiḥ*—by his own hands; *acalān*—hills; *mṛdhe*—in the battlefield; *aṅghripān*—trees; *utkṣipya*—after uprooting; *vegāt*—with great force; *abhidhāvataḥ*—of he who was running very forcefully; *yudhi*—in the battlefield; *bhujān*—all the arms; *kuṭhāreṇa*—by his axe; *kaṭhora-neminā*—which was very sharp; *ciccheda*—cut to pieces; *rāmaḥ*—Lord Paraśurāma; *prasabham*—with great force; *tu*—but; *ahaḥ iva*—just like the hoods of a serpent.

TRANSLATION

When his arrows were cut to pieces, Kārtavīryārjuna uprooted many trees and hills with his own hands and again rushed strongly toward Lord Paraśurāma to kill him. But Paraśurāma then used his axe with great force to cut off Kārtavīryārjuna's arms, just as one might lop off the hoods of a serpent.

TEXTS 35–36

कृत्तबाहोः शिरस्तस्य गिरेः शृङ्गमिवाहरत् ।
हते पितरि तत्पुत्रा अयुतं दुद्रुवुर्भयात् ॥३५॥
अग्निहोत्रीमुपावर्त्य सवत्सां परवीरहा ।
समुपेत्याश्रमं पित्रे परिक्लिष्टां समर्पयत् ॥३६॥

kṛtta-bāhoḥ śiras tasya
gireḥ śṛṅgam ivāharat
hate pitari tat-putrā
ayutaṁ dudruvur bhayāt

agnihotrīm upāvartya
savatsāṁ para-vīra-hā
samupetyāśramaṁ pitre
parikliṣṭāṁ samarpayat

kṛtta-bāhoḥ—of Kārtavīryārjuna, whose arms were cut off; *śiraḥ*—the head; *tasya*—of him (Kārtavīryārjuna); *gireḥ*—of a mountain; *śṛṅgam*—the peak; *iva*—like; *āharat*—(Paraśurāma) cut from his body; *hate pitari*—when their father was killed; *tat-putrāḥ*—his sons; *ayutam*—ten thousand; *dudruvuḥ*—fled; *bhayāt*—out of fear; *agnihotrīm*—the *kāmadhenu; upāvartya*—bringing near; *sa-vatsām*—with her calf; *para-vīra-hā*—Paraśurāma, who could kill the heroes of the enemies; *samupetya*—after returning; *āśramam*—to the residence of his father; *pitre*—unto his father; *parikliṣṭām*—which had undergone extreme suffering; *samarpayat*—delivered.

TRANSLATION

Thereafter, Paraśurāma cut off like a mountain peak the head of Kārtavīryārjuna, who had already lost his arms. When Kārtavīryārjuna's ten thousand sons saw their father killed, they all fled in fear. Then Paraśurāma, having killed the enemy, released the kāmadhenu, which had undergone great suffering, and brought it back with its calf to his residence, where he gave it to his father, Jamadagni.

TEXT 37

स्वकर्म तत्कृतं रामः पित्रे भ्रातृभ्य एव च ।
वर्णयामास तच्छ्रुत्वा जमदग्निरभाषत ॥३७॥

sva-karma tat kṛtaṁ rāmaḥ
pitre bhrātṛbhya eva ca
varṇayām āsa tac chrutvā
jamadagnir abhāṣata

sva-karma—his own activities; *tat*—all those deeds; *kṛtam*—which had been performed; *rāmaḥ*—Paraśurāma; *pitre*—unto his father; *bhrātṛbhyaḥ*—unto his brothers; *eva ca*—as well as; *varṇayām āsa*—described; *tat*—that; *śrutvā*—after hearing; *jamadagniḥ*—the father of Paraśurāma; *abhāṣata*—said as follows.

TRANSLATION

Paraśurāma described to his father and brothers his activities in killing Kārtavīryārjuna. Upon hearing of these deeds, Jamadagni spoke to his son as follows.

TEXT 38

राम राम महाबाहो भवान् पापमकारषीत् ।
अवधीन्नरदेवं यत् सर्वदेवमयं वृथा ॥३८॥

rāma rāma mahābāho
bhavān pāpam akāraṣīt
avadhīn naradevaṁ yat
sarva-devamayaṁ vṛthā

rāma rāma—my dear son Paraśurāma; *mahābāho*—O great hero; *bhavān*—you; *pāpam*—sinful activities; *akāraṣīt*—have executed; *avadhīt*—have killed; *naradevam*—the king; *yat*—who is; *sarva-deva-mayam*—the embodiment of all the demigods; *vṛthā*—unnecessarily.

TRANSLATION

O great hero, my dear son Paraśurāma, you have unnecessarily killed the king, who is supposed to be the embodiment of all the demigods. Thus you have committed a sin.

TEXT 39

वयं हि ब्राह्मणास्तात क्षमयार्हणतां गताः ।
यया लोकगुरुर्देवः पारमेष्ठ्यमगात् पदम् ॥३९॥

vayaṁ hi brāhmaṇās tāta
kṣamayārhaṇatāṁ gatāḥ
yayā loka-gurur devaḥ
pārameṣṭhyam agāt padam

vayam—we; *hi*—indeed; *brāhmaṇāḥ*—are qualified *brāhmaṇas; tāta*—O my dear son; *kṣamayā*—with the quality of forgiveness; *arhaṇatām*—the position of being worshiped; *gatāḥ*—we have achieved; *yayā*—by this qualification; *loka-guruḥ*—the spiritual master of this universe; *devaḥ*—Lord Brahmā; *pārameṣṭhyam*—the supreme person within this universe; *agāt*—achieved; *padam*—the position.

TRANSLATION

My dear son, we are all brāhmaṇas and have become worshipable for the people in general because of our quality of forgiveness. It is because of this quality that Lord Brahmā, the supreme spiritual master of this universe, has achieved his post.

TEXT 40

क्षमया रोचते लक्ष्मीर्ब्राह्मी सौरी यथा प्रभा ।
क्षमिणामाशु भगवांस्तुष्यते हरिरीश्वरः ॥४०॥

kṣamayā rocate lakṣmīr
brāhmī saurī yathā prabhā
kṣamiṇām āśu bhagavāṁs
tuṣyate harir īśvaraḥ

kṣamayā—simply by forgiving; *rocate*—becomes pleasing; *lakṣmīḥ*—the goddess of fortune; *brāhmī*—in connection with brahminical qualifications; *saurī*—the sun-god; *yathā*—as; *prabhā*—the sunshine; *kṣamiṇām*—unto the *brāhmaṇas*, who are so forgiving; *āśu*—very soon; *bhagavān*—the Supreme Personality of Godhead; *tuṣyate*—becomes pleased; *hariḥ*—the Lord; *īśvaraḥ*—the supreme controller.

TRANSLATION

The duty of a brāhmaṇa is to culture the quality of forgiveness, which is illuminating like the sun. The Supreme Personality of Godhead, Hari, is pleased with those who are forgiving.

PURPORT

Different personalities become beautiful by possessing different qualities. Cāṇakya Paṇḍita says that the cuckoo bird, although very black, is beautiful because of its sweet voice. Similarly, a woman becomes beautiful by her chastity and faithfulness to her husband, and an ugly person becomes beautiful when he becomes a learned scholar. In the same way, *brāhmaṇas, kṣatriyas, vaiśyas* and *śūdras* become beautiful by their qualities. *Brāhmaṇas* are beautiful when they are forgiving, *kṣatriyas* when they are heroic and never retreat from fighting, *vaiśyas* when they enrich cultural activities and protect cows, and *śūdras* when they are faithful in the discharge of duties pleasing to their masters. Thus everyone becomes beautiful by his special qualities. And the special quality of the *brāhmaṇa*, as described here, is forgiveness.

TEXT 41

राज्ञो मूर्धाभिषिक्तस्य वधो ब्रह्मवधाद् गुरुः ।
तीर्थसंसेवया चांहो जह्यङ्गाच्युतचेतनः ॥४१॥

rājño mūrdhābhiṣiktasya
vadho brahma-vadhād guruḥ
tīrtha-saṁsevayā cāṁho
jahy aṅgācyuta-cetanaḥ

rājñaḥ—of the king; *mūrdha-abhiṣiktasya*—who is noted as the emperor; *vadhaḥ*—the killing; *brahma-vadhāt*—than killing a *brāhmaṇa; guruḥ*—more severe; *tīrtha-saṁsevayā*—by worshiping the holy places; *ca*—also; *aṁhaḥ*—the sinful act; *jahi*—wash out; *aṅga*—O my dear son; *acyuta-cetanaḥ*—being fully Kṛṣṇa conscious.

TRANSLATION

My dear son, killing a king who is an emperor is more severely sinful than killing a brāhmaṇa. But now, if you become Kṛṣṇa conscious and worship the holy places, you can atone for this great sin.

PURPORT

One who fully surrenders to the Supreme Personality of Godhead is freed from all sins (*ahaṁ tvāṁ sarva-pāpebhyo mokṣayiṣyāmi*). From the very day or moment he fully surrenders to Śrī Kṛṣṇa, even the most sinful person is freed. Nonetheless, as an example, Jamadagni advised his son Paraśurāma to worship the holy places. Because an ordinary person cannot immediately surrender to the Supreme Personality of Godhead, he is advised to go from one holy place to another to find saintly persons and thus gradually be released from sinful reactions.

Thus end the Bhaktivedanta purports of the Ninth Canto, Fifteenth Chapter, of the Śrīmad-Bhāgavatam, *entitled "Paraśurāma, the Lord's Warrior Incarnation."*

CHAPTER SIXTEEN

Lord Paraśurāma Destroys the World's Ruling Class

When Jamadagni was killed by the sons of Kārtavīryārjuna, as described in this chapter, Paraśurāma rid the entire world of *kṣatriyas* twenty-one times. This chapter also describes the descendants of Viśvāmitra.

When Jamadagni's wife, Reṇukā, went to bring water from the Ganges and saw the King of the Gandharvas enjoying the company of Apsarās, she was captivated, and she slightly desired to associate with him. Because of this sinful desire, she was punished by her husband. Paraśurāma killed his mother and brothers, but later, by dint of the austerities of Jamadagni, they were revived. The sons of Kārtavīryārjuna, however, remembering the death of their father, wanted to take revenge against Lord Paraśurāma, and therefore when Paraśurāma was absent from the *āśrama,* they killed Jamadagni, who was meditating on the Supreme Personality of Godhead. When Paraśurāma returned to the *āśrama* and saw his father killed, he was very sorry, and after asking his brothers to take care of the dead body, he went out with determination to kill all the *kṣatriyas* on the surface of the world. Taking up his axe, he went to Māhiṣmatī-pura, the capital of Kārtavīryārjuna, and killed all of Kārtavīryārjuna's sons, whose blood became a great river. Paraśurāma, however, was not satisfied with killing only the sons of Kārtavīryārjuna; later, when the *kṣatriyas* became disturbing, he killed them twenty-one times, so that there were no *kṣatriyas* on the surface of the earth. Thereafter, Paraśurāma joined the head of his father to the dead body and performed various sacrifices to please the Supreme Lord. Thus Jamadagni got life again in his body, and later he was promoted to the higher planetary system known as Saptarṣi-maṇḍala. Paraśurāma, the son of Jamadagni, still lives in Mahendra-parvata. In the next *manvantara,* he will become a preacher of Vedic knowledge.

In the dynasty of Gādhi, the most powerful Viśvāmitra took birth. By dint of his austerity and penance, he became a *brāhmaṇa.* He had 101 sons, who were celebrated as the Madhucchandās. In the sacrificial arena of Hariścandra, the son of Ajīgarta named Śunaḥśepha was meant to be sacrificed, but by the mercy of the Prajāpatis he was released. Thereafter, he became Devarāta in the dynasty of Gādhi. The fifty elder sons of Viśvāmitra, however, did not accept Śunaḥśepha as their elder brother, and therefore Viśvāmitra cursed them to become *mlecchas*, unfaithful to the Vedic civilization. Viśvāmitra's fifty-first son, along with his younger brothers, then accepted Śunaḥśepha as their eldest brother, and their father, Viśvāmitra, being satisfied, blessed them. Thus Devarāta was accepted in the dynasty of Kauśika, and consequently there are different divisions of that dynasty.

TEXT 1

श्रीशुक उवाच
पित्रोपशिक्षितो रामस्तथेति कुरुनन्दन ।
संवत्सरं तीर्थयात्रां चरित्वाश्रममाव्रजत् ॥ १ ॥

śrī-śuka uvāca
pitropaśikṣito rāmas
tatheti kuru-nandana
saṁvatsaraṁ tīrtha-yātrāṁ
caritvāśramam āvrajat

śrī-śukaḥ uvāca—Śrī Śukadeva Gosvāmī said; *pitrā*—by his father; *upaśikṣitaḥ*—thus advised; *rāmaḥ*—Lord Paraśurāma; *tathā iti*—let it be so; *kuru-nandana*—O son of the Kuru dynasty, Mahārāja Parīkṣit; *saṁvatsaram*—for one complete year; *tīrtha-yātrām*—traveling to all the holy places; *caritvā*—after executing; *āśramam*—to his own residence; *āvrajat*—returned.

TRANSLATION

Śukadeva Gosvāmī said: My dear Mahārāja Parīkṣit, son of the Kuru dynasty, when Lord Paraśurāma was given this order by his father, he immediately agreed, saying, "Let it be so." For one complete year he traveled to holy places. Then he returned to his father's residence.

TEXT 2

कदाचिद् रेणुका याता गङ्गायां पद्ममालिनम् ।
गन्धर्वराजं क्रीडन्तमप्सरोभिरपश्यत ॥ २ ॥

kadācid reṇukā yātā
gaṅgāyāṁ padma-mālinam
gandharva-rājaṁ krīḍantam
apsarobhir apaśyata

kadācit—once upon a time; *reṇukā*—Jamadagni's wife, the mother of Lord Paraśurāma; *yātā*—went; *gaṅgāyām*—to the bank of the River Ganges; *padma-mālinam*—decorated with a garland of lotus flowers; *gandharva-rājam*—the King of the Gandharvas; *krīḍantam*—sporting; *apsarobhiḥ*—with the Apsarās (heavenly society girls); *apaśyata*—she saw.

TRANSLATION

Once when Reṇukā, the wife of Jamadagni, went to the bank of the Ganges to get water, she saw the King of the Gandharvas, decorated with a garland of lotuses and sporting in the Ganges with celestial women [Apsarās].

TEXT 3

विलोकयन्ती क्रीडन्तमुदकार्थं नदीं गता ।
होमवेलां न सस्मार किञ्चिच्चित्ररथस्पृहा ॥ ३ ॥

vilokayantī krīḍantam
udakārthaṁ nadīṁ gatā
homa-velāṁ na sasmāra
kiñcic citraratha-spṛhā

vilokayantī—while looking at; *krīḍantam*—the King of the Gandharvas, engaged in such activities; *udaka-artham*—for getting some water; *nadīm*—to the river; *gatā*—as she went; *homa-velām*—the time for performing the *homa,* fire sacrifice; *na sasmāra*—did not remember; *kiñcit*—very little; *citraratha*—of the King of the Gandharvas, known as Citraratha; *spṛhā*—did desire the company.

TRANSLATION

She had gone to bring water from the Ganges, but when she saw Citraratha, the King of the Gandharvas, sporting with the celestial girls, she was somewhat inclined toward him and failed to remember that the time for the fire sacrifice was passing.

TEXT 4

कालात्ययं तं विलोक्य मुनेः शापविशङ्किता ।
आगत्य कलशं तस्थौ पुरोधाय कृताञ्जलिः ॥ ४ ॥

kālātyayaṁ taṁ vilokya
muneḥ śāpa-viśaṅkitā
āgatya kalaśaṁ tasthau
purodhāya kṛtāñjaliḥ

kāla-atyayam—passing the time; *tam*—that; *vilokya*—observing; *muneḥ*—of the great sage Jamadagni; *śāpa-viśaṅkitā*—being afraid of the curse; *āgatya*—returning; *kalaśam*—the waterpot; *tasthau*—stood; *purodhāya*—putting in front of the sage; *kṛta-añjaliḥ*—with folded hands.

TRANSLATION

Later, understanding that the time for offering the sacrifice had passed, Reṇukā feared a curse from her husband. Therefore when she returned she simply put the waterpot before him and stood there with folded hands.

TEXT 5

व्यभिचारं मुनिर्ज्ञात्वा पत्न्याः प्रकुपितोऽब्रवीत् ।
घ्नतैनां पुत्रकाः पापामित्युक्तास्ते न चक्रिरे ॥ ५ ॥

vyabhicāraṁ munir jñātvā
patnyāḥ prakupito 'bravīt
ghnataināṁ putrakāḥ pāpām
ity uktās te na cakrire

vyabhicāram—adultery; *muniḥ*—the great sage Jamadagni; *jñātvā*—could understand; *patnyāḥ*—of his wife; *prakupitaḥ*—he became angry; *abravīt*—he said; *ghnata*—kill; *enām*—her; *putrakāḥ*—my dear sons; *pāpām*—sinful; *iti uktāḥ*—being thus advised; *te*—all the sons; *na*—did not; *cakrire*—carry out his order.

TRANSLATION

The great sage Jamadagni understood the adultery in the mind of his wife. Therefore he was very angry and told his sons, "My dear sons, kill this sinful woman!" But the sons did not carry out his order.

TEXT 6

रामः सञ्चोदितः पित्रा भ्रातॄन् मात्रा सहावधीत् ।
प्रभावज्ञो मुनेः सम्यक् समाधेस्तपसश्च सः ॥ ६ ॥

rāmaḥ sañcoditaḥ pitrā
bhrātṝn mātrā sahāvadhīt
prabhāva-jño muneḥ samyak
samādhes tapasaś ca saḥ

rāmaḥ—Lord Paraśurāma; *sañcoditaḥ*—being encouraged (to kill his mother and brothers); *pitrā*—by his father; *bhrātṝn*—all his brothers; *mātrā saha*—with the mother; *avadhīt*—killed immediately; *prabhāva-jñaḥ*—aware of the prowess; *muneḥ*—of the great sage; *samyak*—completely; *samādheḥ*—by meditation; *tapasaḥ*—by austerity; *ca*—also; *saḥ*—he.

TRANSLATION

Jamadagni then ordered his youngest son, Paraśurāma, to kill his brothers, who had disobeyed this order, and his mother, who

had mentally committed adultery. Lord Paraśurāma, knowing the power of his father, who was practiced in meditation and austerity, killed his mother and brothers immediately.

PURPORT

The word *prabhāva-jñaḥ* is significant. Paraśurāma knew the prowess of his father, and therefore he agreed to carry out his father's order. He thought that if he refused to carry out the order he would be cursed, but if he carried it out his father would be pleased, and when his father was pleased, Paraśurāma would ask the benediction of having his mother and brothers brought back to life. Paraśurāma was confident in this regard, and therefore he agreed to kill his mother and brothers.

TEXT 7

वरेणच्छन्दयामास प्रीतः सत्यवतीसुतः ।
वव्रे हतानां रामोऽपि जीवितं चास्मृतिं वधे ॥ ७ ॥

vareṇa cchandayām āsa
prītaḥ satyavatī-sutaḥ
vavre hatānāṁ rāmo 'pi
jīvitaṁ cāsmṛtiṁ vadhe

vareṇa cchandayām āsa—asked to take a benediction as he liked; *prītaḥ*—being very pleased (with him); *satyavatī-sutaḥ*—Jamadagni, the son of Satyavatī; *vavre*—said; *hatānām*—of my dead mother and brothers; *rāmaḥ*—Paraśurāma; *api*—also; *jīvitam*—let them be alive; *ca*—also; *asmṛtim*—no remembrance; *vadhe*—of their having been killed by me.

TRANSLATION

Jamadagni, the son of Satyavatī, was very much pleased with Paraśurāma and asked him to take any benediction he liked. Lord Paraśurāma replied, "Let my mother and brothers live again and not remember having been killed by me. This is the benediction I ask."

TEXT 8

उत्तस्थुस्ते कुशलिनो निद्रापाय इवाञ्जसा ।
पितुर्विद्वांस्तपोवीर्यं रामश्चक्रे सुहृद्वधम् ॥ ८ ॥

uttasthus te kuśalino
nidrāpāya ivāñjasā
pitur vidvāṁs tapo-vīryaṁ
rāmaś cakre suhṛd-vadham

uttasthuḥ—got up immediately; *te*—Lord Paraśurāma's mother and brothers; *kuśalinaḥ*—being happily alive; *nidrā-apāye*—at the end of sound sleep; *iva*—like; *añjasā*—very soon; *pituḥ*—of his father; *vidvān*—being aware of; *tapaḥ*—austerity; *vīryam*—power; *rāmaḥ*—Lord Paraśurāma; *cakre*—executed; *suhṛt-vadham*—killing of his family members.

TRANSLATION

Thereafter, by the benediction of Jamadagni, Lord Paraśurāma's mother and brothers immediately came alive and were very happy, as if awakened from sound sleep. Lord Paraśurāma had killed his relatives in accordance with his father's order because he was fully aware of his father's power, austerity and learning.

TEXT 9

येऽर्जुनस्य सुता राजन् स्मरन्तः स्वपितुर्वधम् ।
रामवीर्यपराभूता लेभिरे शर्म न क्वचित् ॥ ९ ॥

ye 'rjunasya sutā rājan
smarantaḥ sva-pitur vadham
rāma-vīrya-parābhūtā
lebhire śarma na kvacit

ye—those who; *arjunasya*—of Kārtavīryārjuna; *sutāḥ*—sons; *rājan*—O Mahārāja Parīkṣit; *smarantaḥ*—always remembering; *sva-pituḥ vadham*—their father's having been killed (by Paraśurāma);

rāma-vīrya-parābhūtāḥ—defeated by the superior power of Lord Paraśurāma; *lebhire*—achieved; *śarma*—happiness; *na*—not; *kvacit*—at any time.

TRANSLATION

My dear King Parīkṣit, the sons of Kārtavīryārjuna, who were defeated by the superior strength of Paraśurāma, never achieved happiness, for they always remembered the killing of their father.

PURPORT

Jamadagni was certainly very powerful due to his austerities, but because of a slight offense by his poor wife, Reṇukā, he ordered that she be killed. This certainly was a sinful act, and therefore Jamadagni was killed by the sons of Kārtavīryārjuna, as described herein. Lord Paraśurāma was also infected by sin because of killing Kārtavīryārjuna, although this was not very offensive. Therefore, whether one be Kārtavīryārjuna, Lord Paraśurāma, Jamadagni or whoever one may be, one must act very cautiously and sagaciously; otherwise one must suffer the results of sinful activities. This is the lesson we receive from Vedic literature.

TEXT 10

एकदाश्रमतो रामे सभ्रातरि वनं गते ।
वैरं सिषाधयिषवो लब्धच्छिद्रा उपागमन् ॥१०॥

ekadāśramato rāme
sabhrātari vanaṁ gate
vairaṁ siṣādhayiṣavo
labdha-cchidrā upāgaman

ekadā—once upon a time; *āśramataḥ*—from the *āśrama* of Jamadagni; *rāme*—when Lord Paraśurāma; *sa-bhrātari*—with his brothers; *vanam*—into the forest; *gate*—having gone; *vairam*—revenge for past enmity; *siṣādhayiṣavaḥ*—desiring to fulfill; *labdha-chidrāḥ*—taking the opportunity; *upāgaman*—they came near the residence of Jamadagni.

TRANSLATION

Once when Paraśurāma left the āśrama for the forest with Vasumān and his other brothers, the sons of Kārtavīryārjuna took the opportunity to approach Jamadagni's residence to seek vengeance for their grudge.

TEXT 11

दृष्ट्वाग्न्यागार आसीनमावेशितधियं मुनिम् ।
भगवत्युत्तमश्लोके जघ्नुस्ते पापनिश्चयाः ॥११॥

dṛṣṭvāgny-āgāra āsīnam
āveśita-dhiyaṁ munim
bhagavaty uttamaśloke
jaghnus te pāpa-niścayāḥ

dṛṣṭvā—by seeing; *agni-āgāre*—at the place where the fire sacrifice is performed; *āsīnam*—sitting; *āveśita*—completely absorbed; *dhiyam*—by intelligence; *munim*—the great sage Jamadagni; *bhagavati*—unto the Supreme Personality of Godhead; *uttama-śloke*—who is praised by the best of selected prayers; *jaghnuḥ*—killed; *te*—the sons of Kārtavīryārjuna; *pāpa-niścayāḥ*—determined to commit a greatly sinful act, or the personified sins.

TRANSLATION

The sons of Kārtavīryārjuna were determined to commit sinful deeds. Therefore when they saw Jamadagni sitting by the side of the fire to perform yajña and meditating upon the Supreme Personality of Godhead, who is praised by the best of selected prayers, they took the opportunity to kill him.

TEXT 12

याच्यमानाः कृपणया राममात्रातिदारुणाः ।
प्रसह्य शिर उत्कृत्य निन्युस्ते क्षत्रबन्धवः ॥१२॥

yācyamānāḥ kṛpaṇayā
rāma-mātrātidāruṇāḥ
prasahya śira utkṛtya
ninyus te kṣatra-bandhavaḥ

yācyamānāḥ—being begged for the life of her husband; *kṛpaṇayā*—by the poor unprotected woman; *rāma-mātrā*—by the mother of Lord Paraśurāma; *ati-dāruṇāḥ*—very cruel; *prasahya*—by force; *śiraḥ*—the head of Jamadagni; *utkṛtya*—having separated; *ninyuḥ*—took away; *te*—the sons of Kārtavīryārjuna; *kṣatra-bandhavaḥ*—not *kṣatriyas,* but the most abominable sons of *kṣatriyas.*

TRANSLATION

With pitiable prayers, Reṇukā, the mother of Paraśurāma and wife of Jamadagni, begged for the life of her husband. But the sons of Kārtavīryārjuna, being devoid of the qualities of kṣatriyas, were so cruel that despite her prayers they forcibly cut off his head and took it away.

TEXT 13

रेणुका दुःखशोकार्ता निघ्नन्त्यात्मानमात्मना ।
राम रामेति तातेति विचुक्रोशोच्चकैः सती ॥१३॥

reṇukā duḥkha-śokārtā
nighnanty ātmānam ātmanā
rāma rāmeti tāteti
vicukrośoccakaiḥ satī

reṇukā—Reṇukā, the wife of Jamadagni; *duḥkha-śoka-artā*—being very much aggrieved in lamentation (over her husband's death); *nighnantī*—striking; *ātmānam*—her own body; *ātmanā*—by herself; *rāma*—O Paraśurāma; *rāma*—O Paraśurāma; *iti*—thus; *tāta*—O my dear son; *iti*—thus; *vicukrośa*—began to cry; *uccakaiḥ*—very loudly; *satī*—the most chaste woman.

TRANSLATION

Lamenting in grief for the death of her husband, the most chaste Reṇukā struck her own body with her hands and cried very loudly, "O Rāma, my dear son Rāma!"

TEXT 14

तदुपश्रुत्य दूरस्था हा रामेत्यार्तवत्स्वनम् ।
त्वरयाश्रममासाद्य ददृशुः पितरं हतम् ॥१४॥

tad upaśrutya dūrasthā
hā rāmety ārtavat svanam
tvarayāśramam āsādya
dadṛśuḥ pitaraṁ hatam

tat—that crying of Reṇukā; *upaśrutya*—upon hearing; *dūra-sthāḥ*—although staying a long distance away; *hā rāma*—O Rāma, O Rāma; *iti*—thus; *ārta-vat*—very aggrieved; *svanam*—the sound; *tvarayā*—very hastily; *āśramam*—to the residence of Jamadagni; *āsādya*—coming; *dadṛśuḥ*—saw; *pitaram*—the father; *hatam*—killed.

TRANSLATION

Although the sons of Jamadagni, including Lord Paraśurāma, were a long distance from home, as soon as they heard Reṇukā loudly calling "O Rāma, O my son," they hastily returned to the āśrama, where they saw their father already killed.

TEXT 15

ते दुःखरोषामर्षार्तिशोकवेगविमोहिताः ।
हा तात साधो धर्मिष्ठ त्यक्त्वास्मान्स्वर्गतो भवान् ॥१५॥

te duḥkha-roṣāmarṣārti-
śoka-vega-vimohitāḥ

hā tāta sādho dharmiṣṭa
tyaktvāsmān svar-gato bhavān

te—all the sons of Jamadagni; *duḥkha*—of grief; *roṣa*—anger; *amarṣa*—indignation; *ārti*—affliction; *śoka*—and lamentation; *vega*—with the force; *vimohitāḥ*—bewildered; *hā tāta*—O father; *sādho*—the great saint; *dharmiṣṭha*—the most religious person; *tyaktvā*—leaving; *asmān*—us; *svaḥ-gataḥ*—have gone to the heavenly planets; *bhavān*—you.

TRANSLATION

Virtually bewildered by grief, anger, indignation, affliction and lamentation, the sons of Jamadagni cried, "O father, most religious, saintly person, you have left us and gone to the heavenly planets!"

TEXT 16

विलप्यैवं पितुर्देहं निधाय भ्रातृषु स्वयम् ।
प्रगृह्य परशुं रामः क्षत्रान्ताय मनो दधे ॥१६॥

vilapyaivaṁ pitur dehaṁ
nidhāya bhrātṛṣu svayam
pragṛhya paraśuṁ rāmaḥ
kṣatrāntāya mano dadhe

vilapya—lamenting; *evam*—like this; *pituḥ*—of his father; *deham*—the body; *nidhāya*—entrusting; *bhrātṛṣu*—to his brothers; *svayam*—personally; *pragṛhya*—taking; *paraśum*—the axe; *rāmaḥ*—Lord Paraśurāma; *kṣatra-antāya*—to put an end to all the *kṣatriyas;* *manaḥ*—the mind; *dadhe*—fixed.

TRANSLATION

Thus lamenting, Lord Paraśurāma entrusted his father's dead body to his brothers and personally took up his axe, having decided to put an end to all the kṣatriyas on the surface of the world.

TEXT 17

गत्वा माहिष्मतीं रामो ब्रह्मघ्नविहतश्रियम् ।
तेषां स शीर्षभी राजन् मध्ये चक्रे महागिरिम् ॥१७॥

gatvā māhiṣmatīṁ rāmo
brahma-ghna-vihata-śriyam
teṣāṁ sa śīrṣabhī rājan
madhye cakre mahā-girim

gatvā—going; *māhiṣmatīm*—to the place known as Māhiṣmatī; *rāmaḥ*—Lord Paraśurāma; *brahma-ghna*—because of the killing of a *brāhmaṇa; vihata-śriyam*—doomed, bereft of all opulences; *teṣām*—of all of them (the sons of Kārtavīryārjuna and the other *kṣatriya* inhabitants); *saḥ*—he, Lord Paraśurāma; *śīrṣabhiḥ*—by the heads cut off from their bodies; *rājan*—O Mahārāja Parīkṣit; *madhye*—within the jurisdiction of Māhiṣmatī; *cakre*—made; *mahā-girim*—a great mountain.

TRANSLATION

O King, Lord Paraśurāma then went to Māhiṣmatī, which was already doomed by the sinful killing of a brāhmaṇa. In the midst of that city he made a mountain of heads, severed from the bodies of the sons of Kārtavīryārjuna.

TEXTS 18–19

तद्रक्तेन नदीं घोरामब्रह्मण्यभयावहाम् ।
हेतुं कृत्वा पितृवधं क्षत्रेऽमङ्गलकारिणि ॥१८॥
त्रिःसप्तकृत्वः पृथिवीं कृत्वा निःक्षत्रियां प्रभुः ।
समन्तपञ्चके चक्रे शोणितोदान् ह्रदान् नव ॥१९॥

tad-raktena nadīṁ ghorām
abrahmaṇya-bhayāvahām
hetuṁ kṛtvā pitṛ-vadhaṁ
kṣatre 'maṅgala-kāriṇi

triḥ-sapta-kṛtvaḥ pṛthivīṁ
kṛtvā niḥkṣatriyāṁ prabhuḥ
samanta-pañcake cakre
śoṇitodān hradān nava

tat-raktena—by the blood of the sons of Kārtavīryārjuna; *nadīm*—a river; *ghorām*—fierce; *abrahmaṇya-bhaya-āvahām*—causing fear to the kings who had no respect for brahminical culture; *hetum*—cause; *kṛtvā*—accepting; *pitṛ-vadham*—the killing of his father; *kṣatre*—when the whole royal class; *amaṅgala-kāriṇi*—was acting very inauspiciously; *triḥ-sapta-kṛtvaḥ*—twenty-one times; *pṛthivīm*—the entire world; *kṛtvā*—making; *niḥkṣatriyām*—without a *kṣatriya* dynasty; *prabhuḥ*—the Supreme Lord, Paraśurāma; *samanta-pañcake*—at the place known as Samanta-pañcaka; *cakre*—he made; *śoṇita-udān*—filled with blood instead of water; *hradān*—lakes; *nava*—nine.

TRANSLATION

With the blood of the bodies of these sons, Lord Paraśurāma created a ghastly river, which brought great fear to the kings who had no respect for brahminical culture. Because the kṣatriyas, the men of power in government, were performing sinful activities, Lord Paraśurāma, on the plea of retaliating for the murder of his father, rid all the kṣatriyas from the face of the earth twenty-one times. Indeed, in the place known as Samanta-pañcaka he created nine lakes filled with their blood.

PURPORT

Paraśurāma is the Supreme Personality of Godhead, and his eternal mission is *paritrāṇāya sādhūnāṁ vināśāya ca duṣkṛtām*—to protect the devotees and annihilate the miscreants. To kill all the sinful men is one among the tasks of the incarnation of Godhead. Lord Paraśurāma killed all the *kṣatriyas* twenty-one times consecutively because they were disobedient to the brahminical culture. That the *kṣatriyas* had killed his father was only a plea; the real fact is that because the *kṣatriyas*, the ruling class, had become polluted, their position was inauspicious. Brahminical culture is enjoined in the *śāstra*, especially in *Bhagavad-gītā* (*cātur-varṇyaṁ mayā sṛṣṭaṁ guṇa-karma-vibhāgaśaḥ*). According to the laws of nature, whether at the time of Paraśurāma or at the present, if the government becomes irresponsible and sinful, not caring for brahminical culture, there will certainly be an incarnation of God like Paraśurāma to create a devastation by fire, famine, pestilence or some other calamity. Whenever the government disrespects the supremacy of the Personality of Godhead and fails to protect the institution of *varṇāśrama-dharma*, it will certainly have to face such catastrophes as formerly brought about by Lord Paraśurāma.

TEXT 20

पितुः कायेन सन्धाय शिर आदाय बर्हिषि ।
सर्वदेवमयं देवमात्मानमयजन्मखैः ॥२०॥

pituḥ kāyena sandhāya
śira ādāya barhiṣi
sarva-devamayaṁ devam
ātmānam ayajan makhaiḥ

pituḥ—of his father; *kāyena*—with the body; *sandhāya*—joining; *śiraḥ*—the head; *ādāya*—keeping; *barhiṣi*—upon *kuśa* grass; *sarva-deva-mayam*—the all-pervading Supreme Personality of Godhead, the master of all the demigods; *devam*—Lord Vāsudeva; *ātmānam*—who is present everywhere as the Supersoul; *ayajat*—he worshiped; *makhaiḥ*—by offering sacrifices.

TRANSLATION

Thereafter, Paraśurāma joined his father's head to the dead body and placed the whole body and head upon kuśa grass. By offering sacrifices, he began to worship Lord Vāsudeva, who is the all-pervading Supersoul of all the demigods and of every living entity.

TEXTS 21–22

दद‍ौ प्राचीं दिशं होत्रे ब्रह्मणे दक्षिणां दिशम् ।
अध्वर्यवे प्रतीचीं वै उद्गात्रे उत्तरां दिशम् ॥२१॥
अन्येभ्योऽवान्तरदिशः कश्यपाय च मध्यतः ।
आर्यावर्तमुपद्रष्ट्रे सदस्येभ्यस्ततः परम् ॥२२॥

dadau prācīṁ diśaṁ hotre
brahmaṇe dakṣiṇāṁ diśam
adhvaryave pratīcīṁ vai
udgātre uttarāṁ diśam

anyebhyo 'vāntara-diśaḥ
kaśyapāya ca madhyataḥ
āryāvartam upadraṣṭre
sadasyebhyas tataḥ param

dadau—gave as a gift; *prācīm*—eastern; *diśam*—direction; *hotre*—unto the priest known as *hotā; brahmaṇe*—unto the priest known as *brahmā; dakṣiṇām*—southern; *diśam*—direction; *adhvaryave*—unto the priest known as *adhvaryu; pratīcīm*—the western side; *vai*—indeed; *udgātre*—unto the priest known as *udgātā; uttarām*—northern; *diśam*—side; *anyebhyaḥ*—unto the others; *avāntara-diśaḥ*—the different corners (northeast, southeast, northwest and southwest); *kaśyapāya*—unto Kaśyapa Muni; *ca*—also; *madhyataḥ*—the middle portion; *āryāvartam*—the portion known as Āryāvarta; *upadraṣṭre*—unto the *upadraṣṭā*, the priest acting as overseer to hear and check the *mantras; sadasyebhyaḥ*—unto the *sadasyas*, the associate priests; *tataḥ param*—whatever remained.

TRANSLATION

After completing the sacrifice, Lord Paraśurāma gave the eastern direction to the hotā as a gift, the south to the brahmā, the west to the adhvaryu, the north to the udgātā, and the four corners—northeast, southeast, northwest and southwest—to the other priests. He gave the middle to Kaśyapa and the place known

as Āryāvarta to the upadraṣṭā. Whatever remained he distributed among the sadasyas, the associate priests.

PURPORT

The tract of land in India between the Himalaya Mountains and the Vindhya Hills is called Āryāvarta.

TEXT 23

ततश्चावभृथस्नानविधूताशेषकिल्बिषः ।
सरस्वत्यां महानद्यां रेजे व्यब्भ्र इवांशुमान् ॥२३॥

tataś cāvabhṛtha-snāna-
vidhūtāśeṣa-kilbiṣaḥ
sarasvatyāṁ mahā-nadyāṁ
reje vyabbhra ivāṁśumān

tataḥ—thereafter; *ca*—also; *avabhṛtha-snāna*—by bathing after finishing the sacrifice; *vidhūta*—cleansed; *aśeṣa*—unlimited; *kilbiṣaḥ*—whose reactions of sinful activities; *sarasvatyām*—on the bank of the great river Sarasvatī; *mahā-nadyām*—one of the biggest rivers in India; *reje*—Lord Paraśurāma appeared; *vyabbhraḥ*—cloudless; *iva aṁśumān*—like the sun.

TRANSLATION

Thereafter, having completed the ritualistic sacrificial ceremonies, Lord Paraśurāma took the bath known as the avabhṛtha-snāna. Standing on the bank of the great river Sarasvatī, cleared of all sins, Lord Paraśurāma appeared like the sun in a clear, cloudless sky.

PURPORT

As stated in *Bhagavad-gītā* (3.9), *yajñārthāt karmaṇo 'nyatra loko 'yaṁ karma-bandhanaḥ:* "Work done as a sacrifice for Viṣṇu has to be performed, otherwise work binds one to this material world." *Karma-bandhanaḥ* refers to the repeated acceptance of one material body after another. The whole problem of life is this repetition of birth and death. Therefore one is advised to work to perform *yajña* meant for satisfying Lord Viṣṇu. Although Lord Paraśurāma was an incarnation of the Supreme Personality of Godhead, he had to account for sinful activities. Anyone in this material world, however careful he may be, must commit some sinful activities, even though he does not want to. For example, one may trample many small ants and other insects while walking on the street and kill many living beings unknowingly. Therefore the Vedic principle of *pañca-yajña*, five kinds of recommended sacrifice, is compulsory. In this age of Kali, however, there is a great concession given to people in general. *Yajñaiḥ saṅkīrtana-prāyair yajanti hi sumedhasaḥ:* we may worship Lord Caitanya, the hidden incarnation of Kṛṣṇa. *Kṛṣṇa-varṇaṁ tviṣākṛṣṇam:* although He is Kṛṣṇa Himself, He always chants Hare Kṛṣṇa and preaches Kṛṣṇa consciousness. One is recommended to worship this incarnation by chanting, the *saṅkīrtana-yajña.* The performance of *saṅkīrtana-yajña* is a special concession for human society to save people from being affected by known or unknown sinful activities. We are surrounded by unlimited sins, and therefore it is compulsory that one take to Kṛṣṇa consciousness and chant the Hare Kṛṣṇa *mahā-mantra.*

TEXT 24

स्वदेहं जमदग्निस्तु लब्ध्वा संज्ञानलक्षणम् ।
ऋषीणां मण्डले सोऽभूत् सप्तमो रामपूजितः ॥२४॥

sva-dehaṁ jamadagnis tu
labdhvā saṁjñāna-lakṣaṇam
ṛṣīṇāṁ maṇḍale so 'bhūt
saptamo rāma-pūjitaḥ

sva-deham—his own body; *jamadagniḥ*—the great sage Jamadagni; *tu*—but; *labdhvā*—regaining; *saṁjñāna-lakṣaṇam*—showing full symptoms of life, knowledge and remembrance; *ṛṣīṇām*—of the great *ṛṣis; maṇḍale*—in the group of seven stars; *saḥ*—he, Jamadagni; *abhūt*—later became; *saptamaḥ*—the seventh; *rāma-pūjitaḥ*—because of being worshiped by Lord Paraśurāma.

TRANSLATION

Thus Jamadagni, being worshiped by Lord Paraśurāma, was brought back to life with full remembrance, and he became one of the seven sages in the group of seven stars.

PURPORT

The seven stars revolving around the polestar at the zenith are called *saptarṣi-maṇḍala.* On these seven stars, which form the topmost part of our planetary system, reside seven sages: Kaśyapa, Atri, Vasiṣṭha, Viśvāmitra, Gautama, Jamadagni and Bharadvāja. These seven stars are seen every night, and they each make a complete orbit around the polestar within twenty-four hours. Along with these seven stars, all the others stars also orbit from east to west. The upper portion of the universe is called the north, and the lower portion is called the south. Even in our ordinary dealings, while studying a map, we regard the upper portion of the map as north.

TEXT 25

जामदग्न्योऽपि भगवान् रामः कमललोचनः ।
आगामिन्यन्तरे राजन् वर्तयिष्यति वै बृहत् ॥२५॥

jāmadagnyo 'pi bhagavān
rāmaḥ kamala-locanaḥ
āgāminy antare rājan
vartayiṣyati vai bṛhat

jāmadagnyaḥ—the son of Jamadagni; *api*—also; *bhagavān*—the Personality of Godhead; *rāmaḥ*—Lord Paraśurāma; *kamala-locanaḥ*—whose eyes are like lotus petals; *āgāmini*—coming; *antare*—in the *manvantara,* the time of one Manu; *rājan*—O King Parīkṣit; *vartayiṣyati*—will propound; *vai*—indeed; *bṛhat*—Vedic knowledge.

TRANSLATION

My dear King Parīkṣit, in the next manvantara the lotus-eyed Personality of Godhead Lord Paraśurāma, the son of Jamadagni,

will be a great propounder of Vedic knowledge. In other words, he will be one of the seven sages.

TEXT 26

आस्तेऽद्यापि महेन्द्राद्रौ न्यस्तदण्डः प्रशान्तधीः ।
उपगीयमानचरितः सिद्धगन्धर्वचारणैः ॥२६॥

āste 'dyāpi mahendrādrau
nyasta-daṇḍaḥ praśānta-dhīḥ
upagīyamāna-caritaḥ
siddha-gandharva-cāraṇaiḥ

āste—is still existing; *adya api*—even now; *mahendra-adrau*—in the hilly country known as Mahendra; *nyasta-daṇḍaḥ*—having given up the weapons of a *kṣatriya* (the bow, arrows and axe); *praśānta*—now fully satisfied as a *brāhmaṇa; dhīḥ*—in such intelligence; *upagīyamāna-caritaḥ*—being worshiped and adored for his exalted character and activities; *siddha-gandharva-cāraṇaiḥ*—by such celestial persons as the inhabitants of Gandharvaloka, Siddhaloka and Cāraṇaloka.

TRANSLATION

Lord Paraśurāma still lives as an intelligent brāhmaṇa in the mountainous country known as Mahendra. Completely satisfied, having given up all the weapons of a kṣatriya, he is always worshiped, adored and offered prayers for his exalted character and activities by such celestial beings as the Siddhas, Cāraṇas and Gandharvas.

TEXT 27

एवं भृगुषु विश्वात्मा भगवान् हरिरीश्वरः ।
अवतीर्य परं भारं भुवोऽहन् बहुशो नृपान् ॥२७॥

evaṁ bhṛguṣu viśvātmā
bhagavān harir īśvaraḥ
avatīrya paraṁ bhāraṁ
bhuvo 'han bahuśo nṛpān

evam—in this way; *bhṛguṣu*—in the dynasty of Bhṛgu; *viśva-ātmā*—the soul of the universe, the Supersoul; *bhagavān*—the Supreme Personality of Godhead; *hariḥ*—the Lord; *īśvaraḥ*—the supreme controller; *avatīrya*—appearing as an incarnation; *param*—great; *bhāram*—the burden; *bhuvaḥ*—of the world; *ahan*—killed; *bahuśaḥ*—many times; *nṛpān*—kings.

TRANSLATION

In this way the supreme soul, the Supreme Personality of Godhead, the Lord and the supreme controller, descended as an incarnation in the Bhṛgu dynasty and released the universe from the burden of undesirable kings by killing them many times.

TEXT 28

गाधेरभून्महातेजाः समिद्ध इव पावकः ।
तपसा क्षात्रमुत्सृज्य यो लेभे ब्रह्मवर्चसम् ॥२८॥

gādher abhūn mahā-tejāḥ
samiddha iva pāvakaḥ
tapasā kṣātram utsṛjya
yo lebhe brahma-varcasam

gādheḥ—from Mahārāja Gādhi; *abhūt*—was born; *mahā-tejāḥ*—very powerful; *samiddhaḥ*—inflamed; *iva*—like; *pāvakaḥ*—fire; *tapasā*—by austerities and penances; *kṣātram*—the position of a *kṣatriya; utsṛjya*—giving up; *yaḥ*—one who (Viśvāmitra); *lebhe*—achieved; *brahma-varcasam*—the quality of a *brāhmaṇa.*

TRANSLATION

Viśvāmitra, the son of Mahārāja Gādhi, was as powerful as the flames of fire. From the position of a kṣatriya, he achieved the position of a powerful brāhmaṇa by undergoing penances and austerities.

PURPORT

Now, having narrated the history of Lord Paraśurāma, Śukadeva Gosvāmī begins the history of Viśvāmitra. From the history of

Paraśurāma we can understand that although Paraśurāma belonged to the brahminical group, he circumstantially had to work as a *kṣatriya.* Later, after finishing his work as a *kṣatriya,* he again became a *brāhmaṇa* and returned to Mahendra-parvata. Similarly, we can see that although Viśvāmitra was born in a *kṣatriya* family, by austerities and penances he achieved the position of a *brāhmaṇa.* These histories confirm the statements in *śāstra* that a *brāhmaṇa* may become a *kṣatriya,* a *kṣatriya* may become a *brāhmaṇa* or *vaiśya,* and a *vaiśya* may become a *brāhmaṇa,* by achieving the required qualities. One's status does not depend upon birth. As confirmed in *Śrīmad-Bhāgavatam* (7.11.35) by Nārada:

yasya yal lakṣaṇaṁ proktaṁ
puṁso varṇābhivyañjakam
yad anyatrāpi dṛśyeta
tat tenaiva vinirdiśet

"If one shows the symptoms of being a *brāhmaṇa, kṣatriya, vaiśya* or *śūdra,* even if he has appeared in a different class, he should be accepted according to those symptoms of classification." To know who is a *brāhmaṇa* and who is a *kṣatriya,* one must consider a man's quality and work. If all the unqualified *śūdras* become so-called *brāhmaṇas* and *kṣatriyas,* social order will be impossible to maintain. Thus there will be discrepancies, human society will turn into a society of animals, and the situation all over the world will be hellish.

TEXT 29

विश्वामित्रस्य चैवासन् पुत्रा एकशतं नृप ।
मध्यमस्तु मधुच्छन्दा मधुच्छन्दस एव ते ॥२९॥

viśāmitrasya caivāsan
putrā eka-śataṁ nṛpa
madhyamas tu madhucchandā
madhucchandasa eva te

viśvāmitrasya—of Viśvāmitra; *ca*—also; *eva*—indeed; *āsan*—there were; *putrāḥ*—sons; *eka-śatam*—101; *nṛpa*—O King Parīkṣit;

madhyamaḥ—the middle one; *tu*—indeed; *madhucchandāḥ*—known as Madhucchandā; *madhucchandasaḥ*—named the Madhucchandās; *eva*—indeed; *te*—all of them.

TRANSLATION

O King Parīkṣit, Viśvāmitra had 101 sons, of whom the middle one was known as Madhucchandā. In relation to him, all the other sons were celebrated as the Madhucchandās.

PURPORT

In this connection, Śrīla Viśvanātha Cakravartī Ṭhākura quotes this statement from the *Vedas: tasya ha viśvāmitrasyaika-śataṁ putrā āsuḥ pañcāśad eva jyāyāṁso madhucchandasaḥ pañcāśat kanīyāṁsaḥ.* "Viśvāmitra had 101 sons. Fifty were older than Madhucchandā and fifty younger."

TEXT 30

पुत्रं कृत्वा शुनःशेफं देवरातं च भार्गवम् ।
आजीगर्तं सुतानाह ज्येष्ठ एष प्रकल्प्यताम् ॥३०॥

putraṁ kṛtvā śunaḥśephaṁ
devarātaṁ ca bhārgavam
ājīgartaṁ sutān āha
jyeṣṭha eṣa prakalpyatām

putram—a son; *kṛtvā*—accepting; *śunaḥśepham*—whose name was Śunaḥśepha; *devarātam*—Devarāta, whose life was saved by the demigods; *ca*—also; *bhārgavam*—born in the Bhṛgu dynasty; *ājīgartam*—the son of Ajīgarta; *sutān*—to his own sons; *āha*—ordered; *jyeṣṭhaḥ*—the eldest; *eṣaḥ*—Śunaḥśepha; *prakalpyatām*—accept as such.

TRANSLATION

Viśvāmitra accepted the son of Ajīgarta known as Śunaḥśepha, who was born in the Bhṛgu dynasty and was also known as Devarāta, as one of his own sons. Viśvāmitra ordered his other sons to accept Śunaḥśepha as their eldest brother.

TEXT 31

यो वै हरिश्चन्द्रमखे विक्रीतः पुरुषः पशुः ।
स्तुत्वा देवान् प्रजेशादीन् मुमुचे पाशबन्धनात् ॥३१॥

yo vai hariścandra-makhe
vikrītaḥ puruṣaḥ paśuḥ
stutvā devān prajeśādīn
mumuce pāśa-bandhanāt

yaḥ—he who (Śunaḥśepha); *vai*—indeed; *hariścandra-makhe*—in the sacrifice performed by King Hariścandra; *vikrītaḥ*—was sold; *puruṣaḥ*—man; *paśuḥ*—sacrificial animal; *stutvā*—offering prayers; *devān*—to the demigods; *prajā-īśa-ādīn*—headed by Lord Brahmā; *mumuce*—was released; *pāśa-bandhanāt*—from being bound with ropes like an animal.

TRANSLATION

Śunaḥśepha's father sold Śunaḥśepha to be sacrificed as a man-animal in the yajña of King Hariścandra. When Śunaḥśepha was brought into the sacrificial arena, he prayed to the demigods for release and was released by their mercy.

PURPORT

Here is a description of Śunaḥśepha. When Hariścandra was to sacrifice his son Rohita, Rohita arranged to save his own life by purchasing Śunaḥśepha from Śunaḥśepha's father to be sacrificed in the *yajña.* Śunaḥśepha was sold to Mahārāja Hariścandra because he was the middle son, between the oldest and the youngest. It appears that the sacrifice of a man as an animal in *yajña* has been practiced for a very long time.

TEXT 32

यो रातो देवयजने देवैर्गाधिषु तापसः ।
देवरात इति ख्यातः शुनःशेफस्तु भार्गवः ॥३२॥

yo rāto deva-yajane
devair gādhiṣu tāpasaḥ

deva-rāta iti khyātaḥ
śunaḥśephas tu bhārgavaḥ

yaḥ—he who (Śunaḥśepha); *rātaḥ*—was protected; *deva-yajane*—in the arena for worshiping the demigods; *devaiḥ*—by the same demigods; *gādhiṣu*—in the dynasty of Gādhi; *tāpasaḥ*—advanced in executing spiritual life; *deva-rātaḥ*—protected by the demigods; *iti*—thus; *khyātaḥ*—celebrated; *śunaḥśephaḥ tu*— as well as Śunaḥśepha; *bhārgavaḥ*—in the dynasty of Bhṛgu.

TRANSLATION

Although Śunaḥśepha was born in the Bhārgava dynasty, he was greatly advanced in spiritual life, and therefore the demigods involved in the sacrifice protected him. Consequently he was also celebrated as the descendant of Gādhi named Devarāta.

TEXT 33

ये मधुच्छन्दसो ज्येष्ठाः कुशलं मेनिरे न तत् ।
अशपत् तान्मुनिः क्रुद्धो म्लेच्छा भवत दुर्जनाः ॥३३॥

ye madhucchandaso jyeṣṭhāḥ
kuśalaṁ menire na tat
aśapat tān muniḥ kruddho
mlecchā bhavata durjanāḥ

ye—those who; *madhucchandasaḥ*—sons of Viśvāmitra, celebrated as the Madhucchandās; *jyeṣṭhāḥ*—eldest; *kuśalam*—very good; *menire*—accepting; *na*—not; *tat*—that (the proposal that he be accepted as the eldest brother); *aśapat*—cursed; *tān*—all the sons; *muniḥ*—Viśvāmitra Muni; *kruddhaḥ*—being angry; *mlecchāḥ*—disobedient to the Vedic principles; *bhavata*—all of you become; *durjanāḥ*—very bad sons.

TRANSLATION

When requested by their father to accept Śunaḥśepha as the eldest son, the elder fifty of the Madhucchandās, the sons of

Viśvāmitra, did not agree. Therefore Viśvāmitra, being angry, cursed them. "May all of you bad sons become mlecchas," he said, "being opposed to the principles of Vedic culture."

PURPORT

In Vedic literature there are names like *mleccha* and *yavana*. The *mlecchas* are understood to be those who do not follow the Vedic principles. In former days, the *mlecchas* were fewer, and Viśvāmitra Muni cursed his sons to become *mlecchas*. But in the present age, Kali-yuga, there is no need of cursing, for people are automatically *mlecchas*. This is only the beginning of Kali-yuga, but at the end of Kali-yuga the entire population will consist of *mlecchas* because no one will follow the Vedic principles. At that time the incarnation Kalki will appear. *Mleccha-nivaha-nidhane kalayasi kara-bālam.* He will kill all the *mlecchas* indiscriminately with his sword.

TEXT 34

स होवाच मधुच्छन्दाः सार्धं पञ्चाशता ततः ।
यन्नो भवान् संजानीते तस्मिंस्तिष्ठामहे वयम् ॥३४॥

sa hovāca madhucchandāḥ
sārdhaṁ pañcāśatā tataḥ
yan no bhavān sañjānīte
tasmiṁs tiṣṭhāmahe vayam

saḥ—the middle son of Viśvāmitra; *ha*—indeed; *uvāca*—said; *madhucchandāḥ*—Madhucchandā; *sārdham*—with; *pañcāśatā*—the second fifty of the sons known as the Madhucchandās; *tataḥ*—then, after the first half were thus cursed; *yat*—what; *naḥ*—unto us; *bhavān*—O father; *sañjānīte*—as you please; *tasmin*—in that; *tiṣṭhāmahe*—shall remain; *vayam*—all of us.

TRANSLATION

When the elder Madhucchandās were cursed, the younger fifty, along with Madhucchandā himself, approached their father and

agreed to accept his proposal. "Dear father," they said, "we shall abide by whatever arrangement you like."

TEXT 35

ज्येष्ठं मन्त्रदृशं चक्रुस्त्वामन्वञ्चो वयं स्म हि ।
विश्वामित्रः सुतानाह वीरवन्तो भविष्यथ ।
ये मानं मेऽनुगृह्णन्तो वीरवन्तमकर्त माम् ॥३५॥

jyeṣṭhaṁ mantra-dṛśaṁ cakrus
tvām anvañco vayaṁ sma hi
viśvāmitraḥ sutān āha
vīravanto bhaviṣyatha
ye mānaṁ me 'nugṛhṇanto
vīravantam akarta mām

jyeṣṭham—the eldest; *mantra-dṛśam*—a seer of *mantras; cakruḥ*—they accepted; *tvām*—you; *anvañcaḥ*—have agreed to follow; *vayam*—we; *sma*—indeed; *hi*—certainly; *viśvāmitraḥ*—the great sage Viśvāmitra; *sutān*—to the obedient sons; *āha*—said; *vīra-vantaḥ*—fathers of sons; *bhaviṣyatha*—become in the future; *ye*—all of you who; *mānam*—honor; *me*—my; *anugṛhṇantaḥ*—accepted; *vīra-vantam*—the father of good sons; *akarta*—you have made; *mām*—me.

TRANSLATION

Thus the younger Madhucchandās accepted Śunaḥśepha as their eldest brother and told him, "We shall follow your orders." Viśvāmitra then said to his obedient sons, "Because you have accepted Śunaḥśepha as your eldest brother, I am very satisfied. By accepting my order, you have made me a father of worthy sons, and therefore I bless all of you to become the fathers of sons also."

PURPORT

Of the one hundred sons, half disobeyed Viśvāmitra by not accepting Śunaḥśepha as their eldest brother, but the other half accepted his order.

Therefore the father blessed the obedient sons to become the fathers of sons. Otherwise they too would have been cursed to be sonless *mlecchas.*

TEXT 36

एष वः कुशिका वीरो देवरातस्तमन्वित ।
अन्ये चाष्टकहारीतजयक्रतुमदादयः ॥३६॥

eṣa vaḥ kuśikā vīro
devarātas tam anvita
anye cāṣṭaka-hārīta-
jaya-kratumad-ādayaḥ

eṣaḥ—this (Śunaḥśepha); *vaḥ*—like you; *kuśikāḥ*—O Kuśikas; *vīraḥ*—my son; *devarātaḥ*—he is known as Devarāta; *tam*—him; *anvita*—just obey; *anye*—others; *ca*—also; *aṣṭaka*—Aṣṭaka; *hārīta*—Hārīta; *jaya*—Jaya; *kratumat*—Kratumān; *ādayaḥ*—and others.

TRANSLATION

Viśvāmitra said, "O Kuśikas [descendants of Kauśika], this Devarāta is my son and is one of you. Please obey his orders." O King Parīkṣit, Viśvāmitra had many other sons, such as Aṣṭaka, Hārīta, Jaya and Kratumān.

TEXT 37

एवं कौशिकगोत्रं तु विश्वामित्रैः पृथग्विधम् ।
प्रवरान्तरमापन्नं तद्धि चैवं प्रकल्पितम् ॥३७॥

evaṁ kauśika-gotraṁ tu
visvāmitraiḥ pṛthag-vidham
pravarāntaram āpannaṁ
tad dhi caivaṁ prakalpitam

evam—in this way (some sons having been cursed and some blessed); *kauśika-gotram*—the dynasty of Kauśika; *tu*—indeed; *viśvāmitraiḥ*—by the sons of Viśvāmitra; *pṛthak-vidham*—in different varieties; *pravara-*

antaram—differences between one another; *āpannam*—obtained; *tat*—that; *hi*—indeed; *ca*—also; *evam*—thus; *prakalpitam*—ascertained.

TRANSLATION

Viśvāmitra cursed some of his sons and blessed the others, and he also adopted a son. Thus there were varieties in the Kauśika dynasty, but among all the sons, Devarāta was considered the eldest.

Thus end the Bhaktivedanta purports of the Ninth Canto, Sixteenth Chapter, of the Śrīmad-Bhāgavatam, *entitled "Lord Paraśurāma Destroys the World's Ruling Class."*

Appendixes

The Author

His Divine Grace A. C. Bhaktivedanta Swami Prabhupāda appeared in this world in 1896 in Calcutta, India. He first met his spiritual master, Śrīla Bhaktisiddhānta Sarasvatī Gosvāmī, in Calcutta in 1922. Bhaktisiddhānta Sarasvatī, a prominent devotional scholar and the founder of sixty-four Gauḍīya Maṭhas (Vedic institutes), liked this educated young man and convinced him to dedicate his life to teaching Vedic knowledge. Śrīla Prabhupāda became his student, and eleven years later (1933) at Allahabad he became his formally initiated disciple.

At their first meeting, in 1922, Śrīla Bhaktisiddhānta Sarasvatī Ṭhākura requested Śrīla Prabhupāda to broadcast Vedic knowledge through the English language. In the years that followed, Śrīla Prabhupāda wrote a commentary on the *Bhagavad-gītā*, assisted the Gauḍīya Maṭha in its work and, in 1944, without assistance, started an English fortnightly magazine, edited it, typed the manuscripts and checked the galley proofs. He even distributed the individual copies freely and struggled to maintain the publication. Once begun, the magazine never stopped; it is now being continued by his disciples in the West.

Recognizing Śrīla Prabhupāda's philosophical learning and devotion, the Gauḍīya Vaiṣṇava Society honored him in 1947 with the title "Bhaktivedanta." In 1950, at the age of fifty-four, Śrīla Prabhupāda retired from married life, and four years later he adopted the *vānaprastha* (retired) order to devote more time to his studies and writing. Śrīla Prabhupāda traveled to the holy city of Vṛndāvana, where he lived in very humble circumstances in the historic medieval temple of Rādhā-Dāmodara. There he engaged for several years in deep study and writing. He accepted the renounced order of life (*sannyāsa*) in 1959. At Rādhā-Dāmodara, Śrīla Prabhupāda began work on his life's masterpiece: a multivolume translation and commentary on the eighteen thousand verse *Śrīmad-Bhāgavatam* (*Bhāgavata Purāṇa*). He also wrote *Easy Journey to Other Planets.*

After publishing three volumes of *Bhāgavatam*, Śrīla Prabhupāda came to the United States, in 1965, to fulfill the mission of his spiritual master. Since that time, His Divine Grace has written over forty volumes of authoritative translations, commentaries and summary studies of the philosophical and religious classics of India.

In 1965, when he first arrived by freighter in New York City, Śrīla Prabhupāda was practically penniless. It was after almost a year of great difficulty that he established the International Society for Krishna Consciousness in July of 1966. Under his careful guidance, the Society has grown within a decade to a worldwide confederation of almost one hundred *āśramas*, schools, temples, institutes and farm communities.

In 1968, Śrīla Prabhupāda created New Vṛndāvana, an experimental Vedic community in the hills of West Virginia. Inspired by the success of New Vṛndāvana, now a thriving farm community of more than one thousand acres, his students have since founded several similar communities in the United States and abroad.

In 1972, His Divine Grace introduced the Vedic system of primary and secondary education in the West by founding the Gurukula school in Dallas, Texas. The school began with 3 children in 1972, and by the beginning of 1975 the enrollment had grown to 150.

Śrīla Prabhupāda has also inspired the construction of a large international center at Śrīdhāma Māyāpur in West Bengal, India, which is also the site for a planned Institute of Vedic Studies. A similar project is the magnificent Kṛṣṇa-Balarāma Temple and International Guest House in Vṛndāvana, India. These are centers where Westerners can live to gain firsthand experience of Vedic culture.

Śrīla Prabhupāda's most significant contribution, however, is his books. Highly respected by the academic community for their authoritativeness, depth and clarity, they are used as standard textbooks in numerous college courses. His writings have been translated into eleven languages. The Bhaktivedanta Book Trust, established in 1972 exclusively to publish the works of His Divine Grace, has thus become the world's largest publisher of books in the field of Indian religion and philosophy. Its latest project is the publishing of Śrīla Prabhupāda's most recent work: a seventeen-volume translation and commentary—completed by Śrīla Prabhupāda in only eighteen months—on the Bengali religious classic *Śrī Caitanya-caritāmṛta.*

In the past ten years, in spite of his advanced age, Śrīla Prabhupāda has circled the globe twelve times on lecture tours that have taken him to six continents. In spite of such a vigorous schedule, Śrīla Prabhupāda continues to write prolifically. His writings constitute a veritable library of Vedic philosophy, religion, literature and culture.

References

The purports of *Śrīmad-Bhāgavatam* are all confirmed by standard Vedic authorities. The following authentic scriptures are specifically cited in this volume:

Bhagavad-gītā, 6, 10–11, 25, 35, 36, 40, 41, 51, 60, 66–67, 75–76, 76, 80–81, 95, 108, 123, 160, 172, 207, 208, 219, 220, 224, 232, 233, 261, 263

Brahma-saṁhitā, 9, 29, 50, 68, 119, 188, 230

Caitanya-candrodaya-nāṭaka, 43

Caitanya-caritāmṛta, 38, 171

Mahābhārata, 236–238

Skanda Purāṇa, 60–61

Śrīmad-Bhāgavatam, 6, 7, 8, 25, 29, 45, 97, 104–105, 119, 160, 176, 187, 198, 210, 223, 224, 268

Śvetāśvatara Upaniṣad, 120–121

GENEALOGICAL TABLES

CHART ONE
Sun Dynasty from Aṁśumān up to Kuśa

This second volume of the Ninth Canto continues from the preceeding volume the description of the dynasty which began with the sun-god Vivasvān and his son Śrāddhadeva Manu. The dynasty of the moon-god Soma is also traced up to the appearance of Lord Paraśurāma.

CHART ONE (Chapters 9–11)   The descendants of Aṁśumān up through Lord Rāmacandra, His brothers and Their sons.

CHART TWO (Chapter 12)   The dynasty from Kuśa, younger son of Rāmacandra, up to Bṛhadbala, last king of the succession born before Śukadeva Gosvāmī spoke *Śrīmad-Bhāgavatam* to Parīkṣit.

CHART THREE (Chapter 12)   Śukadeva's prediction of kings yet to come in Kali-yuga, up to the end of the sun dynasty with Sumitra.

CHART FOUR (Chapter 13)   The kings of Mithilā, starting with the city's founder Janaka (Vaideha), the son of Nimi, up to the second Janaka (Sīradhvaja), father of mother Sītā.

CHART FIVE (Chapter 13)   Continuing the kings of Mithilā, up to Mahāvaśī.

CHART SIX (Chapters 14–16)   The moon dynasty, up to Lord Paraśurāma and the sons of Viśvāmitra Muni.

+ indicates marriage ties

Aṁśumān
|
Dilīpa
|
Bhagīratha
|
Śruta
|
Nābha
|
Sindhudvīpa
|
Ayutāyu
|
Ṛtūparṇa
|
Sarvakāma
|
Sudāsa
|
Saudāsa + Damayantī
(Madayantī)   (by Vasiṣṭha Muni)
|
Aśmaka
|
Bālika
(Nārīkavaca, Mūlaka)
|
Daśaratha
|
Aiḍaviḍi
|
Viśvasaha
|
Khaṭvāṅga
|
Dīrghabāhu
|
Raghu
|
Aja
|
Daśaratha + Kausalyā & Sumitrā & Kaikeyī

RĀMACANDRA + Sītā   LAKṢMAṆA   ŚATRUGHNA   BHARATA

Lava   Kuśa   Aṅgada   Citraketu   Subāhu   Śrutasena   Takṣa   Puṣkala

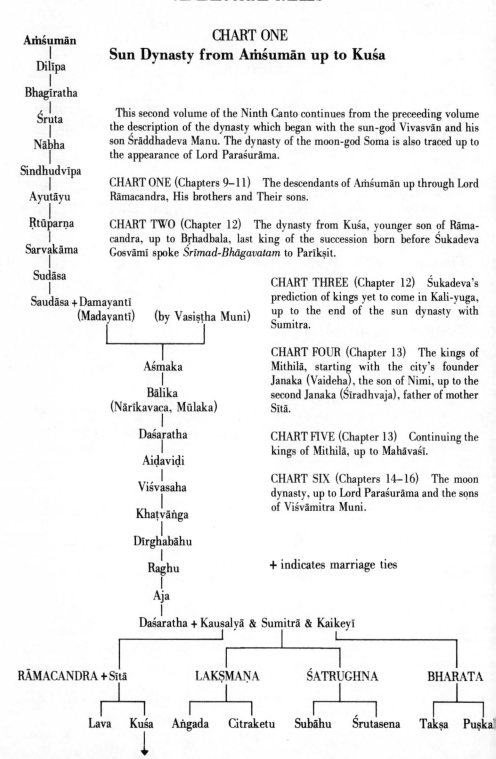

CHART TWO
Sun Dynasty from Kuśa up to Bṛhadbala

Kuśa
Atithi
Niṣadha
Nabha
Puṇḍarīka
Kṣemadhanvā
Devānīka
Anīha
Pāriyātra
Balasthala
Vajranābha
Sagaṇa
Vidhṛti
Hiraṇyanābha
Puṣpa
Dhruvasandhi
Sudarśana
Agnivarṇa
Śīghra
Maru
Prasuśruta
Sandhi
Amarṣaṇa
Mahasvān
Viśvabāhu
Prasenajit
Takṣaka
Bṛhadbala
↓

CHART THREE
Predicted Kings of Sun Dynasty in Kali-yuga

Bṛhadbala
Bṛhadraṇa
Ūrukriya
Vatsavṛddha
Prativyoma
Bhānu
Divāka
Sahadeva
Bṛhadaśva
Bhānumān
Pratīkāśva
Supratīka
Marudeva
Sunakṣatra
Puṣkara
Antarikṣa
Sutapā
Amitrajit
Bṛhadrāja
Barhi
Kṛtañjaya
Raṇañjaya
Sañjaya
Śākya
Śuddhoda
Lāṅgala
Prasenajit
Kṣudraka
Raṇaka
Suratha
Sumitra
(end of dynasty)

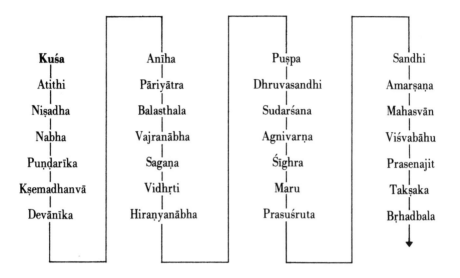

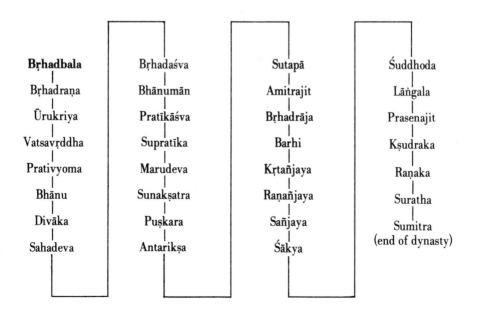

CHART FOUR
Dynasty of Nimi, the Kings of Mithilā (Part One)

- **Vivasvān**
  - Śrāddhadeva Manu
    - Ikṣvāku
      - Nimi
        - Janaka (Vaideha, Mithila)
          - Udāvasu
            - Nandivardhana
              - Suketu
                - Devarāta
                  - Bṛhadratha
                    - Mahāvīrya
                      - Sudhṛti
                        - Dhṛṣṭaketu
                          - Haryaśva
                            - Maru
                              - Pratīpaka
                                - Kṛtaratha
                                  - Devamīḍha
                                    - Viśruta
                                      - Mahādhṛti
                                        - Kṛtirāta
                                          - Mahāromā
                                            - Svarṇaromā
                                              - Hrasvaromā
                                                - Śīradhvaja (Janaka) ↓

CHART FIVE
Kings of Mithilā (Part Two)

- **Śīradhvaja (Janaka)**
  - Kuśadhvaja
    - Dharmadhvaja
      - Kṛtadhvaja
        - Keśidhvaja
          - Bhānumān
            - Śatadyumna
              - Śuci
                - Sanadvāja
                  - Ūrjaketu
                    - Aja
                      - Purujit
                        - Ariṣṭanemi
                          - Śrutāyu
                            - Supārśvaka
                              - Citraratha
                                - Kṣemādhi
                                  - Samaratha
                                    - Satyaratha
                                      - Upaguru
                                        - Upagupta
                                          - Vasvananta
                                            - Yuyudha
                                              - Subhāṣaṇa
                                                - Śruta
                                                  - Jaya
                                                    - Vijaya
                                                      - Ṛta
                                                        - Śunaka
                                                          - Vītahavya
                                                            - Dhṛti
                                                              - Bahulāśva
                                                                - Kṛti
                                                                  - Mahāvaśī
      - Mitadhvaja
        - Khāṇḍikya
  - Sītā (wife of Rāmacandra)

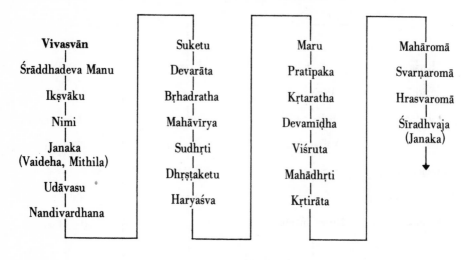

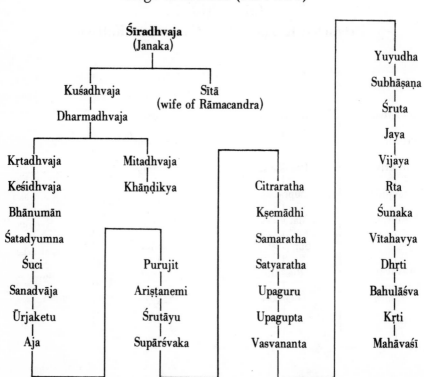

CHART SIX
Dynasty of the Moon-God Soma

- **Viṣṇu**
  - Brahmā
    - Atri + Anasūyā
      - Dattātreya
      - Soma + Tārā (kidnapped)
        - Budha + Ilā (Sudyumna)
          - Purūravā + Urvaśī
            - Āyu
            - Śrutāyu
              - Vasumān
            - Satyāyu
              - Śrutañjaya
            - Raya
              - Eka
            - Vijaya
              - Bhīma
                - Kāñcana
                  - Hotraka
                    - Jahnu
                      - Puru
                        - Balāka
                          - Ajaka
                            - Kuśa
                              - Kuśāmbu
                                - Gādhi
                                  - Viśvāmitra Muni
                                    - Śunaḥśepha (adopted)
                                    - 49 elder sons
                                    - Madhucchandā
                                    - 50 younger sons
                                  - Ṛcīka Muni + Satyavatī
                                    - Jamadagni + Reṇukā
                                      - Vasumān
                                      - (other sons)
                                      - PARAŚURĀMA
                              - Tanaya
                              - Vasu
                              - Kuśanābha
            - Jaya
              - Amita
      - Durvāsā

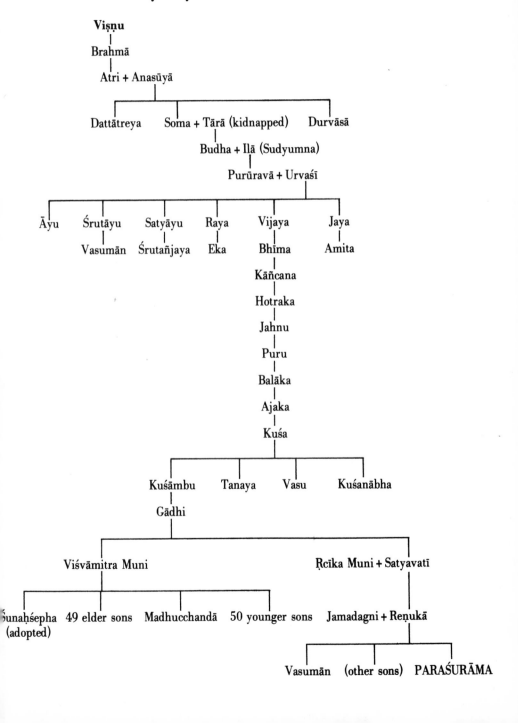

Glossary

A

Ācārya—a spiritual master who teaches by example.

Ahaṅgraha-upāsanā—self-worship, not recommended for anyone other than God.

Aṇimā—the mystic perfection of becoming smaller than the smallest.

Ārati—a ceremony for greeting the Lord with offerings of food, lamps, fans, flowers and incense.

Arcanā—the devotional process of Deity worship.

Artha—economic development.

Āsana—a sitting posture in *yoga* practice.

Āśrama—the four spiritual orders of life: celibate student, householder, retired life and renounced life.

Asuras—atheistic demons.

Avatāra—a descent of the Supreme Lord.

B

Bhagavad-gītā—the basic directions for spiritual life spoken by the Lord Himself.

Bhakta—a devotee.

Bhakti-yoga—linking with the Supreme Lord by devotional service.

Brahmacarya—celibate student life; the first order of Vedic spiritual life.

Brahman—the Absolute Truth; especially the impersonal aspect of the Absolute.

Brāhmaṇa—one wise in the *Vedas* who can guide society; the first Vedic social order.

Brahmarṣi—a title meaning "sage among the *brāhmaṇas.*"

D

Dharma—eternal occupational duty; religious principles.

E

Ekādaśī—a special fast day for increased remembrance of Kṛṣṇa, which comes on the eleventh day of both the waxing and waning moon.

G

Goloka (Kṛṣṇaloka)—the highest spiritual planet, containing Kṛṣṇa's personal abodes, Dvārakā, Mathurā and Vṛndāvana.

Gopīs—Kṛṣṇa's cowherd girl friends, His most confidential servitors.

Gṛhastha—regulated householder life; the second order of Vedic spiritual life.

Guru—a spiritual master.

H

Hare Kṛṣṇa mantra—*See: Mahā-mantra*

Hlādinī—the Lord's pleasure potency.

J

Jīvan-mukta—one liberated even in this life by practical engagement in devotional service.

Jīva-tattva—the living entities, atomic parts of the Lord.

Jñāna—theoretical knowledge.

Jñānī—one who cultivates knowledge by empirical speculation.

K

Kali-yuga (Age of Kali)—the present age, characterized by quarrel; it is last in the cycle of four and began five thousand years ago.

Kalpa—daytime of Brahmā, 4,320,000,000 years.

Kāma—lust.

Kāmadhenu—spiritual cows, in the spiritual world, which yield unlimited quantities of milk.

Kaniṣṭha-adhikārīs—neophyte devotees.

Karatālas—hand cymbals used in *kīrtana.*

Karma—fruitive action, for which there is always reaction, good or bad.

Karmī—a person satisfied with working hard for flickering sense gratification.

Kīrtana—chanting the glories of the Supreme Lord.

Kṛṣṇaloka—*See:* Goloka

Kṣatriyas—a warrior or administrator; the second Vedic social order.

Kuśa—auspicious grass used in Vedic rituals.

L

Laghimā—the yogic power to become as light as a feather.

M

Mahā-mantra—the great chanting for deliverance:
Hare Kṛṣṇa, Hare Kṛṣṇa, Kṛṣṇa Kṛṣṇa, Hare Hare
Hare Rāma, Hare Rāma, Rāma Rāma, Hare Hare.

Mantra—a sound vibration that can deliver the mind from illusion.

Marakata-maṇi—an emerald.

Mathurā—Lord Kṛṣṇa's abode, surrounding Vṛndāvana, where He took birth and later returned to after performing His Vṛndāvana pastimes.

Māyā—illusion; forgetfulness of one's relationship with Kṛṣṇa.

Māyāvādīs—impersonal philosophers who say that the Lord cannot have a transcendental body.

Mokṣa—liberation into the spiritual effulgence surrounding the Lord.

Mṛdaṅga—a clay drum used for congregational chanting.

P

Parambrahma—the Supreme Absolute Truth, Kṛṣṇa.

Paramparā—the chain of spiritual masters in disciplic succession.

Pātāla—the lowest of the universe's fourteen planetary systems.

Prakaṭa-līlā—the manifestation on earth of the Lord's pastimes.

Prasāda—food spiritualized by being offered to the Lord.

R

Rājarṣi—a great saintly king.

Rasātala—the lowest planet in the Pātāla system (*see above*).

S

Sac-cid-ānanda-vigraha—the Lord's transcendental form, which is eternal, full of knowledge and bliss.

Saṅkīrtana—public chanting of the names of God, the approved *yoga* process for this age.

Sannyāsa—renounced life; the fourth order of Vedic spiritual life.

Śāpa—a *brāhmaṇa's* curse.
Śāstras—revealed scriptures.
Śravaṇaṁ kīrtanaṁ viṣṇoḥ—the devotional processes of hearing and chanting about Lord Viṣṇu.
Śūdra—a laborer; the fourth of the Vedic social orders.
Surabhi cows—*See:* Kāmadhenu.
Svāmī—one who controls his mind and senses; title of one in the renounced order of life.
Svāyambhuva-manvantara—the duration of Svāyambhuva Manu's reign, approximately 308,500,000 years.

T

Tapasya—austerity; accepting some voluntary inconvenience for a higher purpose.
Tilaka—auspicious clay marks that sanctify a devotee's body as a temple of the Lord.

V

Vaidurya-maṇi—a spiritual gem which can display different colors.
Vaikuṇṭha—the spiritual world.
Vaiṣṇava—a devotee of Lord Viṣṇu, Kṛṣṇa.
Vaiśyas—farmers and merchants; the third Vedic social order.
Vānaprastha—one who has retired from family life; the third order of Vedic spiritual life.
Varṇa—the four occupational divisions of society: the intellectual class, the administrative class, the mercantile class, and the laborer class.
Varṇāśrama—the Vedic social system of four social and four spiritual orders.
Vedas—the original revealed scriptures, first spoken by the Lord Himself.
Viṣṇu, Lord—Kṛṣṇa's expansion for the creation and maintenance of the material universes.
Viṣṇu-tattva—the original Personality of Godhead's primary expansions, each of whom is equally God.
Viṣṇu-yajña—a sacrifice performed for the satisfaction of Lord Viṣṇu.
Vṛndāvana—Kṛṣṇa's personal abode, where He fully manifests His quality of sweetness.

Vyāsadeva—Kṛṣṇa's incarnation, at the end of Dvāpara-yuga, for compiling the *Vedas.*

Y

Yajña—sacrifice; work done for the satisfaction of Lord Viṣṇu.

Yavana—a lowborn person who does not follow Vedic regulations.

Yogī—a transcendentalist who, in one way or another, is striving for union with the Supreme.

Yugas—ages in the life of a universe, occurring in a repeated cycle of four.

Sanskrit Pronunciation Guide

Vowels

अ a आ ā इ i ई ī उ u ऊ ū ऋ ṛ ॠ ṝ
ऌ ḷ ए e ऐ ai ओ o औ au

ं ṁ *(anusvāra)* ः ḥ *(visarga)*

Consonants

Gutturals:	क ka	ख kha	ग ga	घ gha	ङ ṅa
Palatals:	च ca	छ cha	ज ja	झ jha	ञ ña
Cerebrals:	ट ṭa	ठ ṭha	ड ḍa	ढ ḍha	ण ṇa
Dentals:	त ta	थ tha	द da	ध dha	न na
Labials:	प pa	फ pha	ब ba	भ bha	म ma
Semivowels:	य ya	र ra	ल la	व va	
Sibilants:	श śa	ष ṣa	स sa		
Aspirate:	ह ha	ऽ ' *(avagraha)* – the apostrophe			

The numerals are: १ २ ३ ४ ५ ६ ७ ८ ९ ०

The vowels above should be pronounced as follows:

a – like the *a* in org*a*n or the *u* in b*u*t.
ā – like the *a* in f*a*r but held twice as long as short *a*.
i – like the *i* in p*i*n.
ī – like the *i* in p*i*que but held twice as long as short *i*.

u – like the *u* in p*u*sh.
ū – like the *u* in r*u*le but held twice as long as short *u*.
ṛ – like the *ri* in *ri*m.
ṝ – like *ree* in *ree*d.
ḷ – like *l* followed by *r* (*lr*).
e – like the *e* in th*ey*.
ai – like the *ai* in *ai*sle.
o – like the *o* in g*o*.
au – like the *ow* in h*ow*.
ṁ (*anusvāra*) – a resonant nasal like the *n* in the French word *bon*.
ḥ (*visarga*) – a final *h*-sound: *aḥ* is pronounced like *aha; iḥ* like *ihi*.

The vowels are written as follows after a consonant:

ा ā ि i ी ī ु u ू ū ृ ṛ ॄ ṝ े e ै ai ो o ौ au

For example: क ka का kā कि ki की kī कु ku कू kū
कृ kṛ कॄ kṝ के ke कै kai को ko कौ kau

The vowel "a" is implied after a consonant with no vowel symbol.

The symbol virāma (्) indicates that there is no final vowel: क्

The consonants are pronounced as follows:

k – as in *k*ite
kh – as in Ec*kh*art
g – as in *g*ive
gh – as in di*g-h*ard
ṅ – as in si*ng*
c – as in *ch*air
ch – as in staun*ch-h*eart
j – as in *j*oy
jh – as in he*dgeh*og
ñ – as in ca*ny*on
ṭ – as in *t*ub
ṭh – as in ligh*t-h*eart
ḍ – as in *d*ove
ḍha- as in re*d-h*ot
ṇ – as r*na* (prepare to say the *r* and say *na*).

Cerebrals are pronounced with tongue to roof of mouth, but the following dentals are pronounced with tongue against teeth:

t – as in *t*ub but with tongue against teeth.
th – as in ligh*t-h*eart but with tongue against teeth.

d – as in *d*ove but with tongue against teeth.
dh – as in re*d-h*ot but with tongue against teeth.
n – as in *n*ut but with tongue between teeth.
p – as in *p*ine
ph – as in u*ph*ill (not *f*)
b – as in *b*ird
bh – as in ru*b-h*ard
m – as in *m*other
y – as in *y*es
r – as in *r*un
l – as in *l*ight
v – as in *v*ine
ś (palatal) – as in the *s* in the German word *sprechen*
ṣ (cerebral) – as the *sh* in *sh*ine
s – as in *s*un
h – as in *h*ome

Generally two or more consonants in conjunction are written together in a special form, as for example: क्ष kṣa त्र tra

There is no strong accentuation of syllables in Sanskrit, or pausing between words in a line, only a flowing of short and long (twice as long as the short) syllables. A long syllable is one whose vowel is long (ā, ī, ū, e, ai, o, au), or whose short vowel is followed by more than one consonant (including anusvāra and visarga). Aspirated consonants (such as kha and gha) count as only single consonants.

Index of Sanskrit Verses

This index constitutes a complete listing of the first and third lines of each of the Sanskrit poetry verses of this volume of *Śrīmad-Bhāgavatam*, arranged in English alphabetical order. The first column gives the Sanskrit transliteration, and the second and third columns, respectively, list the chapter-verse reference and page number for each verse.

U

V

Y

General Index

Numerals in boldface type indicate references to translations of the verses of *Śrīmad-Bhāgavatam.*

C

D

M

P

T

U

V